Eco, Ego, Eros: Essays on Philosophy, Spiri

C000121214

ARAMIS PRESS

Photography by Aramis Photography

ISBN: 978-0-578-11868-0

Foreword

By virtue of picking up this book and starting to read, you are probably what I call a "romantic rationalist." That is, you are interested in understanding the world on the basis of science, mathematics and philosophy, but are also looking for a larger meaning within this unfolding universe that you find yourself in. Or, perhaps you have had a spiritual experience and are seeking to integrate such a transformative experience within a scientific worldview.

I recently had the privilege of spending time with His Holiness, the 14th Dalai Lama, in a monastery in India. Of all the wise things he said, one struck me the most, as it was so unexpected for a religious leader: "Any moral ethics must come from intellect and knowledge, not faith." What he meant is that in the construction of a secular ethics that will allow all of humanity to lead a mindful, virtuous and compassionate life, the rational analysis of ultimate reality has to take precedence over blind faith in a God or the laws that this God has allegedly laid down in some sacred text.

By reading *Eco, Ego, Eros*, you are about to embark on such a voyage of discovery that uses rational analysis by some of the greatest Western thinkers, combined with the experimental and theoretical investigation of nature, to make sense of the riddle of our existence. Authored by Tam Hunt, an environmental lawyer and philosopher, this series of short chapters, reflecting their origin in a regular online column, has a magnificent writ. Starting out with panpsychism, the ancient teaching that all creatures and, indeed, all matter, are to a smaller and larger extent conscious, the book covers quantum mechanics, relativity theory, evolution by natural selection, the origin of life, scholars from Descartes to contemporary philosophers of mind, Gödel and the limits of mathematics, Western, Hindu and Buddhist ideas about mind, and the author's own mystical experience when smoking dope in the Pacific Northwest.

The book keeps on returning to its central thesis – that all matter is endowed with consciousness, that every outside in the universe has an inside, only accessible to the system itself. That "inside" is what it feels like to be that system, whether it's a human brain with roughly 100 billion nerve cells, or the 100 million of the mouse or the nervous system of the tiny round worm *C. elegans*, no larger than the letter 'I', with 302 nerve cells. Of course, what the system is capable of experiencing will scale somehow with the complexity of the chunk of excitable matter that gives rise to the mind in the first place.

Spirituality also fits into this grandiose vision of life. To see how, you must now turn over this page and start *Eco, Ego, Eros*.

Christof Koch

February 3, 2013

Seattle, USA

Chief Scientific Officer, Allen Institute for Brain Science, and Victor and Lois Troendle Professor of Cognitive and Behavioral Biology, California Institute of Technology. Author of *The Quest for Consciousness: A Neurobiological Approach* and *Consciousness: Confessions of a Romantic Reductionist*.

Preface

Who reads philosophy anymore? Well, you do. And the world is a better place for it. Some Greek guy said once that the unexamined life is not worth living and I tend to agree. I'm compelled to examine not only my own life but what it means to be alive, to look for patterns, purpose, meaning. This is the stuff of philosophy and the examined life.

This book is a collection of the first three years of my column for the *Santa Barbara Independent*, under the same name: *Eco, Ego, Eros*. This title stands, roughly, for the world/environment, consciousness, and spirituality/philosophy. These are generally the topics I treat here, and there is a thread that runs through them all. This is intentional: I began the column after I'd already largely written two other books that described my preferred theory of consciousness, a version of panpsychism (the view that all matter has some type of consciousness associated with it), and the scientific, spiritual and philosophical consequences of panpsychism.

More generally, most of my writing, and all of the writings included in this volume, are my personal attempt to make sense of it all, to "grok" reality. It seems to me that the intersection of science, philosophy and spirituality is where the real action is in this new millennium. And integrating the various viewpoints we find in the world today is the key task of our time. This book is an attempt to make my ideas on these issues digestible in column-size chunks. Granted, these chunks are still fairly large at times, but try hard and they'll go down.

Philosophy is, particularly relevant in today's era because of the dramatic decline in religious belief in the US and the developed world more generally, and, at the same time, the rise of an overly dogmatic type of materialism as the common basis for much of the natural sciences and philosophy. As I write in "Buddha, Evolving," an essay toward the end of this collection, we are in the midst of a profound shift away from organized religion. Philosophy and more scientifically-minded flavors of spirituality can and should fill the religion-shaped hole this shift is leaving.

My hope is that a panpsychism-based philosophy and accompanying spirituality can provide a satisfying fit for this societal and psychic void.

Part 1

On Matters Philosophical

We can't help ourselves. The gift of words requires that we use these tools to understand, to find meaning, in the world around us and our place in it. We'll never have the final answers, but this shouldn't stop us from trying. And even though words are ultimately an endless rabbit hole, it can be a fun ride down that hole.

Chapter 1

Absent-minded Science, Part 1

We learn from an early age that "to be scientific" means avoiding attributing to nature human-like tendencies such as mind or purpose. To be "anthropomorphic" in science is a cardinal sin.

Modern science, with its amazing successes in improving human understanding, did in fact spring in part from this tendency, made clear with Descartes' philosophical separation of reality into two categories: physical stuff and mental stuff. The mental stuff is the realm of spirit and this is God's domain. The physical stuff is also God's handiwork but it works according to identifiable rules (laws) that humankind may discern through careful observation and experiment.

However, as with most big ideas, Descartes's idea was overly simplistic and, we now know, inaccurate. Very few modern scientists or philosophers would argue in favor of Cartesian dualism, though this view is still fairly common among more religious-minded people. However, dualism's residue today is "reductionist materialism," which simply ignores the mental/spiritual realm that Descartes proposed and attempts, instead, to explain everything as simply matter in motion. The recent challenge to Cartesian dualism and reductionist materialism, from a non-religious perspective, comes from thinkers like Galen Strawson, David Chalmers, and David Ray Griffin, who realize that modern science went astray long ago by trying to expunge mind from its explanations.

The problem becomes apparent when we try to explain mind itself within the "scientific" method that does its best to ignore mind in nature. The prevailing theory of mind argues that mind emerges from mindless matter when a certain level of complexity is reached, in both evolutionary history and in each organism. That is, at some point in the history of life on our planet, a mind appeared for the first time where it was wholly absent before. In this view, the constituents of matter are completely devoid of mind, whether physicists decide that matter is ultimately comprised of quarks and other little chunks, energy, fields, strings, or what have you – until the required level of complexity is reached.

But here's the deeper problem: it seems to be impossible for mind to spring forth from that which is defined as being wholly devoid of mind.

What does mind look like?

Some clarity may be provided if we envision the ultimate constituents of matter as akin to little billiard balls. (This is not an accurate notion, even in terms of the prevailing views of matter, but it is accurate in terms of my point here). No matter how we arrange any number of little billiard balls, the collection of little billiard balls will never give rise to any type of mind – unless there is some type of mind contained in the billiard balls from the get-go. And the prevailing theory of mind today denies that there is any mind at all in the little billiard balls or in any of the ultimate constituents of matter.

To bring the problem closer to home, imagine your own development in your mother's womb. You – originally a single cell – developed steadily in complexity and size. Your body grew and your nervous system differentiated itself from other types of cells in your little body. Nerve cells grew, lengthened, interconnected and eventually formed your brain, spinal chord, etc. Every step of this process was incremental, small change after small change. At what point did your mind emerge? At what point did it suddenly pop into existence where it was wholly absent before? And if it did suddenly emerge, why at a particular point in time and not a moment earlier or later?

Here's one more way of thinking about the problem: imagine observing a brain surgery. You are able to peer into the brain from the outside through a hole cut in the skull. You have a microscope that allows you to peer into the structure of the brain. Let's imagine you could even go further than modern technology allows and you could look into the living brain with such detail that individual dendrites and synapses are distinguishable. Where is the mind? All we will ever see by looking at a brain and its components from the outside are the electrochemical energy flows that comprise the brain's activities. We will never see the mind. Yet we know, more than we know anything else, based on our own experience as thinking beings, that it's there.

Toward resolution

There seem to be two options here: 1) accept that the prevailing view that mind mysteriously emerges from mindless matter is not much different than the religious notion of a soul attaching to the fertilized egg or at some later point in its development; 2) accept that mind is inherent in all matter to some degree and that there is a tiny sort of mind in the fertilized egg (and even tinier minds in the constituents of the egg) and that as the egg complexifies into you, so your mind complexifies.

This second view is known as panpsychism, a view fleshed out to some degree by Greek and Indian philosophers thousands of years ago and developed significantly since then. David Skrbina's *Panpsychism in the West* is a wonderful history of these ideas and more. Panpsychism, while out of fashion for much of the 20th Century is coming back into fashion in the 21st Century as more and more thinkers realize that the prevailing "emergence" theory of mind, a type of reductionist materialism, fails as a matter of principle.

Schopenhauer, the surly German 19th century philosopher perhaps said it best: "Materialism is the philosophy of the subject (consciousness) that forgets to take account of itself." Panpsychism, to the contrary, holds that mind is the inside of matter, no matter how simple, so while we can only see the outside of objects available to our senses, like the neurons and dendrites of our hypothetical brain surgery patient, we know from our own direct experience that matter also has an inside and this is what we call mind. The inside of matter is only directly accessible to itself, such that my mind is knowable only to me, as is the case with every human, cat, bat, rat, gnat, and so on down the chain of complexity.

This "absent-minded science" that is a key feature of reductionist materialism is not a problem just in cognitive science and philosophy of mind. It's also a major problem in biology. The prevailing view of evolution, known as adaptationism or the Modern Synthesis, holds that we must avoid ascribing any purpose to the evolutionary process, either at the organismic level or higher levels. Indeed, the view that nature is completely devoid of purpose is a widely held and explicit assumption for the majority of biologists today. Talk about "design" and "intention," when these terms are used by mainstream biologists, is always to be considered short-hand and tongue-in-cheek for processes that are wholly devoid of purpose or mind.

Yet here we are, humans with minds and intentions, trying to explain how we got here. Our purpose in devising theories of evolution is to explain key aspects of nature, including ourselves, in terms of our history and our place in the universe. Thus, if we are indeed part of nature – as we surely are – then the mere fact of our presence in the universe demonstrates unequivocally that mind is very much part of nature. And if there is mind in us, and by extension in all matter to some degree, then mind surely has had a role in the evolution of life from the very beginning. Sewall Wright, a well-known American evolutionary biologist, stated it well in a 1977 article: "[E]mergence of mind from no mind is sheer magic."

The evolution of life has not, then, been a mindless process of random mutation and natural selection. Rather, the evolution of life has surely been a multi-faceted process with both random and purposeful elements from the get-go. Lamarck wasn't entirely wrong in supposing that acquired traits can sometimes be heritable, and nor was Darwin or his successors in supposing that random mutation of germ-lines were the only cause of variation. The Modern Synthesis is at this time being extended into a new synthesis that recognizes a broader and richer view of evolution that encompasses both Darwin and Lamarck. Eva Jablonka and Marion Lamb's excellent *Evolution in Four Dimensions* delves into some of these ideas, exploring the epigenetic, behavioral and symbolic dimensions of evolution, in addition to the traditional genetic dimension, as well as ways in which some acquired traits can indeed be heritable (a later essay in this series will explore these ideas in more depth).

It is clear, then, that we must no longer ignore mind in nature. Moreover, it is time for science and philosophy to wholly repudiate Cartesian dualism, and its slightly less damaging cousin reductionist materialism, and acknowledge that matter and mind are an undivided whole. Science has progressed far by expunging mind from its explanations. Anthropomorphism can indeed be a lazy philosophical position if we simply extend various human attributes reflexively (and unreflectively) into the universe around us. But to go further than today's impasse we need to re-embrace mind, and ourselves, as an inherent part of nature.

"Mind" doesn't have to be human-like mind – and most of the minds that exist in the universe are surely very little like human minds because of an almost total lack of complexity in the physical substrate that is the objective aspect of each mind. But a simple mind is still a mind. The panpsychist view is that each little speck of matter throughout the universe is both a speck of matter and a speck of mind. And as matter complexifies, so mind complexifies.

This is not anthropomorphism as much as it is a legitimate "psychomorphism" because we realize that mind must indeed be part of the very fabric of reality if we are to explain our very existence as human beings. We are here. We have minds – or, to be accurate, we are mind. What we call matter and mind are two aspects of the same thing, the outside and inside of matter, respectively. We are part of nature.

Ergo: mind is part and parcel of the unbroken fabric of reality and is literally ubiquitous. To ignore these facts is to misunderstand nature and ourselves.

Chapter 2
Absent-Minded Science, Part II:

The Zombie Defense

Here's a head-scratcher for you: Can zombies argue that they don't exist? Empirical evidence suggests they can. Or does it?

The philosophy of mind is a thriving field in recent decades, with new books and articles appearing with increasing frequency. This article is the second in a series on the role of mind in the universe and, thus, in science.

Strangely, modern science is dominated by the idea that to be scientific means to remove consciousness from our explanations, in order to be "objective." This was, of course, the rationale behind behaviorism, a now-dead theory of psychology that took this trend to a perverse extreme. Behaviorists like John B. Watson and B.F. Skinner scrupulously avoided any discussion of what their subjects thought, intended or wanted and focused, instead, entirely on behavior. They thought that because thoughts in other peoples' heads, or in animals, are impossible to know with certainty, we should simply ignore them in our theories. We can only be truly scientific, they asserted, if we focus solely on what can be directly observed and measured: behavior.

This point of view is known most generally as "positivism," which asserts that only those things we can measure directly should be part of our theories in science. Positivism has held sway in various branches of science to varying degrees over the last couple of centuries. Einstein was in his early career strongly inspired by Ernst Mach's version of positivism, creating his special theory of relativity in 1905 partly as a response to this philosophy (and thus expelling the luminiferous ether from physics as "superfluous"). But Einstein learned better, rejecting positivism by the middle of his career as inadequate. A great passage from Walter Isaacson's biography of Einstein is very telling:

"We cannot observe electron orbits inside the atom," Heisenberg said [to Einstein]. "A good theory must be based on directly observable magnitudes."

"But you don't seriously believe," Einstein protested, "that none but observable magnitudes must go into a physical theory?"

"Isn't that precisely what you have done with relativity?" Heisenberg asked with some surprise.

"Possibly I did use this kind of reasoning," Einstein admitted, "but it is nonsense all the same."

In other words, Einstein's approach had evolved.

Einstein had a similar conversation with his friend in Prague, Philipp Frank. "A new fashion has arisen in physics," Einstein complained, which declares that certain things cannot be observed and therefore should not be ascribed reality.

"But the fashion you speak of," Frank protested, "was invented by you in 1905!"

Replied Einstein: "A good joke should not be repeated too often."

21st Century scientists and philosophers are steadily beginning to realize that Einstein was right in this regard and most physicists have generally abandoned a strong positivist stance. But modern science still suffers in many ways from its own version of cognitive dissonance by maintaining what is essentially a behaviorist/positivist stance in, of all places, the philosophy of mind - and in biology, the focus of my next installment in this series.

Erwin Schrödinger, one of the key architects of quantum mechanics in the early part of the 20th Century, labeled this approach in 1954 the "principle of objectivation" and expressed it clearly:

> By [the principle of objectivation] I mean ... a certain simplification which we adopt in order to master the infinitely intricate problem of nature. Without being aware of it and without being rigorously systematic about it, we exclude the Subject of Cognizance from the domain of nature that we endeavor to understand. We step with our own person back into the part of an onlooker who does not belong to the world, which by this very procedure becomes an objective world.

Schrödinger did, however, identify both the problem and the solution. He recognized that "objectivation" is just a simplification that is a temporary step in the progress of science in understanding the natural world. We are now at the point where we must abandon, where appropriate, the principle of objectivation – and so gain a more complete understanding of reality, and thus ourselves.

Now back to the zombies... In defending positivism and a radical materialist view of consciousness, some writers have argued that consciousness is an illusion, a view described as "eliminativism" because it attempts to resolve the problem of explaining consciousness by arguing that it doesn't really exist. Once we have explained what brains do, under this view, we have said all there is to say about consciousness. So "mind" and subjectivity reduces to what the brain does, which is just matter and energy in motion. Daniel Dennett, W.V.O. Quine, Douglas Hofstadter and Susan Blackmore all arguably fall into this camp. These writers argue, accordingly, that they themselves, as subjective beings, don't exist. Let's call this the "zombie defense."

A zombie, in the philosophy of mind, is a person who looks and acts exactly the same as a real person. But the zombie lacks any inner life, any consciousness. Eliminativists, who argue that mind can be explained entirely as electrochemical signals in the brain, are arguing, effectively, that they are themselves zombies, and so is everyone else.

Now, my description here isn't entirely fair, because no philosopher has, to my knowledge, argued literally that she is a zombie. But arguing that consciousness itself is an illusion amounts to the same thing. Words are important, obviously, so this strange state of affairs should prompt us to re-examine our terms – and more closely examine the writings of the eliminativists.

Dennett is the most well-known of these philosophers and he has argued that once we explain the processes of consciousness there is nothing left to explain. But he also states in a key 1988 article: "I don't deny the reality of conscious experience." So Dennett's position is arguably contradictory. The better interpretation is, however, that Dennett's key argument is primarily directed against any type of Cartesian dualism, under which there is a special substance that we can call mind, spirit or soul that is distinct from matter. We find, in examining the works of Dennett, Blackmore, etc., that the most reasonable reading of their work is not: a) consciousness itself is an illusion (even though they may actually state this or something like this), but, rather: b) the "self," as some kind of permanent or semi-permanent entity or "soul" is an illusion.

The tension in Dennett's position is that by acknowledging (necessarily, it would seem) the reality of conscious experience, Dennett can't also argue that purely externalist objective explanations of consciousness say all that can be said about conscious experience. Rather, if conscious experience is real, it is surely different than simply describing – in as much detail as one likes – the electrochemical processes of a human brain. No matter how much detail we provide about electrochemical processes, such descriptions will never say anything at all about the quality of the subjective experience. This is the whole point of accepting an epistemological dualism between the "inside" and "outside" of things – which Dennett say he does accept.

Materialism, under this line of reasoning, reduces to what I label "crypto-panpsychism." This is the case because if we accept that subjectivity is the most real thing we know, and that it springs from matter, then we have the view that all matter has some degree of mind or subjectivity – panpsychism under a different name. To be even more geeky, we can give this position a more complete label of "panpsychist materialism," and this is what philosopher David Ray Griffin has done in his excellent book *Unsnarling the World-Knot* (though he uses the similar phrase "panexperiential physicalism").

To sum up, by ignoring mind in nature we ignore the only way we know the world – because the "world" is, for each of us, wholly a creation of our own mind, based on the imperfect sense data we receive from the objective world – but we also ignore the more complete science made possible by accepting mind as present in all of nature. Human minds are, then, a natural product of the evolution of mind and matter, which are just two aspects of the same thing. Human minds represent the most complex form of mind in this corner of our universe. We are, then, special in the complexity of our minds, but we are not distinct in a qualitative sense from the rest of nature, and the infinite number of far less complex minds that constitute nature – the world all around us.

In the last analysis, Teilhard de Chardin, another panpsychist, had it right and, as always, expressed the thought beautifully in his 1959 book, *The Phenomenon of Man*: "To decipher man is essentially to try to find out how the world was made and how it ought to go on making itself."

Chapter 3
Absent-Minded Science, Part III:

On Solidity

For those of us who are contemplative, there is a tendency when encountering a philosophical system that is initially appealing to become overly excited. It is *the* system, *the* approach to explaining all of *this* (arms out-stretched), which we have been looking for and failed to find for so many years.

This happened to me a few years ago when I first encountered Alfred North Whitehead's ideas. I've read widely in philosophy for two decades now, but it was only when I was sufficiently inspired to write down my own ideas, my own theory of *this*, that I got serious about examining other serious theories. Whitehead was a British mathematician, logician, physicist and philosopher. He spent the last decade or so of his academic life at the Harvard philosophy department and became, ironically, a key part of the American 20th Century philosophic tradition, along with William James, Charles Peirce, Josiah Royce, etc. Before then, he spent many years at Cambridge University in England, where he famously collaborated with Bertrand Russell on the three-volume *Principia Mathematica*, a *tour de force* that attempted to reduce all of mathematics to simple logic. It failed, ultimately, but that's a different story.

Whitehead is best-known today for what is known as "process philosophy," also known as the "philosophy of organism." The basic idea of process philosophy, as with all Buddhist schools of thought, is that all of *this* is impermanent, flux, constant change – process. Whitehead wrote a number of books in the last phase of his career that fleshed out his incredibly rich philosophy. None is more rich – or more difficult – than his *Process and Reality*, which first appeared in 1929. This book presents Whitehead's theory of everything and situates it within the Western tradition of John Locke, Spinoza, Kant, Hegel, Schopenhauer, Hume, and others.

Whitehead's system is compelling for a number of reasons, not least of which are its adequacy to the facts of human experience, its logical consistency, and the pedigree of its creator (I don't find this last criterion necessarily compelling, but a lot of people do put stock in it, so I list it here). It's hard to find someone more qualified than Whitehead to create a comprehensive philosophical system, due to his background in mathematics, logic and physics at the highest levels of academia.

After digging into *Process and Reality* and related works, I became a little infatuated with Whitehead and his intellectual successors David Ray Griffin (author of the incredibly good *Unsnarling the World-Knot*, which was my first serious introduction to Whitehead's ideas and I highly recommend this book as the starting point for those interested in learning Whitehead), John Cobb, Jr., Charles Hartshorne, etc. Here's why.

Perhaps the primary purpose of philosophy is to explain the objective world and how we fit into it. When we look around us, feel around us, sense around us, in the most general sense, we detect solidity. The chair I'm in right now stops me from falling to the ground because of its solidity. The ground more generally stops me, and you, from falling through the Earth because of its solidity. The stars in the heavens are detectable to our telescopes because of their presumed solidity. And the microbes and electrons we see in our microscopes are detectable because of their solidity. So what is this solidity?

Physics is of course the science of solidity and "matter" is what we generally call most of the stuff that collectively comprises solidity. Most non-physicists – and perhaps many physicists also – presume that modern physics has in fact pinned down solidity. But it hasn't. Physics still has no idea what matter really is. Many theories abound and most physicists, when pressed to really drill down deep, would suggest that matter is comprised of fields, which are themselves comprised of energy, or vice versa. Quantum field theory is one of the crown jewels in modern physics, which successfully combined quantum mechanics with special relativity. (See Max Jammer's excellent book, *Concepts of Matter*).

The far more difficult task of reconciling general relativity (the prevailing theory of gravity, space and time) with quantum mechanics (the prevailing theory of matter) has yet to be achieved. String theory is the most well-known reconciliation attempt and this theory, or actually "set of theories" because there are a huge number of related theories, suggests that all matter/energy/fields are really tiny strings vibrating in many dimensions. There are many problems, however, with string theory, as described by Lee Smolin in his 2006 book, *The Trouble With Physics*.

My point here is not, however, to survey all the candidates for a "general unified theory." Rather, my point is to highlight that we really don't know – still – what the heck matter is.

But there is a solution. The solution is more philosophical than physical, even though there's really not a separation between these two endeavors because philosophy's role is to truly generalize science. And we don't need to get hung up on the terms – matter, energy, fields, strings, etc. – to get to the solution.

For example, if we consider energy to be the most fundamental reality behind the apparent solidity of matter, it becomes very difficult to define what energy "really" is. Ultimately, this discussion becomes just a word game. We can define energy by using yet more words. But what we're trying to do is to explain the apparent solidity around us, the apparent solidity that our senses present to us. We can label the apparent solidity around us "matter," as is the usual convention. Or we can label it "condensed energy," or we can use both terms. Or we can describe it as "really" tiny vibrating strings, when we look all the way down. We could even label the "true" reality behind our senses "Ideas," as Plato did and many Idealist philosophers since Plato have done. What really matters, however, is not the terminology but the conceptual placeholder. What are we trying to explain? In this case we're trying to explain the apparent solidity of the objective world.

Philosophers like Alfred North Whitehead and Arthur Koestler, the Hungarian polymath, have realized this difficulty and have opted to use more general terms that will remain accurate and useful no matter what terms our current physical theories prefer. For Whitehead, the ultimate constituents of reality are "actual entities." An actual entity is just another name, but it's very different than traditional views of "matter" or "energy." An actual entity is a general description for an event. An event is a happening, a process, a becoming, from the very smallest happening, like a photon or electron, to the largest, like the universe as a whole. So the actual entity is very different than the traditional notions of matter or energy. An actual entity never exists outside of time. It's a process, not a thing. Time – duration – is built into the definition.

Whitehead's "actual entity" is thus a more complete description of fundamental reality because it necessarily implies that no physical thing exists outside of time. All actual things, to be actual, which means they are perceivable or "physical," must exist in time. We can conceptually freeze objects. We can image an arrow frozen in mid-flight, hanging in space. But this is just a reflection of our imaginations, not a reflection of reality. Similarly, modern physics often imagines that the ultimate constituents of matter could in actuality be frozen in place and given a name, independent of time. Physics takes the approach of asking the universe to "just please hold still for a second so that we can study you." But it never does. The universe is always in motion, always becoming. Time is always proceeding forward. It is, then, a mistake to conceptually separate matter from time and to believe that this conceptual separation is indicative of reality.

Arthur Koestler coined another term that is perhaps even more general than Whitehead's actual entities. Koestler described a "holon" as a universal unit of organization that is both a part and a whole. Koestler writes:

> A part, as we generally use the word, means something fragmentary and incomplete, which by itself would have no legitimate existence. On the other hand, there is a tendency among holists to use the word 'whole' or 'Gestalt' as something complete in itself which needs no further explanation. But wholes and parts in this absolute sense do not exist anywhere, either in the domain of living organisms or of social organizations. What we find are intermediary structures on a series of levels in ascending order of complexity, each of which has two faces looking in opposite directions: the face turned toward the lower levels is that of an autonomous whole, the one turned upward that of a dependent part.

Koestler's holon is a very useful explanatory concept that can be used to describe any level of reality. It can also be used outside of physics to describe social organization or biological structures.

Holons and actual entities are, then, the most general of terms to explain the apparent solidity around us. A highly important corollary to these terms is that all actual entities and all (physical) holons have an accompanying experience, that is, at least a rudimentary consciousness or mind. This is, then, much more than a re-labeling of "matter." Holons and actual entities do a far better job of explaining the solidity around us because they also explain our relationship, as conscious beings, to that solidity.

Each actual entity is, according to Whitehead, a "drop of experience." If all things are actual entities, then all things have experience. Ergo: experience goes all the way down. And up. This is where we return to the theme of this series of articles: absent-minded science. Today's prevailing physical theories have such a hard time explaining consciousness because they subscribe to a view of matter that from the outset *excludes* mind.

Whitehead, Koestler, Griffin and other panpsychists realized that our explanations of solidity had to be revised in order to adequately explain our place in that solidity, the universe around us. These philosophers have some good company. David Bohm, a highly influential American physicist, wrote in 1987: "Even the electron is informed with a certain level of mind." Similarly, Freeman Dyson, another American physicist, wrote: "[T]he processes of human consciousness differ only in degree but not in kind from the processes of choice between quantum states which we call 'chance' when made by electrons."

Now, back to my opening theme. I'm still enamored of Whitehead because his ideas are, as mentioned, logically coherent, empirically adequate, and come from such a respected intellect. But I've realized since my initial infatuation that Whitehead is one in a long line of comprehensive thinkers that includes Heraclitus, Aristotle, Plato, Plotinus, Spinoza, Leibniz, Kant, Schopenhauer, Locke, Russell, James, Royce, etc., all the way to the modern era with such key figures as Ken Wilber, David Ray Griffin, Galen Strawson, David Chalmers, Christof Koch, etc. But I've also realized that thinkers who I at first dismissed as silly, such as the idealists Berkeley, Hegel, Schelling, etc., were actually arriving at many of the same truths. They generally just use different language. Obviously, there are many important differences, but there are many commonalities when we look past the disparate terminology.

The terms don't matter as much as what these terms point to. Whether we call our philosophy "idealism" or "materialism" or "panpsychism," we are trying to explain the same thing: reality, *this*. Some approaches are better than others, but our criteria are themselves necessarily subjective. I have highlighted empirical adequacy, logical consistency, and intellectual pedigree here. But other criteria could be used and different conclusions reached.

I'm still highly partial to Whitehead and his co-thinkers because I see process philosophy as the most sophisticated philosophical system around, but my love has been extended to other great thinkers and my understanding is better off for it.

Chapter 4

Absent-Minded Science, Part IV:

The "C word" and Emergence

At a talk I attended at UC Santa Barbara in 2011, Professor Marcus Raichle, one of the pioneers of brain imaging, jokingly referred to consciousness as the "C word." His little joke highlighted the fact that for many working neuroscientists and others who think about the brain, trying to explain what consciousness actually is – as opposed to explaining the various functions of brains – is still a bit frowned upon.

It also seems that many neuroscientists who do think about the "hard problem" of consciousness – the mind/body problem by a different name – believe that once we explain the functions of brains there's really not much, if anything, left to explain about consciousness itself.

I find in my discussions on consciousness that arguments about "emergence," well, *emerge* as a response from critics time and time again. Consciousness is, in this view, simply an emergent property of complex biological structures like brains.

I've long been a defender of the alternative panpsychist view of consciousness. The type of panpsychism I find compelling, as mentioned in my last essay, is that developed into a comprehensive system by Alfred North Whitehead, Henri Bergson, Charles Hartshorne, David Ray Griffin and many others during the 20th Century. Panpsychist theories are growing in popularity, but still a minority view.

The basic idea is that all components of the universe have at least some rudimentary type of consciousness or experience, which are just different words for subjectivity or awareness. The key question for panpsychist theories of consciousness is why some aggregations of matter contain unitary subjects and others don't (saying "unitary subject" is actually redundant but I want to be entirely clear).

For example, no modern panpsychist that I know of argues that a chair or a rock is conscious – despite the bad jokes often lobbed at panpsychists. Rather, the molecules that *comprise* the chair or rock presumably have a very rudimentary type of consciousness but the larger objects themselves (again, presumably) lack the kind of interconnections required to become unitary subjects.

The subjects we know best are humans – each of us, in fact, knows exactly one subject intimately: ourselves. Clearly, then, some aggregates of matter do in fact produce a complex unitary subject and we call this our "mind."

The "hard problem" of consciousness is figuring out the relationship between mind and matter and why some matter gives rise to unitary subjects and why others don't? Why am I conscious, and you, and my cat, but not the chair or the rock?

We have literally no certainty as to what objects in the universe, other than ourselves, are also subjects because we can only know our own self as a subject. We must, then, use reasonable inference to determine what other objects in the universe are also subjects.

And it is through reasonable inference that we can conclude that panpsychism is a better solution to the hard problem than its competitors. This is a strong statement, to be sure, but I have presented numerous lines of reasoning to support this assertion in previous essays and present some additional lines below.

Does Mind Emerge?

The prevailing position with respect to the hard problem seems to be some type of "emergence" theory. The basic idea is that mind simply emerges from matter in certain complex forms, just like wetness or solidity or color emerge from matter in certain situations. Jeffrey Goldstein provides a concise and clear definition of emergence in a 1999 paper: "the arising of novel and coherent structures, patterns, and properties during the process of self-organization in complex systems." (In Corning, Peter A. (2002), "The Re-Emergence of "Emergence": A Venerable Concept in Search of a Theory", *Complexity* 7 (6): 18–30.) There are many other definitions, of course, but this one is good for present purposes.

So, is mind like wetness or other emergent physical properties? To my mind (pardon the pun), the answer is a resounding "no."

There is a crucial difference. Let's take liquidity. Liquidity is indeed a new feature of molecules that isn't present until the right conditions are present. Hydrogen and oxygen molecules aren't themselves liquid at room temperature. And yet the liquidity of water is entirely explicable by looking at how these molecules interact with each other. There is really no mystery (well, surely some, but not much) in how these molecules combine to form dipolar molecules that attract each other more loosely than in a solid but less loosely than in the constituent gases. In other words, liquidity is pretty predictable, or at least explicable, when we consider the constituents of any given liquid. We're dealing with "outsides" at every step in this process – first the outsides of the individual molecules and then the outsides of the combination of molecules in the liquid.

We can strengthen the point further by considering the fact that both hydrogen and oxygen become liquids of their own if we cool them enough. Liquid hydrogen "emerges" from gaseous hydrogen at -423 degrees Fahrenheit. Liquid oxygen emerges from gaseous oxygen at the comparatively balmy temperature of -297 degrees. Liquidity thus emerges at different temperatures as a relatively straightforward shift in the types of bonds between the constituent molecules.

Consciousness is entirely different because we are not talking about relational properties of the outsides of various substances. We are talking about insides, experience, consciousness, phenomena, qualia, and all the other terms we can use for mind or subjectivity. And when we define our physical constituents as wholly lacking in mind, then it is literally impossible for mind to "emerge" from this wholly mindless substrate. Emergence of mind from no-mind is what Strawson calls "radical emergence," and he makes basically the same argument that I've made here as to its impossibility, in "Realistic Monism" and *Consciousness and Its Place In Nature*.

It is "radical" because the emergence of insides from what previously consisted only of outsides would be the spontaneous creation of an entirely new category of reality. And it is philosophically profligate to suggest that this kind of thing can happen when there are other more plausible alternatives.

Now, maybe impossibility is too strong a word. At this level of abstraction we can't prove anything (can anything be proved, period?). I can't prove that it is impossible for mind to emerge from matter where it was wholly absent before. So perhaps a better word would be "implausible." It is highly implausible, then, that the inside of matter (mind, consciousness) would suddenly emerge at some arbitrary midpoint in the history of the universe. Sewall Wright, a well-known American evolutionary biologist, stated it well in a 1977 article: "[E]mergence of mind from no mind is sheer magic." (Wright, S. (1977) Panpsychism and Science, in Cobb, J.B. & Griffin, D.R. (eds.), *Mind in Nature: Essays on the Interface of Science and Philosophy*, Lanham, MD: University Press of America.)

Colin McGinn, a British philosopher, states perhaps even more forcefully why emergentism fails:

[W]e do not know how consciousness might have arisen by natural processes from antecedently existing material things. Somehow or other sentience sprang from pulpy matter, giving matter an inner aspect, but we have no idea how this leap was propelled. . . . One is tempted, however reluctantly, to turn to divine assistance: for only a kind of miracle could produce this from that. It would take a supernatural magician to extract consciousness from matter. Consciousness appears to introduce a sharp break in the natural order -- a point at which scientific naturalism runs out of steam.

(McGinn, C. (1991) *The Problem of Consciousness: Essays Toward a Resolution*, Malden, MA: Blackwell, p. 45.)

In light of these arguments, isn't it far more plausible that mind is simply present where matter is present instead of emerging for the first time at a seemingly arbitrary midpoint in the history of our universe?

This is the panpsychist position: Where there is matter there is also mind – they are two aspects of the same thing. As matter complexifies, so mind complexifies. (The details become far more complex than this, but this is the basic position).

Alan Watts said it best: "For every inside there is an outside, and for every outside there is an inside; though they are different, they go together."

It seems, then, that today's prevailing theory that advocates mind as a purely emergent phenomenon has major problems. But what about those thinkers who come at the hard problem from a less dogmatic or materialistic position?

Ken Wilber, an increasingly well-known American philosopher and social critic who is no materialist, to be sure, argues in his monumental 1995 work *Sex, Ecology, Spirituality: The Spirit of Evolution* that mind is in fact a case of "novel emergence." Wilber elaborates in great detail Arthur Koestler's original idea that all of reality is comprised of holons, which are part/wholes. Holons are parts when they look upward in whatever hierarchy they belong to and are wholes when they look downward. Wilber at times argues for what seems to be panpsychism, and he clearly has strong sympathies with this position.

Yet he also argues for the emergence of mind and the nöosphere more generally. He suggests (p. 100 of *Sex, Ecology, Spirituality*) that mind and the nöosphere arise through "novel emergence." And in footnote 13 (p. 540), he explicitly criticizes the panpsychist position that even the most fundamental constituents of reality have some type of mind, writing: "Do atoms possess an actual prehension (Whitehead) or perception (Leibniz)? I don't know; that seems a bit much."

It seems, then, that Wilber is not entirely of one mind on this issue. We can argue, however, for the same reasons presented above that it is implausible to suggest that mind is a case of "novel emergence." Surely if all of reality is comprised of holons, as Wilber assiduously argues, and all holons have an outside and an inside, then this "inside" must entail some degree of mind. If it isn't mind, then what is it?

In footnote 13, Wilber states that the inside should be described as "depth" rather than mind per se. But this isn't much help. Framing inside as depth seems like an empty well unless we agree that depth is synonymous with mentality. And in other parts of SES, Wilber does suggest exactly this (footnote 25, p. 548, for example): "Forms of consciousness do indeed emerge (as forms of matter do), but consciousness itself is simply alongside all along, as the interior of whatever form is there (from the moment of creation)."

Plausibility Versus Possibility

In closing, I want to reiterate that there can be no certainty in this discussion. If we are intellectually honest, the best we can say is "position x seems better than position y because of a, b, c reasons." And this is the nature of philosophy more generally – and of science, for that matter, even if this truth is not widely acknowledged.

Yet, for the many reasons I've set forth in this series of essays, it does indeed seem that the panpsychist position is better at explaining the hard problem of consciousness than the various types of emergence arguments. And "better" in this case simply means "more plausible."

This means that for people like me who enjoy the exchange of ideas, the C word will be the subject of much spirited debate for many years to come.

Chapter 5

Absent-Minded Science, Part V:

Sex, Psyche and Evolution

The sight of a feather in a peacock's tail, whenever I gaze at it, makes me sick!

Charles Darwin in a letter to Asa Grey

Most people now realize that sexual attraction is in the mind, even though we often forget this insight in practice. The growth of phone sex and online sex is testament to the ability of imagination to titillate as much or more than actual human contact. And the presence of pornography in all cultures throughout history is an ongoing reminder that people can be turned on by the strangest things and certainly don't need a live human being for this purpose.

There is a much deeper principle at work here, however; one that is highly relevant to this series of essays on "absent-minded science" (which is what I call the modern habit in a number of different fields of expelling mind from legitimate scientific explanations). Sex is central to human existence and other animals. But its centrality extends far beyond the animal world. This is the key theme of this fifth installment of this series.

Why is sex so central to our lives? The facile answer is that it's because we need sex to reproduce. But this is only partly true. Many species reproduce without sex, including some complex vertebrates like lizards and fish. So why do we have sex? No one really knows the answer to this question, but there are many theories. I won't delve much into why our species reproduces sexually; rather, I'm going to delve into what sex is, as a general principle, and the role of sex in evolution.

Natural selection is the key agent in Darwinian evolution. Natural selection is the label we give to the idea that traits that confer some survival advantage will obviously spread. But Darwin didn't stop there. His second major book focused in part on sexual selection, another agent of evolution. "Sexual selection" is the bridge between Darwin and Lamarck and sexual selection is Lamarckian through and through. This is not generally acknowledged by today's biologists and it may in fact be a novel interpretation. (Darwin was a Lamarckian in many ways, but this is not commonly known).

Sexual selection is the term Darwin gave to the idea that certain traits appear to be detrimental to survival and/or foraging for food – such as the peacock's tail. However, if such traits help an organism find more mates and have more offspring the trait may still spread because its reproductive benefits outweigh its survival disadvantages. Mate choice, primarily female choice because males are generally the aggressors in most sexually-reproducing species, is key to sexual selection.

Natural selection is supposed to be a general theory of evolution, which means that it should be applicable in all times and all places and tell us something about how and why populations and species evolve.

To be a general theory of evolution, however, it seems that a theory must possess at least the following features: 1) applicability in all times and places; 2) capability to make predictions that are testable; 3) falsifiability, which means that if predictions are tested and found to be false then the theory as a whole may eventually be rejected under the weight of sufficient counter-evidence.

Sexual selection is arguably a more general theory than natural selection. Historically, these two selective forces have sometimes been presented by biologists as parallel forces, but with natural selection as by far the more important force. In recent decades, sexual selection is generally framed as part of the broader process of natural selection. In reality, of course, there is no "force" behind natural selection. It's just physics and chemistry in action, so when we talk about natural selection as a force or an agent, it's reification of a sort at work. Rather than being an actual force, natural selection is just a label for the collective forces of nature acting on organisms.

Sexual selection is different, however, because there really is supposed to be a selective agent (a force of a sort) at work, which may not be explained wholly through physical and chemical forces – if these forces ignore mind in nature. This goes back to Parts I through IV of this series of essays, however, because contemplating these ideas requires that we consider whether mind (and thus choices made by minds) can in fact be explained through current physical and chemical theories.

I argued earlier in this series of essays that current physical theories cannot, in principle, explain mind because the constituents of matter are defined by modern physics as wholly mindless. We are thus left with a system of physics that excludes that which is most real to each of us – ourselves, our own minds, subjectivity itself – which surely should be included in an adequate theory of physics and, by extension, biology. I argued that this impasse requires the inclusion of mind, in a highly rudimentary form, in all forms of matter, a view known as panpsychism or panexperientialism.

Panpsychism holds that as matter complexifies, the tiny bit of mind in each tiny piece of matter complexifies and eventually reaches our highly complex type of mind due to the highly complex matter that comprises our brains and bodies.

This raises the question: how did we, and other life forms like us, reach such a high level of complexity? How did we evolve? This is where evolutionary biology and the philosophy of mind intersect.

If we acknowledge that all matter has some degree of mind, no matter how small, we realize that choice must be inherent in all matter. This is the case because the essence of mind is the selection (choice) between alternatives made available through perception. One of today's preeminent physicists, Freeman Dyson (Professor Emeritus at Princeton's Institute for Advanced Study, the same institution where Einstein resided for a number of years before his death in 1955) makes this point explicit: "[T]he processes of human consciousness differ only in degree but not in kind from the processes of choice between quantum states which we call 'chance' when made by electrons."

Dyson is saying that what physicists normally interpret in electron behavior as pure chance – randomness – is better interpreted as choice. Choices can be fickle, so what seems to be random is in fact a result of unpredictable choices by these tiny entities. Thus, even electrons make choices – but very very simple choices compared to the infinity of choices possible to our advanced human consciousness. Choice at the level of the electron is apparently limited to how the electron will manifest and move in the next moment. Particles such as electrons are not static, timeless entities. Thinking of the fundamental constituents of reality as unchanging particles is the fallacy of "substantialism," which Whitehead's panpsychist "process philosophy," attempts to correct.

If a type of rudimentary choice is inherent even at the level of electrons, a universal principle of evolution is made apparent. I call this universal principle "generalized sexual selection." The essence of sexual selection is choice – generally female choice, as Darwin described in his 1871 book, The Descent of Man. Darwin recognized that many traits, such as the peacock's tail, could not be explained strictly through natural selection. Rather, Darwin argued that female choice resulted over many generations in pronounced features in males who compete vigorously for female attention.

To be entirely clear, the peacock's tail is not considered adaptive because its weight and size make it harder for male peacocks to escape predators and to forage for food. But if its disadvantages are outweighed by increased mating opportunities for the male who carries the showy burden, it will continue as a trait in male peacocks.

Darwin's division of natural selection and sexual selection into two distinct agents of evolution may not be warranted when we think through the better interpretation of what's really going on.

The simple structure of neo-Darwinian natural selection has just two parts: 1) random variation of traits results from random mutation of genes and through sexual recombination; 2) those traits that confer a survival and reproductive advantage will obviously increase and are thus "selected." (Again, there is not really any "selection" going on, but the end result is "as if" there was some selection process).

What I call "generalized sexual selection" (GSS or "giss"), re-frames this argument as follows: 1) variation in traits comes about through random mutation and through male competition for mating opportunities and striving more generally for self-improvement, which can sometimes be incorporated into the germ line of the male; 2) female choice is the selective agent that leads to greater reproduction of those males with the most desirable traits to the females who choose them, who incorporate the male germ line into their own by mating with them. In other words, variation is not always random – it is sometimes directed, with increasing mating opportunities as a significant motivation, and the urge to survive and other urges surely at work also. Perhaps more importantly, selection is not blind, it is conscious at every level of nature through the choices made mostly by females.

I call this theory "generalized sexual selection" because it applies to situations that don't involve sex in the traditional sense. Most species on our planet don't reproduce sexually. Bacteria, for example, often reproduce asexually, as do protists. And even many vertebrates reproduce asexually, such as certain species of lizards and fish. However, bacteria are constantly exchanging genetic information, which is a rudimentary kind of sex, defined at this level as the mixing of genetic information from at least two entities. This type of sex is known as "horizontal gene transfer" because it occurs without simultaneous reproduction.

But here's why GSS applies beyond traditional sexual reproduction. The terms "male" and "female" are not as clear-cut as we generally assume. And in GSS, "male" refers to any genetic donor and "female" to any genetic recipient – as Lynn Margulis and Dorion Sagan describe in their 1986 book, *The Origins of Sex*. Thus, a bacterium that gives some genetic material to another is a male and the recipient is a female. These roles can and do change on a regular basis, thus the "gender" of each bacterium changes regularly. What is important, then, is not gender, per se, but actions.

The principle extends even deeper, however, when we consider further the panpsychist notion of matter. If all matter has some degree of mind or subjectivity, then GSS applies to literally all matter, not just biological forms. This is the case because the most sophisticated panpsychist thinking, that of Alfred North Whitehead and his intellectual descendants, recognizes that each of the ultimate constituents of matter – what Whitehead calls "actual entities" – contains both "mental" and "physical" aspects. They are two sides of the same coin. Physical and mental aspects of each actual entity (the Whiteheadian "atom") oscillate with each step forward in time.

The mental aspect of each actual entity is informed by the immediately prior physical aspects of all other actual entities available to it. Each actual entity, in its mental aspect, chooses what information to accept and rejects everything else. Thus, the mental aspect of each actual entity can be considered to be "female" insofar as it chooses what information from the universe around it to include in its objective manifestation – like the female bower bird accepting the attention of a hard-working showy male. When the actual entity becomes objective, it becomes "male" insofar as its manifestation now constitutes information for the next round of actual entities to consider in their mental/female aspect. More crudely put, the female aspect receives and the male aspect penetrates. But these aspects oscillate within each actual entity.

Wipe your brow as I wrap up this essay.

GSS is a potentially powerful re-framing of evolution in a way that recognizes the unbroken continuum of the complexity of matter, which should be considered to be experiential through and through. I won't delve into further details about the testability and falsifiability of GSS here, but it is my view that GSS presents a more adequate theory of evolution than the prevailing adaptationist view of natural selection – which generally denies the role of mind and choice in evolution.

Who knew sex was so important?

Chapter 6
Absent-Minded Science, Part VI:

Natural Selection and the Universal Eros

I am conscious that I am in an utterly hopeless muddle. I cannot think that the world, as we see it, is the result of chance; and yet I cannot look at each separate thing as the result of Design.

Charles Darwin, 1860

It has now become more or less respectable to talk of purpose or directedness in ontogeny … but it is still considered heretical to apply the same terms to phylogeny.

Arthur Koestler, 1978

Since the 1970s, there has been a resurgence of critiques against the mainstream Darwinian theory of evolution, which asserts that "natural selection" is the primary agent of evolution. Criticizing Darwin's ideas and the "neo-Darwinian" framework that constitutes the modern theory of evolution is not new. What is new, however, is the fact that we seem to be in the middle of a long-overdue shift in what has become an overly dogmatic "adaptationist" view of evolution, in which all or almost all evolution is thought to occur through natural selection.

This essay continues my extended critique of "absent-minded science," the tendency in modern science to ignore, intentionally or through oversight, the role of mind in nature. I want to be clear up front that I am not a supporter of Intelligent Design or any religiously-motivated critique of natural selection. Rather, I approach these very difficult problems primarily from the point of view of a hard-nosed philosopher and scientist trying to make sense of it all – and finding that many mainstream approaches could be significantly improved.

Charles Darwin is the father of modern biology, completing his world-changing book, *On the Origin of Species*, in 1859, after mulling the issues he wrote about for over 25 years. Darwin's major accomplishment was to present a plausible theory, with oodles of supporting evidence from his observations of pigeons, barnacles, worms and many other creatures, that explained life's complexity and evolution as a result not of divine design but of natural design. That is, design without design, without a conscious agent, supernatural or not. Darwin's theory of evolution was an extended argument that God did not need to be invoked to explain the evolution of life (though Darwin remained agnostic as to whether God needed to be invoked with respect to the origin of life).

Darwin's vision of evolution resulting from various natural forces, independent of a designer, was actually far more pluralist than today's mainstream biologists generally acknowledge. Darwin invoked the use and disuse of organs as a major cause in evolutionary change (mole's eyes have atrophied, for example, because of disuse, as Darwin argued in *Origin*, though this is not generally an accepted explanation today). Darwin also suggested that reproductive competition - sexual selection - was a significant force in evolution, particular in later works. However, Darwin invoked the process of natural selection as the major cause of evolutionary change, which has become the all-encompassing explanatory theme for too many modern biologists. Natural selection is analogous to the artificial selection that Darwin observed in pigeons and other domesticated animals of his day. Rather than a conscious agent (humans) selecting desirable traits, however, nature "selects" traits based on their tendency to result in more offspring. "Selects" is in quotes because the key point of natural selection is that it is akin to conscious selection, but it is not in fact conscious. It happens automatically, without any conscious selection.

Today's mainstream theory of evolution, generally described as the Modern Synthesis or Neo-Darwinism, combines the insights from modern genetics with Darwin's theory of evolution by natural selection. As a consequence, much of modern biology is concerned with molecular change in DNA and RNA, which exist in all cells and guide the production of proteins, which are the building blocks for life, independently of larger questions about natural selection.

Whereas Darwin's vision was "pluralist" because he suggested many agents for evolution, today's mainstream evolutionary theory is generally "adaptationist" in that it invokes natural selection as either the only significant cause of evolution (adaptation) or, at least, its primary agent. ("Genetic drift" and many other agents are also recognized by mainstream biology but the large majority of biologists still stress natural selection as the key agent). Adaptationists see all, or almost all, traits as the result of natural selection acting on the random evolution of different traits.

What does "natural selection" mean?

Now here's the major problem with today's focus on natural selection or adaptationism: natural selection, as a theory, doesn't really do much explaining.

This is a strong claim, to be sure, but it can be demonstrated very clearly. The problem arises from the use of different terms for the same concept. A common way of describing natural selection is "survival of the fittest." This phrase was coined by Herbert Spencer, a British philosopher, but was used by Darwin himself as a synonym for natural selection. Let's look at the content of this phrase and its meaning.

Survival of the fittest means that the fittest organisms survive and thus spread more offspring. This is how natural selection is supposed to work. But we must ask ourselves what these terms mean. What does "the fittest" mean? Well, to be "fit" in this context means that those organisms that manage to survive leave more offspring. But what does "survival" mean? It means the same thing because there is no evolution without reproduction. So it turns out that the phrase "survival of the fittest" really means "survival of those who survive," or "the fittest are the fittest."

"Survival of the fittest" is, then, a tautology that means nothing. It has no explanatory power and no predictive power because it is logically empty. It is akin to saying "evolution happens." While this is obviously true, based on the abundant fossil record showing the development of life on our planet, it does not amount to a theory of how or why evolution happens. And the theory of natural selection purports to be exactly that.

This is not a new critique of natural selection. In fact, Samuel Butler, a well-known critic of Darwin who had an ongoing feud with Darwin while both were alive, made this claim. Many others have made the same argument since, including prominent biologists T.H. Morgan ("For it may be little more than a truism to state that the individuals that are best adapted to survive have a better chance of surviving than those not so well adapted to survive") and C.H.Waddington ("Natural selection turns out on closer inspection to be a tautology, a statement of an inevitable although previously unrecognized relation. It states that the fittest individuals in a population will leave most offspring. Once the statement is made, its truth is apparent."), and prominent philosopher of science Karl Popper (though he later recanted without adequately explaining why).

The response to the tautology claim has varied over the years, with the most common response being silence. But a common response has been something like this: "Even if survival of the fittest is a tautology there are other ways to describe natural selection that aren't tautological." It is very difficult, however, to define natural selection non-tautologically. Here are a few other examples.

Natural selection is often described as "differential reproduction" of those organisms that have more adaptive traits. This just means some organisms leave more offspring than others ("differential"). But what leads to differential reproduction? Survival of the fittest. And I've just shown that this phrase is tautological. We can state as an empirical fact that some organisms have more offspring than others, but we are left with no additional information or insight if we assert something like: "differential reproduction, or survival of the fittest, was responsible for more offspring." This statement is yet another tautology.

Another way of describing natural selection is by discussing "adaptive traits." A trait is adaptive if it leads to more offspring. But this is also tautological because the only way we have to determine what is adaptive is to examine an organism's reproductive success. How else could we know what is adaptive? To say that a trait is adaptive and thus leads to more offspring is to say that a trait that leads to more offspring is a trait that leads to more offspring. We are back to tautology.

What's going on here? As I mentioned above, what's going on is the use of different terms for the same concept. All these terms: survival, fitness, adaptation, differential reproduction, are referring to exactly the same concept: increased offspring. Thus, to say that natural selection is adaptation through survival of the fittest sounds like it means something, but all this phrase really says is that increased offspring are increased offspring are increased offspring. And while saying that "a rose is a rose is a rose" has some poetic meaning, in biology it's not helpful. (All of these statements I've been discussing can be described as A = A, which is surely true but contains no information).

To those readers who think I'm inaccurate or being unfair, let's look at an actual statement by a leading current evolutionary thinker. Francisco Ayala, a well-known biologist at UC Irvine, wrote in the 2008 book, *Back to Darwin*: "Natural selection – i.e. differential multiplication – can accomplish adaptation because a favorable mutation that has occurred in one individual may thus spread to the whole species in a few generations..." Let's parse this sentence. "Natural selection," "differential multiplication," "favorable," "adaptation," "may thus spread," are all ways of saying exactly the same thing: more offspring are produced in some situations. Even more simply, all these phrases say, essentially: there is some biological change occurring. Ayala's sentence says A = A = A = A = A. It is, thus, true but unhelpful as a theory of evolution.

Natural selection is, in the final analysis, better viewed as a postulate and not a theory. It is the postulate that evolution has happened naturally, without supernatural influence. "Natural selection" stands as the counter to the long-held view of "supernatural selection," that is, the various types of creationism or intelligent design. To be a theory of evolution, however, natural selection theory must say something about *how* historical changes occurred and make meaningful predictions about what kind of changes we may see in the future. And natural selection, as it is generally framed, is sorely lacking in this regard.

What are we to do?

Jerry Fodor and Massimo Piatelli-Palmarini present a critique of natural selection in their 2010 book, *What Darwin Got Wrong*. They also argue that natural selection is empty as a theory, though their arguments are a bit different than what I've presented above. They suggest that the solution to this impasse is an acknowledgement that natural selection should be considered, instead, "natural history." And natural history, like all historical writing and thinking, is "just one damned thing after another." There is some truth to this statement and it is, in fact, largely what many evolutionary biologists do today anyway. In other words, rather than looking to a general theory of how evolution occurs – what natural selection claims to be – biologists and others should (and generally do) focus on describing the actual details of how change seems to have occurred with each species, given the species' environment, traits and observed behaviors.

There are other options available, however, including a set of concepts developed by D'Arcy Wentworth Thompson, a 20th Century British biologist, and Stuart Kauffman, a contemporary American biologist, that focus on "order for free" in nature as a whole. So rather than looking to natural selection as the key agent of change in evolution, these thinkers see order arising spontaneously in all sorts of places around us, such as in snowflakes, crystals, and in extremely complex organisms like ourselves and many other creatures, as a compounding of these more basic sources of order.

Another, more controversial, notion is that there is a driving force behind complexity and evolution. This idea has been championed by various biologists, philosophers and theologians over the centuries. French biologist Jean-Baptiste Lamarck was one of the early and most prominent thinkers who suggested that evolution was being pushed by a "force that perpetually tends to make order." This was one of two agents of evolution that Lamarck proposed. The second is more well-known and considered discredited today: the notion that organisms themselves, through intention, use and disuse, can change their bodies and that some of these changes are inherited. As I mentioned in Part V of this series, however, there is an increasing body of evidence that some evolutionary change is Lamarckian (Ted Steele's books have argued for reacceptance of Lamarckian inheritance of acquired traits).

The final concept I'll mention, which is perhaps the best way of framing a comprehensive theory of evolution, was described well by the American philosopher Gerald Heard. Heard wrote in his classic 1939 essay, *Pain, Sex and Time*, that "from the most primitive forms of life up to the completion of man's physique, the one clear coordinating achievement is heightened awareness." Modern biologists know that there is no *necessary* progression from lower complexity and awareness to higher complexity and awareness in each biological lineage. We have many examples of organisms becoming less complex as they evolve. However, it is undeniable that there is a *general trend*, as Heard describes, toward greater complexity and greater awareness (perception). Teilhard de Chardin has gone further and described evolution as "an ascent toward consciousness."

Recognizing that this trend exists we can propose as a working hypothesis that there is a driving agent behind this trend. This driving agent may reduce to the same "order for free" tendency that Thompson and Kauffman focus on. But Heard suggests, and I agree, that there is more going on here than the simple physical and chemical ordering principles that Thompson and Kauffman focus on. Rather, there seems to be a basic force in all things that leads to greater connection, thus greater complexity, and thus greater awareness of our universe around us.

These concepts can be framed in a highly rigorous and empirical way and, in fact, Alfred North Whitehead and his co-thinkers have done exactly this. Whitehead, a British mathematician, physicist and philosopher who ended his long career at Harvard, as professor of philosophy from 1924 to 1937, described in his later works how the *Eros* of the universe was responsible for creativity and evolution. This seems at first blush to be a fuzzy mystical view - and Whitehead was at times a bit of a mystic. But he created a system that was highly rigorous and viewed creativity itself as foundational, even giving it a capital letter as Creativity. *Eros* is a synonym for Creativity and represents the fundamental desire to perceive and to embrace, which is shared by all actual entities in our universe - according to Whitehead. So *Eros* is fundamentally embodied, not disembodied as a mystical principle. This ground's Whitehead's system.

In other words, Whitehead's ideas rest on the notion that all matter, literally, has some degree of consciousness, of awareness. This view is known as panpsychism or panexperientialism and is an increasingly popular solution to the broad inquiry over the last few decades into the nature of consciousness (Parts I through IV of this series discuss panpsychism in some detail).

It turns out that panpsychism offers not only a powerful solution to the question of "what is consciousness?" but also to the question of "how did life arise and evolve?"

The panpsychist solution is to recognize that mind and thus purpose are inherent in all of nature – but extremely rudimentary in most cases. However, as matter complexifies in macromolecules like amino acids (which form spontaneously in many situations), this innate mind and purpose starts to play an increasingly significant role in evolution. It is, thus, a bootstrapping process that has no end in sight.

Margulis and Sagan, two respected but admittedly non-mainstream contemporary biologists, support this view in their highly readable 1995 book, *What is Life?* They appeal to Samuel Butler, an early critic of absent-minded science in biology (p. 232):

> *Butler brought consciousness back in [to biology] by claiming that, together, so much free will, so much behavior becoming habit, so much engagement of matter in the processes of life, had shaped life, over eons producing visible organisms, including the colonies of cells called human. Power and sentience propagate as organisms. Butler's god is imperfect, dispersed. We find Butler's view - which rejects any single, universal architect - appealing. Life is too shoddy a production, both physically and morally, to have been designed by a flawless Master. And yet life is more impressive and less predictable than any 'thing' whose nature can be accounted for solely by 'forces' acting deterministically.*

In evolution, then, God is indeed in the details – literally. The "dispersed" God that Margulis and Sagan refer to is the mind contained in each thing, in each organism, that exercises some degree of choice – no matter how small – in how it manifests.

This leads us back to the Generalized Sexual Selection I described in Part V, which is an elaboration of Darwin's own ideas on sexual selection. In GSS, all things have male and female aspects and choices made primarily by females have played a strong role in the evolution of life on our planet. Perhaps the starring role. When we combine Thompson and Kauffman's "order for free" with the panpsychist Generalized Sexual Selection, we may arrive at a general theory of evolution that provides a broader approach to explaining evolution in all its guises than the theory of natural selection.

Now, there are ways to define natural selection non-tautologically and I have delved into more detail on these issues in my 2011 peer-reviewed article, "The Middle Way of Evolution."

To sum up this series of essays to this point: we cannot adequately explain matter in physics or evolution in biology without re-naturalizing mind. We needn't appeal to an archaic notion of God as omniscient Designer to provide adequate explanations. Rather, we can appeal to the dispersed god of panpsychism, the god manifested in a million million little pushes from each entity making its own choices (though we shall have a role for a non-dispersed God later in this series of essays).

Mind is inextricably part of nature and if we are to explain this undeniable fact we can no longer ignore mind in our scientific explanations.

Chapter 7

Absent-Minded Science, Part VII:

What Is Life?

Science ... is becoming the study of organisms. Biology is the study of the larger organisms; whereas physics is the study of the smaller organisms.

Alfred North Whitehead, Science and the Modern World (1925)

What is life? Is life something that, like obscenity, we "know it when we see it?" This intuitive approach may be good enough for many people, but science seeks definitions in order to get a better handle on the phenomena being studied. The last couple of essays in this series have discussed theories of evolution without stopping to establish what the heck we are talking about in discussing "life."

Unfortunately, every definition of life provided thus far runs into serious problems. "Grasping the nature of life is like catching a whirling eddy in a stream: the moment you have it in your hands it disappears and leaves you with the matter but not the form." Aristotle perhaps said it best: "Nothing is true of that which is changing." In other words, if all is in flux – as all things are – then static definitions of physical phenomena are literally impossible, including life. This is a fundamental limitation that is too rarely acknowledged in modern science and philosophy. We may carve out generally workable definitions, as rules of thumb (heuristics) for deeper study, but we must always acknowledge that any definition regarding physical phenomena that ignores the truth of flux fails from the outset.

Numerous modern biologists have attempted to answer the question: what is life? J.B.S. Haldane, the 20th Century British biologist, a giant in his field, began a short essay – "What is Life"? – by stating, however: "I am not going to answer this question." He recognized the difficulties and stayed away from any definition. There are also three books from the 20th Century alone, with the same title, which do attempt to answer this eons-old question.

Erwin Schrödinger, a paragon of modern physics well-known for his role in shaping quantum theory, described in his little 1935 masterpiece, *What is Life?*, the concept of negative entropy, or negentropy, as the defining characteristic of life. Contrary to the Second Law of Thermodynamics, which asserts that the general tendency in our universe is for order to decay into disorder – entropy – the tendency of life, indeed the very defining characteristic of life, is the opposite. Schrödinger defines life by its ability to create order out of disorder, to defy the trends that inanimate matter must otherwise inexorably follow.

This definition is intriguing, but modern knowledge about the self-organizing characteristics of what is normally considered inanimate matter renders it problematic as a definition of life as something distinct and qualitatively different from non-living matter. When water freezes it transitions from a less ordered state to a more ordered state. This is negentropy. But is water alive? What about crystals more generally, whether of water, silicon or metal? We shall see below that there isn't really any clear separation from what is negentropic and what is not. If life is defined as what is negentropic, then the whole universe is in some manner negentropic because key parts of the universe are negentropic and perhaps, over time, the whole universe will become negentropic. Hold that thought.

The American Ernst Mayr, was another giant of 20th Century biology. He taught at Harvard for decades and, after he had retired, wrote his encyclopedic overview of biology, *The Growth of Biological Thought*, and many other books. He acknowledged the difficulty in defining life: "Attempts have been made again and again to define 'life.' These endeavors are rather futile since it is now clear that there is no special substance, object, or force that can be identified with life."

Mayr couldn't resist however, proposing his own list of criteria to describe the "process of living," as opposed to "life." Mayr's criteria for living processes were:

- complexity and organization

- chemical uniqueness

- quality

- uniqueness and variability

- a genetic program

- a historical nature

- natural selection

- indeterminacy

I won't go into details regarding Mayr's system except to say that Mayr, despite his own cautions, falls right into the same trap as other biologists, with his criteria for living processes, that he warned about in refusing to define "life." First, Mayr's criteria are, collectively, a definition of life – which he said he wasn't going to provide.

Second, all of Mayr's criteria either fall on a continuum or are arbitrary distinctions proposed intuitively and without a deeper foundational principle. Why must life have a genetic program, and what does this even mean? Does the genetic program have to be DNA? Can it be bits of code in a computer? Mayr's writings on these questions reveal his own lack of resolve on this topic. He suggests that computers and software may contain instructions akin to DNA, but then fails to explain why software "DNA" is qualitatively different than non-software DNA. The same can be said with respect to all of his criteria.

A simpler definition of life is offered by British biologists John Dupre and Maureen A. O'Malley. They discuss the three criteria for life that most modern approaches to defining or characterizing life include:

- Reproduction

- Metabolism

- Spatial boundedness

This definition of life gives rise to the possibility that mechanical or electronic creatures may be considered alive, assuming such creatures will eventually be able to reproduce themselves, as they surely will be able to do in coming years. Personally, I am fine with such an inclusive definition, but most biologists it seems are not. If artificial life is truly to be considered life, then what is the principled distinction between life and non-life?

Dupre and O'Malley raise additional problems with these criteria, including the key fact that almost all organisms rely on other organisms for metabolism and reproduction, challenging the notion that we can point to a particular organism and call it "alive" and pretend that it is entirely distinct from its network of symbionts, parasites, etc.

This broader problem with all attempts to answer "what is life?" becomes even more apparent when we consider the variety of "almost alive" parts of our universe. All of these border-line cases, described below, can be described as satisfying the above three-part definition. Yet none of these borderline cases is generally considered, by modern biologists, to be alive, revealing the problematic approach to "life" that is implicit in today's biology and philosophy of biology.

Viruses are the most well-known member of this group of border-line cases. Viruses are responsible for the common cold and for the flu, as well as many other damaging diseases. Viruses are very simple creatures that consist of merely a protein shell and a dab of RNA (some contain DNA), which is a precursor to DNA. Viruses can't reproduce without invading host cells and co-opting their reproductive machinery. A virus will attach itself to a cell wall, penetrate the wall and transfer its RNA into the cell. The RNA melds itself with the cell's DNA, forcing the cell to create more viruses. It's incredibly ingenious when we look at it with fresh eyes. How on Earth did such complex processes evolve in such tiny and apparently non-complex creatures? It's one of many marvels of life as we know it.

Yet many biologists consider viruses not to be alive. Or, to be more accurate, they consider a virus when it is in its dormant state outside of a host cell to be inert non-living matter. This is the case because the virus can't reproduce itself without invading a host cell. Thus it fails the independent reproduction criterion.

This distinction itself quickly becomes manifestly arbitrary, however, when we ponder why the distinction is drawn between a virus outside of a cell and a virus inside a cell. Once the virus is inside the cell, it loses any independent existence because its RNA (or DNA) melds with the DNA of the host cell. If the virus outside of the cell, with its little protein shell and RNA, is not alive, what suddenly becomes alive when it merges with the host cell? Is it now a virus/host combination entity that is alive? Or is the virus to be considered conceptually distinct even when it is attached to a host cell and its RNA injected into the host cell? If so, why? And at what exact point does the virus suddenly become "alive" as it attaches to a cell and injects its RNA?

Self-replicating RNA is a second type of borderline biological agent. Self-replicating RNA consists of only a strand of RNA. As the name suggests, it's different than normal RNA, which occurs inside cells, in that it can reproduce itself without a cell's help. Self-replicating RNA creates whole new strands of RNA as a free-floating agent outside of a cell. Is this life? Why not?

What about prions? Prions are self-replicating molecules responsible for various diseases such as "mad cow disease." Prions are even simpler than viruses and self-replicating RNA. Prions consist of nothing more than a very simple protein enfolded in a certain way. In fact, some definitions of "prion" refer only to the information about enfolding the protein, rather than the actual protein. Prions – a contraction of "protein infection" – infect normal proteins and cause them to fold in a way that is always lethal. In cows, the prion infects the brain and causes normal proteins to fold in such a way that it ruins the normal functioning of infected cells. Prions are like viruses in that they don't seem to have built-in reproductive machinery (and if the prion is simply information that directs the enfolding process it doesn't, by definition, have any "machinery" at all).

Prion reproduction is a simple transfer of information, consisting of the way the infected protein folds, from a prion to a normal protein. The act of transferring this information, however this is done at the microbiological level, is itself the prion's reproductive act. Indeed, it is the only reproduction possible for such a simple form, for what else would reproduction of a prion, a mere way of protein enfolding, consist of? We see, then, that the prion does in fact have its own reproductive machinery built into its very simple structure. Recent research has also found that prions evolve just like DNA-based life. So is a prion alive? If not, why not? It seems to meet the three-part test.

This is the kind of difficulty that arises from any proposed definition of what is necessarily in flux: life or even the "process of life" that Mayr tried to characterize with his criteria. We can solve this problem by suggesting that all things are alive to some degree. Life is simply the flux of increasingly complex forms, which includes all matter in the universe. As matter becomes more complex, it becomes "more alive." An electron is alive, but just a tiny bit. A molecule of oxygen is alive, but just a little bit. A virus outside a cell is alive, but just a tiny bit, and a prion, and so on. Aristotle wrote, two and a half thousand years ago: "Nature proceeds little by little from things lifeless to animal life in such a way that it is impossible to determine the exact line of demarcation, nor on which side thereof an intermediate form should lie." Dupre and O'Malley reach the same conclusion in their paper, proposing a continuum approach to life that stresses collaboration.

If you can't establish where the line of demarcation for "life" lies it makes little sense to posit any line at all. With no line, life becomes a continuum of more or less life in each particular organism. And all things are "organisms" in this conception of life. As we've seen in previous essays, Whitehead conceived of all matter as "drops of experience." A key feature (perhaps the feature) of this rudimentary experience is will, which includes at its most fundamental level the ability to make choices about how to move and how to manifest in each moment, given the tumult of available information from the surrounding universe. Whitehead, Schopenhauer, David Bohm, Freeman Dyson, David Ray Griffin, and others have suggested that all matter, even subatomic particles, has some freedom of choice over how to move and manifest in each moment. Dyson writes, as mentioned previously, that "the processes of human consciousness differ only in degree but not in kind from the processes of choice between quantum states which we call 'chance' when made by electrons."

It is generally only in highly complex collections of matter, such as in biological life (what we generally mean when we talk about life), that we see the obvious manifestations of this ability to make choices. But the choices are also manifest, as Dyson writes, in forms that we would not traditionally consider alive, such as atoms and subatomic particles. They're just not as obvious.

J.B.S. Haldane, who puckishly refused to answer the question of what life is in his 1947 essay, supported the view that there is no clear demarcation line between what is alive and what is not: "We do not find obvious evidence of life or mind in so-called inert matter...; but if the scientific point of view is correct, we shall ultimately find them, at least in rudimentary form, all through the universe."

More recently, University of Colorado astrobiologist Bruce Jakosky, who has worked with NASA in the search for extraterrestrial life, asked rhetorically: "Was there a distinct moment when Earth went from having no life to having life, as if a switch were flipped? The answer is 'probably not.'" Aristotle, Haldane, Dupre, O'Malley and Jakosky are not alone, however, among eminent scientists in holding this view. Bohr, the Danish physicist who made seminal contributions to quantum mechanics, agreed, stating that the "very definitions of life and mechanics ... are ultimately a matter of convenience.... [T]he question of a limitation of physics in biology would lose any meaning if, instead of distinguishing between living organisms and inanimate bodies, we extended the idea of life to all natural phenomena."

This argument shares many obvious similarities with the argument for panpsychism in earlier essays in this series – the idea that all things have some type of experience that becomes more complex as the organization of matter becomes more complex. We see now that "life" and "consciousness" may be viewed as different terms for the same phenomenon. As matter becomes more complex, it becomes more alive and more conscious. These are simply two ways of saying the same thing.

We reach, with this analysis, a smooth synthesis of physics and biology – as Whitehead suggests in the quote at the beginning of this essay. Physics is the science of fundamental physical forms, organisms, which are just a little bit alive. Biology is, then, simply the science of more complex organisms. The practical dividing line between these two fields becomes arbitrary and a matter of convenience. There is no real dividing line at all.

So what is life? We are led in the final analysis to realize that Schrödinger was right in his assertion that the defining characteristic of life is negentropy – a tendency toward order, toward form. Life is the universal process of creating and maintaining new forms, instead of the opposite tendency to destroy form. Entropy, the second law of thermodynamics is, in this view, a postulate that is in the process of being disproven as we realize that life is all-pervasive. This is another way of stating Schrödinger's insights. This view of life as universal is known as hylozoism or panzoism.

Life is simply shorthand for the complexity of matter and mind – which are two aspects of the same entity. That is, each real thing is both matter and mind. We apply the label of "life" as a matter of convenience to more complex forms of matter and mind. But there is no point at which a particular collection of matter suddenly becomes alive. Life does not "emerge." (Life does, however, disappear rather suddenly, from particular organisms, as we are reminded all too often. Death becomes, in this view of life, a matter of different levels of organization: when a given organism dies, its status as a unitary subject, a unitary organism, disappears even as its constituents may keep on living. I will be fleshing out my thoughts on death in later essays.)

This view of life and consciousness as two terms for the same phenomenon provides a unifying framework for physics, biology and the study of consciousness. While the particular tools for studying phenomena within each field as we know it today will surely remain different in practice, having a unifying philosophical framework like that which I've proposed here can be helpful in reaching new insights.

Chapter 8

Absent-Minded Science, Part VIII:

On Logic

Is logic entirely logical? In a word: no.

Logic is the *sine qua non* of Western science and rationality. We are taught from an early age that the scientific method, with its language of mathematics and logic, can solve all empirical problems. Sure, there are some areas that perhaps science will never shed much light upon – the sphere of values and spirit, better left to philosophy and religion (so the prevailing paradigm holds). But in everything else, science is generally perceived to be an all-purpose toolkit that will eventually unlock all of nature's secrets.

If only it were that easy.

Western science is indeed built upon logic, with the ancient Greek philosopher Aristotle's thoughts on the subject still in many ways at the core of today's system. Aristotelian logic starts with the law of non-contradiction. Something can't be true and false at the same time. Something can't be A and not-A at the same time. This seems like good common sense as well as good scientific method. Surely something can't be itself and something else at the same time. Surely something can't be true and false at the same time.

Aristotle's work focused on deductive logic through the syllogism. Syllogisms have two or more premises, which are given, and a conclusion that follows necessarily from the premises. A classic example (forgive the sexist language):

All men are mortal.

All Greeks are men.

Conclusion: All Greeks are mortal.

Yet the work of Bertrand Russell, Alfred North Whitehead (who partnered on the three-volume *Principia Mathematica* in the early part of the 20th Century), Gottlob Frege and Kurt Gödel, among others, has shown that Aristotle didn't get it quite right. Russell and Whitehead, after being flummoxed by a number of mathematical paradoxes, attempted to fix the increasing number of problems by re-framing all of mathematics in terms of logical propositions (attempting to solve German mathematician David Hilbert's second problem, out of a famous list of 23 problems that Hilbert presented to the world in 1900). Figure 1 shows an example of their work from Principia, in which they prove that 1 + 1 = 2. It only took them 379 pages to establish this proposition!

$$*54\cdot43. \quad \vdash:. \alpha, \beta \in 1 . \supset : \alpha \cap \beta = \Lambda . \equiv . \alpha \cup \beta \in 2$$

Dem.

$$\vdash. *54\cdot26. \supset \vdash:. \alpha = \iota`x . \beta = \iota`y . \supset : \alpha \cup \beta \in 2 . \equiv . x \neq y .$$

$$[*51\cdot231] \qquad\qquad\qquad\qquad\qquad \equiv . \iota`x \cap \iota`y = \Lambda .$$

$$[*13\cdot12] \qquad\qquad\qquad\qquad\qquad \equiv . \alpha \cap \beta = \Lambda \qquad (1)$$

$$\vdash. (1) . *11\cdot11\cdot35 . \supset$$

$$\vdash:. (\exists x, y) . \alpha = \iota`x . \beta = \iota`y . \supset : \alpha \cup \beta \in 2 . \equiv . \alpha \cap \beta = \Lambda \qquad (2)$$

$$\vdash. (2) . *11\cdot54 . *52\cdot1 . \supset \vdash . \text{Prop}$$

From this proposition it will follow, when arithmetical addition has been defined, that $1 + 1 = 2$.

Figure 1. *Volume 1, Page 379, of Principia.*

Russell and Whitehead thought they had succeeded in their decade-long effort to place mathematics on an impregnable foundation of logic but Kurt Gödel, the Austrian mathematician, showed in 1931 that their efforts were doomed to failure. In short, Gödel showed that any "formal system" (Russell and Whitehead's work was a type of formal system) will allow logical propositions that are grammatical but cannot be proved within the formal system itself. This is known as Gödel's "Incompleteness Theorem" and is a major problem with the basis for Western science because proof is the basis for mathematical deduction. Mathematics is, in turn, the basis for Western science (at least the physical sciences). Douglas Hofstadter provides excellent discussions of Gödel's theorem in his books, *Gödel, Escher, Bach: An Eternal Golden Braid*, and *I Am a Strange Loop*.

Before Gödel wreaked havoc on mathematicians' dreams of unassailable logic, Russell had described what is essentially the same problem, in different language, which can be described well with a simple metaphor: There is a town in which a single barber shaves everyone who does not shave himself; who shaves the barber? If the barber shaves himself, by the terms of the scenario just described, he doesn't shave himself. And if he doesn't shave himself he does shave himself. Hence the paradox, known as Russell's Paradox.

Framed in Gödel's language, Russell's Paradox states: "This statement cannot be proved." Thus, if the statement (the sentence itself in quotes) can be proved it cannot be proved and if it cannot be proved it can be proved.

An even simpler version of this paradox has been around since Aristotle's time, known as the Liar's Paradox: "This sentence is false." If it is false it is true; if it is true it is false.

Russell tried to solve this paradox by stating that no class can include itself as a member, but this technical solution fails to solve the more mundane barber paradox as I've just described it and it seems to be a "cheat," in which the problem is allegedly solved by simply limiting its applicability. Russell stated in The Philosophy of Logical Atomism: "You can only get around [the paradox] by observing that the whole question whether a class is or is not a member of itself is nonsense, i.e. that no class either is or is not a member of itself, and that it is not even true to say that, because the whole form of words is just noise without meaning." Russell worked out this suggested solution to the paradox in more detail, with Whitehead, in *Principia*. But Russell's attempted solution highlights the far broader problem of inherent paradox in all conceptual systems – as Gödel resoundingly established in his later refutation of Russell and Whitehead's work.

Aristotle's work, as with modern science, focused generally on deductive logic, as opposed to inductive logic. Inductive logic proceeds from particulars to universal propositions, the opposite of deduction. Induction, however, is arguably as important or more important to modern science than deduction. There is still a thriving debate on the role of induction, with the 20th Century's most famous philosopher of science, Karl Popper, famously criticizing induction as a myth, in his 1959 *magnum opus*, *The Logic of Scientific Discovery*. Popper argued that scientists don't really use inductive methods in their work at all. I don't agree with Popper's critique but I won't delve further into inductive logic in this essay.

Western Logic vs. Eastern Logic?

We in the West find it surprising when we first learn that "dilemmatic" logic, i.e., Aristotle's logic, with only true or false as legitimate conclusions, is not the only type of logic around. The Indian philosophical traditions of Buddhism and Vedanta have long subscribed to "tetralemmatic" logic, known in Sanskrit as the *catuskoti*. (Thomas McEvilley's wonderful 2002 book, *The Shape of Ancient Thought*, discusses in detail commonalities between ancient Greek and Indian philosophy, including the *catuskoti*). Tetralemmatic logic has four legitimate conclusions: true; false; true and false; and neither true nor false. Huh? Is this type of logic used only for dramatic effect or is there more to it?

The hard task of science and philosophy is to craft theories ("truth") that are valid over the broadest swath of space and time. A "general" theory, like Einstein's general theory of relativity, is supposed to be valid over all times and all places. We can never know, of course, if this is really the case, but it is an assertion made with the term "general." There is no real demarcation point between science and philosophy but it is fair to state that the task of philosophy is to, among other things, generalize scientific theories for even broader applicability.

How can something be both true and false at the same time or not true and not false at the same time? In short: it's a matter of perspective. "I am a man" is true right now, for me, but false for my sister, therefore it is both true and false or neither true nor false if we focus on the same time as the key element of our perspective. And if we focus on space as the key element of our perspective, the statement "I am a man" becomes neither true nor false with respect to me because it depends also on the time at which we make such a judgment. I was a boy before I was a man and I was neither a boy nor a man before I was born; ditto for after I am dead ("I" don't exist then). Our perspective in space and time is crucial to judging the truth or falsity of any statement. Truth depends on perspective. This is pretty common sense for most people, but it needs to be stated clearly.

Another example came to me as I was writing this essay. I took a break to take out the trash and noticed the evening star shining brightly as I stepped outside. The Evening Star is another name for the planet Venus, which is also known as the Morning Star when seen in the morning. It's so bright because it's a planet reflecting our sun's light. The planet is always visible on clear nights in the evening and morning because it's so close to the sun when considered from our perspective on our planet. I could say, accurately, when I saw the Evening Star that the "Evening Star is visible." But this would be false if I saw the same planetary object in the morning because it would then be, according to our time-dependent naming conventions, the Morning Star, even though it's actually the same stellar object.

And if we take the broader time perspective of, let's say, a year's duration, the statement "the Evening Star is visible" becomes both true and not true and neither true nor untrue. This is the case because it is sometimes visible and sometimes not during the one-year period. Thus a single statement, "the Evening Star is visible," when considered over this broader time period cannot capture the details of truth or falsity within this time period.

It is only if we fix a point in space and time as our perspective that dilemmatic logic holds. But fixing a perspective in time and space is impossible in actuality. With every moment our perspective necessarily changes in time. Similarly with space: all things are moving, in process.

Can we conceptually fix a point in space and time, if not in actuality? We can, and this is the perspective that led to Plato's postulated realm of ideal forms (what Whitehead calls "eternal objects"). Is the number π a constant that is always a circle's circumference divided by its diameter? Well, yes, it is for Euclidean (flat) space-times. But not for Lobachevskian (curved) space-times. Yet again, it's a matter of perspective. How about a square? Does a square always have four sides? Yes, by definition. Does a cube always have six faces? Yes, by definition.

These last two statements hold in any type of space-time. It seems, then, that definitional statements that are true in any type of space-time constitute a category for which Aristotle's law of non-contradiction holds firm. And that's it, as far as I can tell. It is, unfortunately, a rather narrow category.

Ultimate Reality, Ultimate Truth?

More generally, what is "truth"? And is there an "ultimate truth," discoverable through scientific or spiritual inquiry, or a combination of the two?

"Truth" is used in different ways, but the two primary meanings are: 1) truth as synonymous with "reality"; 2) truth as a set of concepts comprising a single worldview that exactly reflects reality. There is undeniably an "ultimate truth" in the first sense of the word – there is indeed something (an entire universe), which we can call "reality" or any other label we prefer, as opposed to nothing, pure nothingness. Even if we are Idealists in that we view all of reality as essentially mind-like, there is still something that we call reality. We are here, in the universe, after all, questioning it all.

So why use "truth" when we really mean "reality"? All concepts will forever fail to capture the totality of reality because we never know the full extent of what we don't know. We will never know reality in all her intimate details. Reality will always surprise us with new things and all of our concepts and theories shall remain incomplete. Forever.

There is, then, no "ultimate truth" in terms of definition (2) above. Ironically, this statement itself leads to paradox: if there is no ultimate truth, the statement itself is arguably false, thus there is ultimate truth. And if there is ultimate truth, the statement is false. But if it's false, there is ultimate truth… Paradox seems to be inescapable.

This needn't, however, stop us from trying to create better and better models of reality (this is what I'm attempting in this essay, for example, by examining our tools for philosophical and scientific inquiry). It should, instead, lead us to remain humble in the face of mystery and to always remain open to new information and ideas. Truth is relative but it is also asymptotic in terms of the scientific method and, hopefully, for each of our personal quests for our own truths.

Whither Mind?

What happens when we apply this perspectival and "asymptotic truth" approach to mind – the role of perspective (subjectivity) itself within reality? We arrive at, unsurprisingly, different truths, different perspectives. From one perspective, mind is simply the function of complex types of matter like our brains. This perspective, the "reductionistic materialist" approach to mind is, however, a limited perspective because it forgets perspective itself by defining matter as wholly objective. From the reductionistic materialist perspective, a brain is just a brain and it can be described in a wholly objective manner.

Yet from another perspective, the perspective of panpsychism (also known as panexperientialism), all matter has some degree of mind. No "vacuous actuality" is possible, to use Whitehead's phrase. What we think of as being wholly objective, wholly actual – matter – is not, and cannot be, wholly objective from the broader panpsychist perspective. Materialism is, in this view, a "flatland" perspective and panpsychism expands our perspective upwards in an additional dimension.

We can, then, say that the statement "mind is synonymous with matter" is true, false, both true and false, or neither true nor false, depending on one's perspective. The level of reality on which we choose to perch defines our truths.

Logic is Limited

In the last analysis, logic is not entirely logical – and it seems that it never will be. There is a possibility (never say never) that a "meta-logic" will be discovered that transcends these paradoxes. But for now the best we can do in the face of paradox is seek to expand our experiential understanding as broadly as possible– and we should remain forever humble in the face of mystery.

My next installment in this series, *On the Heart*, will explore the balance we must strike between reason and faith in light of the failures of a purely logical approach to the universe.

Chapter 9
Absent-Minded Science, Part IX:

On the Heart

"Excuse me luv," the woman said to me as I walked down the street on my way to the train station. As I turned around to see who was speaking, she picked my scarf up from the ground, which I had evidently just dropped, and handed it to me with a smile.

I was visiting Reading, England, and was always pleasantly surprised, amused and a little perplexed by the familiar "luv" manner of speech in this rainy island where I was born.

The scarf had been given to me about a week earlier, by a very nice woman named Julie who was looking after my grandfather for a few days. The gift was unexpected, as I had never met Julie before then.

The kindness of strangers seems irrational to some people and wouldn't generally be considered economically rational behavior to an economist focused on pure cost/benefit analysis. Thankfully, humans aren't entirely rational creatures, despite the assumptions of economists. We follow our hearts as much or probably more than we do our heads.

This latest essay in my series on absent-minded science continues the exploration of reason and logic begun in my last installment. Part X will conclude the series with a light-hearted examination of why certain explanations are more compelling than others.

A broader insight may be arrived at when we consider what it really means to be "rational." Like a lot of concepts, we think at first blush we know what this word means. But there's really no clear and defensible definition of rational behavior or "rationality" more generally. What time frame are we referring to? How broad are our considerations in making "rational" decisions? These details are key to any conclusion regarding "rational behavior" in any situation, and these details depend on the choices of the person acting in each situation (as discussed in my last essay, truth is perspectival in all situations other than definitions that are independent of any particular space-time).

Paulo Coelho's masterpiece, *The Alchemist*, has much to say about the heart. This amazing little book is a parable about how to live a good life by finding and achieving one's "personal legend." Alchemy is unsurprisingly a consistent theme in the book, meant as a metaphor for personal transformation – looking for one's "personal legend." The book is still on bestseller lists despite its release in the early 1990s.

The book's main character, a young sheepherder from Andalusia, Spain, travels with the Alchemist through the desert of North Africa looking for his personal legend. He asks the Alchemist: "Why do we have to listen to our hearts?"

"Because wherever your heart is, that is where you'll find your treasure."

"But my heart is agitated, the boy said. "It has its dreams, it gets emotional, and it's become passionate over a woman of the desert. It asks things of me, and it keeps me from sleeping many nights, when I'm thinking about her."

"Well, that's good. Your heart is alive. Keep listening to what it has to say."

The boy had a long conversation with his heart there in the desert. He came to understand his heart. "He asked it, please, never to stop speaking to him. He asked that, when he wandered far from his dreams, his heart press him and sound the alarm. The boy swore that, every time he heard the alarm, he would heed its message."

The secret that alchemists have pursued over the centuries, according to Coelho, is known as the "Master Work." The Master Work is written on an emerald and describes how to create the Elixir of Life and the Philosopher's Stone. But the Masterwork, according to the Alchemist, "can't be understood by reason alone. It is a direct passage to the Soul of the World."

This metaphor stands for life in general. Can we grasp life, can we understand our own lives and find meaning, with reason alone? It seems not. Reason is a very powerful tool and it is certainly a good guide to most aspects of life. But reason has limitations. Reason depends on representations, on models of reality. To try and grasp life with reason alone is like trying to describe the most beautiful sunset you've ever seen with words alone. It can't do it justice.

The problems go far deeper, however.

A prominent 2nd Century CE Buddhist philosopher, Nagarjuna, concluded that there is no ultimate truth: all doctrines are ultimately empty. Jan Westerhoff writes in his introduction to Nagarjuna's work (*Nagarjuna's Madhyamaka: A Philosophical Introduction*): "According to [Nagarjuna's] view of truth, there can be no such thing as ultimate truth, a theory describing how things really are, independent of our interests and conceptual resources employed in describing it."

But if there is no ultimate truth, even this doctrine cannot be true, so there is ultimate truth. We end up in paradox, a problem inherent in all logical or conceptual systems, as discussed in more depth in my last essay.

This is a key insight of the Zen Buddhist tradition (which came much later than Nagarjuna's version of Buddhism, but still relies in part on Nagarjuna's thinking): language and concepts ultimately fail in leading us to true understanding. They are, at best, pointers to reality. Hence the use of paradoxical koans as teaching aids, the most famous of which is "what is the sound of one hand clapping?" These mind-twisters have no correct answer – they are intended to show that logic itself is illogical.

Reality is apparently deeper than logic.

Nancy Cartwright, a respected philosopher of science, makes a great case in her 1999 book, *The Dappled World: A Study of the Boundaries of Science*, that science does indeed exist within fairly limiting boundaries. Even our best theories of physics, biology, economics, etc. consist of a "dappled" patchwork of ideas and mathematics. Despite the fact that we have accomplished truly great things over the last few hundred years: modern medicine, powerful computers that fit in our palm, marvels in entertainment, etc., we are just scratching the surface of what the universe has to offer.

Science, while limited, has obviously been tremendously important in helping us to understand the world and create useful technologies. This trend shall certainly continue, probably in perpetuity.

We know with certainty, however, that we will never know the fullness of nature because we never know the full extent of what we don't know. We are like a hiker seeking the top of a mountain who thinks she sees the top not far away only to find as she crests the hill she is on that she sees yet another hill above her, and so on. We will never know where the top is because we don't know the full extent of what we don't know.

To extend the physical metaphor further: this mountain springs from an ocean of unreason, with other islands of reason rising from the ocean's surface in the dappled manner suggested by Cartwright and other thinkers. The best we can hope for is to navigate this vast ocean of unreason and scale the islands of reason we come across with equanimity and grace.

The kindness of strangers often demands this, as does a more complete experience of the universe.

Chapter 10

Absent-Minded Science, Part X:

On Explanations

Tigger: Well, hello there Eeyore, my friend – lovely day isn't it?

Eeyore: Lovely is all relative, isn't it? Compared to yesterday I guess it is fair to say that today is lovely.

Tigger: Er… Yes! It is all relative and today is indeed lovely compared to yesterday. But, you know Mr. Eeyore, this brings to mind a little philosophical problem I've been pondering.

Eeyore: Oh yes? [His large ears perk up as Eeyore loves philosophy almost as much as Owl]. Since when do you like philosophy my bouncy friend?

Tigger: Oh yes! [Tigger bounces on his tail in excitement]. You'll be very interested in this, I have no doubt. I have been pondering … explanations.

Eeyore: Explanations?

Tigger: Yes! Explanations. Why are we convinced of certain explanations and not others? What is it that changes our minds and hearts?

Eeyore: Harrumph. Well, I'll grant you that this is indeed an interesting problem with no ready answer.

Tigger: Exactly! But we can certainly attempt some answers, can we not? I, for one, have come to realize that the most reasonable answer isn't always the most convincing for most people. Reason, while cited by practically all scientists, philosophers, and thinking animals and people more generally, can only take us so far. And I have noticed, as I spend more years bouncing around this little blue planet of ours, that what seems eminently reasonable to one person can seem utterly perplexing to others.

Eeyore: But reason is reason my tiger friend. Everyone knows that that Greek fellow Aristotle established the rules of reason thousands of years ago. Aristotle showed that through basic rules of deductive logic we could discover everything about the world that may be discovered.

Tigger: Oh he did, did he? I should like to meet this fellow some time.

Eeyore: He's dead, you ninny.

Tigger: Oh. Well, that is indeed unfortunate. It seems to me, however, that reason can take us only so far in explaining the world – and perhaps even less far in convincing people to change their views. Owl was telling me about something called paradox, or self-contradiction, as inherent in all logical systems. Some fellow named Guhhhdel established this mathematically, though Owl tells me it can be shown very clearly with the simple statement: "This sentence is false." If it's true, it's false and if it's false it's true. Paradox is inescapabobble.

Eeyore [thinking for a moment as he nibbles some grass]: Oh yes, I vaguely recall Owl telling me about that gentleman. Well, I suppose logic may not be as impregnable as it should be, but it certainly works well enough for me. I haven't come across any such paradoxes in my life.

Tigger: Neither have I! Guhhhdel's theorem doesn't mean science itself is invalid as a tool. But it shows that logic itself is not entirely logical and that science is a limited tool – it's not all-powerful. And, more generally, it seems to me that we rely on logic in our lives less than you are suggesting. It seems to me that most animals and people rely more on stories than logic.

Eeyore: Stories? What the devil are you talking about?

Tigger: We may after all be merely figments of someone else's imagination.

Eeyore: Erm, that thought had occurred to me once in a while. It would be just my luck to not even be real.

Tigger: Ah, but is it so bad to be the product of another's imagination? Are not all of us, after all, the product of a hidden Author? Owl knows another fellow, the Alchemist, who says that all that we see and know of was written by just one hand. Including us. That hand is surely not a tigger's paw, a donkey's hoof, or a human hand, but one hand nonetheless.

Eeyore: I never much liked stories. And I certainly don't like hidden paws, hoofs or hands. I prefer facts.

Tigger: But Eeyore, my dear friend, there are no facts without stories and no stories without facts. In fact, as with so many things there is no sharp dividing line between facts and stories. I would go even further, however, and suggest to you that all facts are nothing but stories. They are mini-stories inside of a larger story. Stories within stories within stories.

Eeyore: Now you're talking nonsense you exuberant naïf. Of course facts are not stories. Facts are facts. I kick this rock with my hoof and establish thus the fact of the rock. [Eeyore winces a little as he does so].

Tigger: Don't hurt yourself my equine friend! The rock is indeed a story that you tell yourself. This doesn't mean the story is fantabobulous – it can be as real as anything, and surely the rock is as real as anything else you care to kick (or merely point to instead if you prefer not to stub your hoof). But the rock is nevertheless a story in the sense I am suggesting because all things are stories. Or perhaps "argument" is a better word: all things are arguments of which we convince ourselves and then try to convince others. Those "facts" that are generally accepted by most people are those stories, those arguments, that most people find believable and nothing more. Mutual and widespread belief is the mark of a good story, is it not?

Eeyore: My, Tigger, haven't you grown? Who have you been talking to lately?

Tigger: I talk to whoever will talk with me and I find almost every animal or person has something of value to share. Even Roo and Piglet, those sweet children. Especially those sweet children. Anyway, evening shall soon fall and I have no guarantee that the sun shall come up again tomorrow, though I certainly hope it shall. I must be off! Until we meet again my furry fellow! [Tigger bounces away whistling loudly].

Eeyore [muttering to himself as Tigger recedes]: Thank heavens. I can only handle so much Tigger at a time. What a strangely exuberant creature he is.

Chapter 11

A Science of Beauty, Part 1

There's no accounting for taste.

Folk saying

Art is the imposing of a pattern on experience, and our aesthetic enjoyment is recognition of the pattern.

Alfred North Whitehead (1943)

A photographer friend of mine told me years ago that the "world just looks better through a camera lens." Indeed it does – to most of us. The camera viewfinder adds a frame to a part of the world and allows the photographer to focus her attention. In short, the camera's frame allows a photographer to create art.

But what the heck is art? What is beauty? Do these questions matter to anyone beyond the photographer, art lover, art historian or philosopher of art?

I'll attempt to show in this two-part essay why these questions – and their answers – should be important to practically every field of human thought.

Art has been around as long as humans have been around and it seems that thinking about art – the philosophy of art – has been too. Plato, as with practically every topic in philosophy or science, had some relevant insights. Though the topic was discussed in many different Platonic dialogues, Plato's idea of art was never clearly spelled out by the master. The simplest summary of Plato's feelings on the matter is that he viewed beauty as the perception of eternal Forms that exist as a substrate to reality. Actual (physical) forms are imperfect reflections of the deeper Forms; the artist enjoys most the art that most fully reveal the Forms. These ideas are strange to us today and this kind of thinking (sometimes known as "essentialism") has been dispelled in most areas of thought over the course of the last couple of centuries.

Kant, the difficult 18th Century German philosopher, presented perhaps the most influential historical theory of art (aesthetics) in his third critique, The Critique of Judgment. For Kant, there was indeed no accounting for taste, but those with good taste would agree on what is good art. So while artistic appreciation is purely subjective for Kant, there are certain principles that make good art universally appreciated.

Time-traveling to the present era for the sake of brevity, I'm going to mention just a couple more modern notions of art.

For Stephen David Ross, a professor of philosophy and literature at SUNY Binghamton, art is all about contrast – "intense contracts," to be more specific. Contrasts are "conjunctions, unifications, syntheses, of dissimilar, opposing constituents." Ross also recognizes that the criteria he describes exist on a spectrum, as a matter of degree, except for the "intensity of contrast." (I'm not clear how "intensity" can be anything but a continuum, but this is Ross's contention.)

The two quotes at the beginning of this essay are better answers, however, to the question: what is art? There is indeed no accounting for taste because taste is so varied, but most of us can also agree with Whitehead's statement as a non-exclusive description of art. We do, in making a judgment about what is art, whether we enjoy it or not, impose our own patterns on the sense impressions provided by the art object.

Visual art is more easily recognized as intended to be art than other mediums – it is far more clearly delineated than music, for example. Paintings have frames. Sculptures have pedestals. It's not hard to figure out what visual art is intended to be art. (Whether the art critic believes the intention is warranted or not is a different question altogether.)

There is a limited audio equivalent of a frame or pedestal: the rather inadequate silences that often begin and end a song or other types of music. As we perceive sound around us, let's say at a loud restaurant or bar, we may have trouble differentiating when we are listening to a song or to conversations, or a mix of both.

But can conversations be art even when not intended as such? Or could a conversation or set of conversations become art simply by being packaged as art by an enterprising artist? Is a cacophony of fruit machines in Las Vegas art because I record it and call it art? Is a conversation itself art when practiced by those skilled at the art of conversation?

Or, for a higher profile debate: is the 1987 photograph Piss Christ (a plastic crucifix suspended in a vat of the artist's urine) art because Serrano (the artist) says it is and was paid to produce it?

Well, under Whitehead's approach to art, even Serrano's highly irreverent creation became art when Serrano imposed a pattern on his experience, and this is aesthetically appreciated when the perceiver recognizes the pattern of experience relevant to the piece. A conversation could be considered art when it is "framed" by the perceiver as being such. So it is indeed in the eye/ear of the beholder and there ain't no accounting for taste. Frames can be, and are, imposed by the creative artist during the course of her craft; but frames are also imposed by anyone, professional artist or not, when a pattern is recognized and appreciated. And this is as much art as that produced by the professional artist.

Art in Nature, Nature in Art

Even though aesthetic enjoyment seems to be hopelessly arbitrary on a case-by-case basis, what if there were at least some possible accounting for taste? Could there be principles of beauty that we can enumerate and examine empirically? In short, is a science of aesthetics, a science of beauty, possible – rather than "merely" a philosophy of art?

I think there is and I'm going to suggest a few ideas in this essay along these lines. While I agree that there's no accounting for individual taste, it seems that there are patterns and tendencies that we can identify at various levels that can form the basis for aesthetic enjoyment and a science of beauty.

I equate aesthetics and beauty even though many artists and philosophers of art wish to distinguish them. They are equivalent for me because there is no legitimate division between what should be considered "merely" beautiful and what should be considered to hold aesthetic/artistic value: it's all about shades of beauty. Beauty is potential art and art is beauty recognized, as I'll explain further below. Aesthetics is all about judgments of beauty, in the broadest sense. Beauty is all about value, quality, and so is aesthetics. To say something is beautiful is equivalent to saying something has aesthetic value.

The first step in creating a science of beauty is to recognize that aesthetic appreciation, an appreciation for beauty, like with almost all things in the universe, exists on a continuum, a spectrum, not as an "all or nothing" phenomenon. Art is not limited to humans. We do in fact have clear evidence of art and aesthetic appreciation in many non-human species. Darwin wrote explicitly in his 1871 book, *The Descent of Man*, that many animals, including birds – with their little bird brains – appear to exhibit aesthetic appreciation: "Birds appear to be the most aesthetic of all animals, excepting of course man, and they have nearly the same taste for the beautiful as we have.... In man, however, when cultivated, the sense of beauty is manifestly a far more complex feeling, and is associated with various intellectual ideas." (P. 307, Plume Concise Edition 2007).

The peacock's tail, to use the most well-known example, is most likely as magnificent as it is merely because peahens (females) like ornate tail feathers in their males – a phenomenon labeled by Darwin as "sexual selection." That is, the peacock's tail has evolved because of the steady selection by peahens, through increased mating opportunities and therefore increased reproduction of males with more impressive feathers. A larger tail is "maladaptive" in terms of survival, because of its weight and size, but it confers a reproductive advantage because of its attractiveness to peahens. (See Part V of my series on "absent-minded science" for more on sexual selection).

Experiments have been conducted on peacocks and have confirmed that peahens do indeed mate more frequently with peacocks that have larger tails and more eye feathers, resulting in more offspring for peacocks with the biggest tails. Does the peahen count eye feathers and compare the various peacocks with each other? Of course not. But a peahen doesn't have to know how to count to be able to appreciate a larger array of feathers, just as humans don't need to think explicitly about symmetry to enjoy facial beauty in other humans and make judgments about who they consider more beautiful (as a personal matter).

Human beauty is in fact another great example for my thesis. Judgments about human beauty are sometimes placed in a different category than more refined artistic appreciation. That is, appreciation of beauty is thought by some to be different in kind than appreciation of art. This is a big mistake. Appreciation is a continuum and there is no real separation between enjoying fine art or a human face – or a human body, for that matter. It's all about attraction or, to be more accurate, degrees of attraction, just as Darwin suggested by recognizing that human aesthetic appreciation is "more complex" than that of birds. Attraction, as with most things, lies on a continuum.

There is certainly a difference, however, to use an extreme example, between appreciation for porn and appreciation for the Mona Lisa as a work of art. But the appreciation is the commonality, even if the type of appreciation is different in important ways. Appreciation is a continuum of increasing complexity as new threads emerge and are woven in at each level of complexity. Similarly, I'll try to demonstrate here that an ant's appreciation for a good meal lies on the same continuum as the highest human artistic appreciation, as does a leech's appreciation for human blood or an electron's appreciation for one path of motion over another. Yes, even non-biological objects are subsumed in this general theory of art.

Here are a few interesting examples of art in the natural world.

Australian cetologists recently made a remarkable discovery: humpback whales enjoy pop songs that change each year. "Our findings reveal cultural change on a vast scale," said the primary researcher Ellen Garland, a graduate student at The University of Queensland. Male whales generally sing just one mating song each year, but it changes over time and more catchy versions spread rapidly to different populations around the world. Interestingly, the songs seem to spread always from west to east.

Why do whales enjoy pop songs that change relatively rapidly? We can never know because enjoyment is a purely individual and internal affair, but it certainly seems reasonable to believe that whales have a fairly complex culture, as Garland suggests, and that their relatively advanced minds can adapt and enjoy different songs over short periods of time, whether or not the primary purpose of these songs is to attract mates.

Is a whale song art? Surely it should be considered such – as much as any human musical creation should be considered art. It seems clear to me, though it is again unprovable, that the same mix of motivations prompts whale song creation as prompts human song creation: sheer desire to create beautiful sounds, desire to attract mates, desire to entertain loved ones, etc.

Similarly, some birds are capable of learning songs that evolve over time: parrots, hummingbirds and songbirds. All other birds are stuck with songs based on their genetic heritage, though this heritage also evolves, just at a slower pace. An interesting recent study found that young male songbirds learn songs more quickly in the presence of female birds. The degree to which this process is "self-conscious" is impossible to know, but through the principle of continuity – the notion that biological and physical change is almost always continuous, not discontinuous – we can have some confidence that there is indeed relatively complex thought present in the little birds, even though there is very likely not much of a sense of self.

At much lower levels of complexity, bacteria create beautiful forms through their own propagation in appropriate media. It is highly unlikely that there is an intention in the individual bacteria to create the pattern – it is, rather, a consequence of the collective behavior that results in a macro-scale pattern that we as human beings can enjoy. Recent research by Eshel Ben-Jacob at Tel Aviv University has suggested, however, that bacteria have a surprising intelligence and far more sophisticated communication abilities than previously thought, which are largely responsible for the amazing patterns observed by Ben-Jacob and others.

Bees create hexagonal honeycombs through an innate desire to be more efficient in constructing cells for their offspring and to store honey. Hexagonal honeycombs sectionalize the volume of the hive most efficiently, in terms of the consumption of wax for walls, though there are many other ways to tile a plane or sectionalize volume (as M. C. Escher amply demonstrated in his work, using what are known more generally as "Penrose tiles" to create very interesting images).

Similar forms occur, without the intervention of any bees or microbial life, in fluids placed in certain conditions. Benard convection cells are generally hexagonal cells that appear in shallow dishes filled with heated liquid. The hexagonal cells form as a result of the heat-induced motion of the molecules comprising the liquid. As the molecules rise up in the fluid column they are pushed aside by other rising cells. As they are pushed aside they meet other molecules pushed from other columns. The dynamic equilibrium state leads to hexagonal cells because this is the lowest energy condition, entirely analogous to honeycombs or soap bubbles joining together.

Where is the dividing line in these examples of nature's complexity and creativity between "unintentional" art and intentional art? Does art require a frame imposed by an "artist," whether it's an actual frame or an analog to a frame such as the pauses between songs? Or can the art appreciator herself impose the frame whenever and wherever she wants? This is, in fact, what a photographer does when turning her lens to any subject she wishes to turn into art. Photography is generally "found art." And we can argue by analogy that any artist working in any medium can impose a frame on her subject and thereby turn it into art. All of these examples are an imposition of pattern on experience and thus the creation of art. It doesn't matter if there is recognition of that pattern by anyone other than the creator herself. And it is important to keep in mind that the appreciator becomes an artist through the very act of appreciation, the very recognition of pattern.

It seems, then, that art is art independent of the process of creation – except for the frame itself. The frame becomes all-important. This is similar to, but even more general, than Whitehead's opening quote: "Art is the imposing of a pattern on experience, and our aesthetic enjoyment is recognition of the pattern." I assert that the pattern is the frame is the pattern is the frame. Art becomes art when a subject imposes her frame on her experience. And that's it. There is no necessary separation between creation by an artist and appreciation by another individual. They can be the same person. Beauty is pervasive. Art is pervasive.

Principles of beauty

Based on this discussion, I propose a brief outline of necessarily general principles of beauty that hold at various levels of reality. These principles constitute a very rudimentary beginning to a science of beauty, but it is nonetheless a beginning:

• Symmetry is beautiful – at all levels of reality. This beauty of symmetry is most likely a consequence of the fact that symmetrical forms are the lowest energy forms, the most stable forms, from the simplest of structures to the most complex, and due to the predictability of symmetry.

- Similarly, symmetry in time (music, for example) is often beautiful, and is generally known as consonance. At higher levels of cognition, consonance gives way to appreciation of more complex temporal patterns, including dissonance.

- At the lowest levels of cognition, simpler types of symmetry are most beautiful, but as cognition complexifies, more complex symmetries like the Golden Ratio become beautiful. At the highest levels of cognition, fractal symmetry (multi-level spatio-temporal symmetry) becomes quite beautiful.

- At higher levels of cognition, unpredictability arising from a base of predictability is beautiful. Symmetry and predictability are generally beautiful, but when more complex consciousness develops (it's a sliding scale), the surprise of novelty can become equally if not more attractive.

- Contrasting and complementary colors are beautiful. No matter the range of vision in the appreciator, contrasting colors introduce additional detail into the world and this is considered attractive at all levels.

- The interpenetration of opposites is beautiful and is known most generally as complementarity; the interpenetration of symmetry and asymmetry (or symmetry building and symmetry breaking, as the biologist Lee Klinger has suggested) is perhaps the primary form.

Part II of this essay will elaborate further on these ideas and suggest a path for fleshing out this proposed science of beauty.

Let me close with a quote from one of my favorite movies, American Beauty (a work of profound beauty in its own right), spoken by one of the main characters, a disturbed yet precociously wise high-school boy who obsessively films the world around him, as he describes a short video of a plastic bag floating rhythmically in the air with a number of dry leaves:

It was one of those days when it's a minute away from snowing and there's this electricity in the air, you can almost hear it. And this bag was, like, dancing with me. Like a little kid begging me to play with it. For fifteen minutes. And that's the day I knew there was this entire life behind things, and ... this incredibly benevolent force, that wanted me to know there was no reason to be afraid, ever. Video's a poor excuse, I know. But it helps me remember... and I need to remember... Sometimes there's so much beauty in the world I feel like I can't take it, like my heart's going to cave in.

Chapter 12

A Science of Beauty, Part II

For he who would proceed aright in this matter ... will create many fair and noble thoughts and notions in boundless love and wisdom; until on that shore he grows and waxes strong, and at last the vision is revealed to him of a single science, which is the science of beauty everywhere.

Plato, Symposium

Science matters because it is the preeminent story of our age, an epic saga about who we are, where we came from, and where we are going.

Michael Shermer

Why do we need a science of beauty? Haven't science and art done just fine in their own domains over the last few millennia? Yes, but...

My attempt, in this and my previous column, to meld science, beauty, and art is prompted by thinking about the nature of mind. I've written a number of essays explaining my view of mind in nature, nature in mind. I highlighted what I view as fatal problems for the prevailing materialist conception of mind, in which mind is regarded as emerging somehow from what is generally viewed as entirely mindless. Mind is, in the alternative panpsychist philosophy that I support, ubiquitous because mind and matter are two aspects of the same thing. Where there is mind there is matter and where there is matter there is mind. As matter complexifies, so mind complexifies.

This vision of mind and matter has important ramifications also for biology and evolution because if mind is ubiquitous we realize that mind must have an important role (perhaps the starring role) in evolution, which is just another word for complexification – even though evolution can lead to simpler forms in some situations. "Sexual selection" was the term Darwin gave to the evolutionary effects of female choice in mate selection and male-male competition for mates. Many traits in the animal kingdom (and probably in other kingdoms also) stem from sexual selection, including the oft-mentioned peacock's tail. This showy and overly large tail, it is thought, resulted not from its role in helping its owner to survive (its effect is the opposite in this regard), but to help it gain more mates and thus spread its genes to the next generation. If its role in producing more offspring outweighs any harm to its owner's survival, it will spread as a trait.

But why would peahens find showy tails attractive? And by extension what is the basis for any female choice with respect to sexual selection? (It's not just female choices, of course, because many species, including our own, exhibit female and male choices in mating; but throughout nature it's generally female choices that make the difference.) I've realized in pondering these issues for some time now that a key to answering these questions is an understanding of aesthetics, of value – which are just different words for beauty.

Mind is, at its root, about information – perception/reception thereof – and a choice based on the information received. Choices are, in turn, all about appreciation, likes, dislikes. In other words, all choices are aesthetic choices, a synonym for value, whether positive or negative. So if mind is ubiquitous, the experience of beauty, of aesthetic appreciation, is ubiquitous. Aesthetic appreciation becomes art, as discussed in Part I, when the observer imposes a frame on her experience, whether literal or metaphorical. Art is, in my framing (pardon the pun), all about beauty. Art doesn't, however, have to be about traditional notions of anthropocentric beauty, and indeed much modern art has explicitly attempted to focus on subjects that are not traditionally beautiful (in the more narrow sense of this term). Again, beauty is for present purposes all about likes and dislikes, value, a process of discernment that is pervasive if mind is pervasive.

Beauty in a traditional sense is a completely arbitrary notion because there is generally no appeal to anything common to all observers. Rather, beauty becomes merely a matter of taste and nothing more. If mind, appreciation, and judgments about beauty exist at every level of nature, however, can we even then say anything about beauty and appreciation other than the bromide: "beauty is in the eye of the beholder"?

It turns out that we can, if we accept that the structure, the form, the patterns that we see throughout nature are the objective manifestation of appreciation, of beauty, by many levels (hierarchies) of non-human minds. Beauty results from a constant process of sensing and objective manifestation, for each little piece of the universe. Beauty is, then, potential art and art is beauty recognized (what constitutes good art is a different matter…). The recognition of beauty that results in art is necessarily recognition by an actual entity at a different level than the beauty being recognized. The entity recognizing beauty, and thus creating art, can itself be recognized as beauty by other entities at different levels, ad infinitum.

As we humans, who possess the most highly developed type of consciousness that we know of, developed our ability to create intentional art, this ubiquitous appreciation for beauty gained immense new levels of complexity. There is indeed no accounting for taste at the human level because of the awesome complexity made possible with our advanced minds, language, and tools – but we can still suggest and explore various principles of beauty that are generally applicable, even if not universally and always true.

The principles of beauty I proposed in Part I are broad principles for establishing what potential experiences are likely to be manifested as beauty and where we may create art through recognition of beauty. This kind of prediction is far easier at the non-human level because minds are so much simpler below the human level of complexity. Certain types of birds will almost always find shiny objects beautiful – and so do many humans, but humans are certainly less predictable in this and all other aspects of beauty because we are more complex and thus freer in our judgment and actions.

Fleshing Out a Science of Beauty

A developed science of beauty – deserving of the name "science" – will allow predictions about the types of structures/form/beauty we can expect to see at various levels of complexity in novel situations. Such predictions will, however, become more and more difficult as complexity increases. But over time, as additional data is collected in numerous situations involving the natural world, evolution, and intentional art, the principles of beauty may increasingly act as a basis for useful predictions in science and for artistic creativity. As with all science, the process of hypothesis, prediction, test, and adjustments will lead to an improved science – with no end in sight.

The principles of beauty I proposed in Part I are meant as suggestions based on my own initial and admittedly far from comprehensive empirical analysis. We have good reasons, for example, to believe that symmetry is beautiful, that contrasting and complementary colors are beautiful, and that at higher levels of cognition the interpenetration of opposites is beautiful. These are commonalities of many objects commonly considered beautiful, such as human faces, birds' tails, mathematical theories, or poetry. I am not suggesting that these principles of beauty hold necessarily in every instance. Rather, judgments at every level of reality are free to some degree and will often depart from any attempt to systematize judgments about beauty. This is the case – an important point – because each subject is to some degree beholden to history. Even at the simplest levels of reality, history exerts some pressure. No parts of our universe exist separate from history because all things are subject to a vast continuum of spatial and temporal causes that limit freedom to various degrees. As matter/mind complexifies, however, free will is in many ways enhanced because we gain the ability to transcend, at least in part, our history.

Getting a little more technical, Whitehead's panpsychism posits that all actualities – "actual entities" – transition from potentiality to actuality by perceiving the universe around them, choosing what perceptions to internalize, and then becoming objective/actual based on those perceptions. This is an iterative process, moment to moment to moment… This process takes place in literally every part of the universe in perpetuity, from subatomic particles to humans to perhaps even more complex structures beyond our current understanding. It is a perpetual oscillation between potentiality and actuality that produces the universe in each moment. Thus potentiality produces perception produces experience produces actuality. Rinse and repeat for all of eternity. This is what I mean by "history" for each subject/actuality.

Beauty is, in the conception I advocate here, objective in the sense of the process of creation for each unit of the universe – all objectified experience is beauty because each entity has taken the potential experience available to it and manifested objectively in the most aesthetically appealing manner possible – but there is no objective basis for supposing that any particular thing is universally beautiful, that is, for all subjects. Beauty judgments, as with all judgments, are still entirely subjective in terms of the freedom of each subject to make an individual choice about beauty in each instance. The utility of this approach consists in its recognition that beauty is still in the eye of the beholder, but also that there are commonalities to every judgment of beauty and a universal process that leads to such judgments.

It is because of this all-encompassing panpsychist view of nature that I see all of nature as manifesting beauty, something that Whitehead merely hints at: "An actual fact is a fact of aesthetic experience. All aesthetic experience is a feeling arising out of the realization of contrast under identity." (Process and Reality, p. 280).

I don't have space to discuss in detail here all that Whitehead had to say about aesthetics and art. However, in order to queue up my future columns on the "Anatomy of God," I'm going to sketch a few of Whitehead's ideas about God in relation to beauty.

God and Beauty

Whitehead's view of God is not traditional. He was not a Christian, nor was he much of a mystic. He does, however, find a strong role for God in his metaphysics. He states of God, using the male pronoun for convenience only, not due to any literal masculinization of God: "He does not create the world, he saves it: or, more accurately, he is the poet of the world, with tender patience leading it by his vision of truth, beauty, and goodness." (Process and Reality, p. 346). Readers familiar with Plato will recognize truth, beauty, and goodness as the preeminent forms or archetypes that had a very prominent place in Plato's metaphysics. Whitehead is well-known for his statement that Western philosophy is "a series of footnotes to Plato." He didn't mean by this statement that Plato had it all figured out. Rather, he meant only that Plato had been systematic in his identification of the issues.

In this particular instance, Whitehead follows Plato in believing that there is indeed a realm of forms, or "eternal objects," which have an integral role in the ongoing and perpetual creation of each subject throughout the universe (I'll describe my own thoughts on forms and eternal objects in later columns). God's role is, for Whitehead, to inject an initial suggestion into each subject as it undergoes its transition from pure potentiality to actuality. Each subject may accept or reject this suggestion – and this is itself key to the ubiquitous free will discussed above. This process is itself what constitutes beauty for each subject, as it considers the full range of data it receives from the universe and manifests objectively. We don't have to accept Plato's or Whitehead's vision of God, however, to accept the notion of beauty as universal.

By bringing God into this discussion, I don't mean to suggest a reflexive mystification of notions of beauty. There's enough mystification already in this area! Rather, I bring up divinity because there is indeed a long tradition of equating strong appreciation, artistic rhapsody, with the divine. And I don't think this is entirely wrong, as I'll explain later…

Beauty Everywhere

What is the end result of this aesthetic vision, this story about art, mind, and the world that I have sketched here? The end result is a realization that there is beauty everywhere, at every level of existence – literally. As Ricky Fitts in American Beauty reminds us: "Sometimes there's so much beauty in the world I feel like I can't take it, like my heart's going to cave in." To those attuned to beauty and art in all its forms, every waking moment can be a moment of enjoyment, of aesthetic appreciation.

This vision of beauty as ubiquitous may, I hope, bring us closer to Plato's own vision "of a single science, which is the science of beauty everywhere."

Chapter 13

In Defense of Philosophy

Philosophy has come under attack by various scientists in recent years, generally because, well, they just don't get it. This little essay is my attempt to show why.

Lawrence Krauss, an American physicist at Arizona State University and author of a number of books, stated recently that "philosophy hasn't progressed in two thousand years." He clarified in an *Atlantic Monthly* interview that he was being purposefully provocative in this statement.

Krauss' point was that whereas science progresses through the creation of hypotheses, experiments and falsification, philosophy amounts to little more than word games that don't really go anywhere. This is unfortunately a rather common attitude among working scientists and even among laypeople. Richard Dawkins, the well-known British evolutionary biologist and author of numerous popular books on evolution, wrote the Afterword for Krauss' book. Dawkins likens Krauss' book to Darwin's On the Origin of Species in terms of its potential importance in de-throning supernatural views of the world in favor of purely naturalistic explanations.

The bottomline is that the boundaries between philosophy and science are rather arbitrary and arguably even illusory. There is, perhaps, a continuum of changes in methodology that separates the two. Science at its best focuses on testable hypotheses, whereas philosophy rests on the twin criteria of logic and adequacy to the facts. But this is a fuzzy boundary, at best.

The *sine qua non* of a good scientific theory is falsifiability, at least in Karl Popper's school of thought, which is prevalent in science today, whether he is acknowledged or not. Falsifiability means that a hypothesis or theory can both be tested and, if the test is failed, result in potentially falsifying (rejecting) the hypothesis or theory at issue.

Philosophy, however, traditionally relies on logical consistency and adequacy to the facts. This latter criterion means that inconvenient facts shouldn't be ignored. This is a weaker version of falsifiability.

What is truly ironic, however, is that Popper himself was a philosopher, primarily a philosopher of science. He has had, contrary to the statements of Krauss and other anti-philosophers, a huge influence on how science is actually done. All debates about scientific method, about how science is and should be done, fall squarely within the rubric of the "philosophy of science." For any working scientist to be ignorant of the philosophy of science, of the work of Popper, Lakatos, Kuhn, Feyerabend and others, is to be a bad scientist, in my view.

In fact, Krauss and Dawkins are both bedfellows with the equally well-known philosopher Daniel Dennett, at Tufts University. Is Dennett's book, *Darwin's Dangerous Idea*, which explains and adds to the literature on the theory of evolution, properly categorized as biology or philosophy? It's clearly both. Is Dennett's most well-known book, *Consciousness Explained*, cognitive science or philosophy? It's both, but this book has had a very substantial impact in neuroscience, cognitive science and the philosophy of mind. Is Dennett, a philosopher, uninfluential *vis a vis* scientists? Clearly not.

David Albert, a philosopher of science, recently reviewed Krauss' book in the *New York Times* and found it wanting in many ways. Krauss' basic claim is that physics can now answer even the most profound of philosophical/religious questions: why is there something rather than nothing? Why does anything exist at all? Krauss' answer: the laws of physics just are, and everything else, including our entire universe, flows from that.

Albert responds to Krauss' ideas:

Where, for starters, are the laws of quantum mechanics themselves supposed to have come from? Krauss is more or less upfront, as it turns out, about not having a clue about that. He acknowledges (albeit in a parenthesis, and just a few pages before the end of the book) that everything he has been talking about simply takes the basic principles of quantum mechanics for granted. "I have no idea if this notion can be usefully dispensed with," he writes, "or at least I don't know of any productive work in this regard." And what if he did know of some productive work in that regard? What if he were in a position to announce, for instance, that the truth of the quantum-mechanical laws can be traced back to the fact that the world has some other, deeper property X? Wouldn't we still be in a position to ask why X rather than Y? And is there a last such question? Is there some point at which the possibility of asking any further such questions somehow definitively comes to an end? How would that work? What would that be like?

Krauss, in his rebuttal in an *Atlantic Monthly* interview, refers to Albert as a "moronic philosopher." (Dawkins has indulged in similarly infelicitous public language on more than one occasion). The moron Krauss refers to is a professor of philosophy at Columbia University who happens to hold a Ph.D in theoretical physics. Albert also runs the M.A. program in the philosophy of physics at Columbia University. I am not suggesting that Albert's views should simply be taken on authority; rather, I'm suggesting that perhaps Krauss should look at himself a little harder for calling such a figure a "moronic philosopher."

More to the point, what Krauss fails to point out is that there is still a lot of room for philosophy, spirituality, religion or science to provide answers to the most basic of questions like "why is there something rather than nothing?" (I've provided some suggestions here and here.) Science has not answered this question, as Krauss suggests in his book it has, and it probably never will because science is supposed to rest on falsifiability. How could a theory about why there is something rather than nothing be tested, let alone be falsified? It seems clear that such a theory couldn't be either tested or falsified because the universe we're in does indeed exist, and we have no way of examining non-existence…

Brute facts are a necessary evil

There is a level of explanation at which "brute facts" rear their ugly head. We simply have to accept certain brute facts as the basis of our preferred system, just as we have to accept Euclid's axioms if we are to use his system of geometry. We can argue about what brute facts are necessary, and that is exactly where philosophy or theology should take over from science. Krauss is arguing that the laws of physics as we know them are the brute facts we should accept as the "nothing" out of which our universe arises. But he's not arguing this explicitly; rather, he seems to mock the suggestion that some people may prefer to go a bit deeper and ask why do the particular laws we observe around us exist. We may never know the answer to this or similarly deep questions, but it is not irrational to speculate about answers. And nor should it be discouraged.

Turning to Dawkins' own book tackling some similar issues, *The God Delusion*, we find equally unconvincing arguments. To be sure, Dawkins makes many good and valuable arguments. I agree with him that organized religion's answers to the big questions are increasingly failing in today's world. And I certainly agree that behaving ethically is a matter quite independent of one's views about the Creator. However, Dawkins' arguments are generally fairly sophomoric in that they fail to engage any of the more rigorous philosophies/spiritualities that adhere to both reason and faith. I'm rather partial to Whitehead's process philosophy, which is just one such approach that is rigorous and compatible with modern science – but also finds room for God (not necessarily as a conscious being, but perhaps even that).

Dawkins key point is that the traditional omnipotent and omniscient Creator God of Christianity conflicts in numerous ways with modern science. And on this I agree. But that traditional notion of God is not the only notion out there. There are many alternative concepts of a higher intelligence or a higher power that rational people can subscribe to. I explore some of these ideas in my in-progress documentary.

Dawkins and Krauss are fairly described as "fundamentalist scientismists," as in "scientism." Scientism, like most isms, takes a single idea too far, to the point where it becomes dogmatic and closes one off to other ideas. Dawkins and Krauss are to MSNBC as Christian fundamentalists and Creationists are to Fox News. They're all way too dogmatic and extreme.

Krauss and Dawkins are bad philosophers

At the end of the day, what Krauss, Dawkins, and other scientists like them who criticize philosophy, are doing is itself philosophy – but it's just very bad philosophy. The claim, for example, that science can answer the question "why is there something rather than nothing," is itself obviously unfalsifiable. So it would seem that Krauss' book falls under the rubric of philosophy, not science. Similarly with Dawkins' book, which claims that science has demonstrated that God very likely does not exist. How could this theory be falsified? If we could demonstrate that God does indeed exist, his theory could be falsified, but as we've seen from a few thousand years of debate no such demonstration is forthcoming.

The basic rules of philosophy are logical coherence and adequacy to the facts. Krauss and Dawkins attempt philosophy, but they break both of these rules in their books. They fail in being logically coherent because they argue against the importance of philosophy while actually engaging in philosophy. And their ideas are not adequate to the facts because they fail to recognize that many questions relevant to human experience cannot be examined from a strictly scientific point of view, at least not the kind of science that focuses on falsifiability. (I've suggested, following Ken Wilber, that a single "deep science," can encompass science and spirituality, but this is not a path Krauss or Dawkins choose to tread.)

There is also an unfortunately common thread in this kind of writing: an obvious lack of any personal deep spiritual experiences that prompt reflection or hesitation at embracing a purely reductionist approach to nature. I can't help but feeling in reading Krauss, Dawkins, Dennett, etc., that these gentlemen would benefit greatly from a week-long silent meditation retreat or some similarly profound experience.

I'll end with the conclusion of Albert's review of Krauss' book:

> When I was growing up, where I was growing up, there was a critique of religion according to which religion was cruel, and a lie, and a mechanism of enslavement, and something full of loathing and contempt for everything essentially human. Maybe that was true and maybe it wasn't, but it had to do with important things — it had to do, that is, with history, and with suffering, and with the hope of a better world — and it seems like a pity, and more than a pity, and worse than a pity, with all that in the back of one's head, to think that all that gets offered to us now, by guys like these, in books like this, is the pale, small, silly, nerdy accusation that religion is, I don't know, dumb.

Amen.

Part II

On Matters Spiritual

What is spirituality? For me, it's about the search for meaning that each of us is compelled to conduct. What is meaning? Simply the narrative we tell ourselves about our relationship to the rest of reality.

Chapter 13

The Mirror of the World:

Toward a Post-Modern Environmentalism

We don't want other worlds, we want mirrors.

Solaris, a 2002 Stephen Soderbergh film

Environmentalism is generally viewed as the movement designed to help protect and preserve the natural world around us, distinct from the artificial world of homes, neighborhoods and cities. This is an overly narrow view. Environmentalism needs to be extended to our inner space, our psyches, as well as the external world, if we are to be effective in tackling pressing environmental problems.

Our global environmental crisis continues, but it is a slow-moving crisis and, therefore, not capable of triggering the appropriate reactions. Problems like biodiversity loss, ocean acidification, deforestation, climate change, etc., all take place on the scale of decades, even centuries, which is far too slow for most of us to really care about these issues. And this is why those who self-identify as environmentalists or, more importantly, work actively to improve any of these problems, are generally a small minority of the population.

Complicating matters in recent years is the worst global recession in decades and justified concerns about jobs and our economy, an ongoing "war on terrorism" that distracts from other issues, and the ascendancy of right-wing media in the U.S. and increasingly in other parts of the world that actively campaign against many environmental causes.

What are we to do, then, in order to tackle these slow-moving environmental crises? There are numerous policy and practical recommendations available for all of these problems. I have written fairly extensively, for example, on renewable energy as a major part of the cure for climate change (and peak oil), and many others have offered sensible solutions to all of the environmental challenges we're facing. And yet none of these major problems is being solved at the pace required – and many are not being solved at all.

What's missing? It seems to me that we need to change ourselves as much or more than we need to change the world. This essay focuses on a few ideas for the cultural/psychological/spiritual shift that seems necessary for us to solve the environmental challenges we face.

Deep Science

"World" used to mean the "universe" in addition to referring to our little blue-green planet. It was the totality, everything. The German philosopher Schopenhauer mused in the 19th Century about "unsnarling the world-knot" – that is, figuring out what the heck all of this is around us. But as our knowledge of the world/universe grew, our vocabulary grew. "Universe" was used throughout the 20th Century to refer to the sum total of planets, stars, nebulas, etc., revealed by our modern telescopes. Nowadays, some use the term "multiverse" rather than universe to refer to the totality, which may include other universes or other dimensions beyond our detection. Brian Greene's The Hidden Realities offers a great overview of this history.

This shift in vocabulary and philosophy is a direct result of the ongoing scientific and mathematical exploration of the reality outside of us. As our knowledge of our surroundings – our environment – has increased, our vocabulary and concepts have evolved. We have grown our worlds by growing ourselves, and vice versa.

The last few centuries have witnessed unprecedented advancements in the study of nature, yielding supercomputers that fit in our palms, space flight, and weapons that can simulate Armageddon if unleashed. But the study of inner space, the human psyche, is an even richer tradition and has been ongoing for millennia. This inner science, or "deep science," has been most pronounced in the traditions of the East, with Hinduism, Buddhism and Taoism. The West has many of its own similar traditions, but it is fair to state that the Eastern traditions have a much longer history and more depth.

Alan Wallace (*Choosing Reality; Hidden Dimensions*, and many other books) has written extensively about this deep science, as has Ken Wilber (*The Marriage of Sense and Soul; Sex, Ecology, Spirituality*, and many others). Both are generally Buddhist in orientation, but you don't have to be a Buddhist to appreciate their writings and wisdom. Wallace's point, convincingly made, is that while the West has been successful in terms of growing GDP and in developing technology over the last few centuries, the Eastern traditions have a many thousand-year tradition of turning inward and studying the human psyche. We have much to learn from these traditions, with meditation as our primary tool for personal inquiry. The deep science that Wilber and Wallace write about offers a means for scientific exploration of one's own mind, conducted through extensive practice and testing.

The western world has in fact sacrificed inner growth in many ways in order to be so successful at building material wealth. When more than one in ten people in the U.S. is on anti-depressant medication, perhaps as many take anti-anxiety medication, and more than one in a hundred people are incarcerated, it is clear that we, in the iconic civilization of the western world, have major issues.

There is a growing awareness that this set of problems stems at least in part from our alienation from nature. E. O. Wilson coined the term "biophilia" for the human love for nature, for life. We do indeed have an affinity for life itself, in all its grandeur and diversity, even though this affinity is so often sublimated in our highly technological modern culture. Wilson argues, and I strongly agree, that by re-acquainting ourselves with the natural world – hiking, camping, studying life, etc. – we may mitigate many of the inner problems we face, individually and collectively.

My fear, however, is that our increasing "technologization" may only exacerbate our separation from nature. Technology is ubiquitous now, particularly personal electronics, and this trend seems very likely to continue rapidly in coming years. I'm no Luddite, to be sure. I love my gadgets (sometimes a little too much, especially my lovely iPhone 4...) But I actively seek time in nature free from technology, and see this as a major component of my peace of mind. The marvels of modern technology are exciting, but are easily rivaled by nature's marvels when we dig a little and start to understand life on our planet.

Mind and Spirit

The inner work we need to complete starts with a recognition that we are indeed special. We are the bleeding edge of consciousness in our corner of the universe. We are, as far as we know, the only game in town in terms of higher self-consciousness, technologically adept consciousness. We have, as human beings, achieved what is tantamount to a quantum leap in intelligence and technology when compared to all other species. We are gods unto ourselves. Unfortunately, we are the kind of Greek gods who often do very unwise things and re-enact all manner of petty human dramas.

Our astounding human achievements have been most pronounced in the modern era, which has its roots in the scientific revolution of the 17th Century. The advent of the modern era is generally characterized by increasing specialization and the immense amounts of new knowledge that springs from specialization. With specialization comes separation. Most people can't possibly understand even a small portion of the totality of human knowledge today. The age of Renaissance men has long been over – there is simply far too much knowledge for any one person to gain even partial mastery. With this specialization we have realized the fruits of technology in all their glory. But the downside has been increasing alienation – from each other, from much of human knowledge, and perhaps most importantly from nature herself.

A post-modern worldview is needed, but not the deconstructive nihilistic post-modernism that has found favor in some quarters. Rather, we need a post-modernism that recognizes our active kinship with all of nature by integrating our humanity seamlessly with the rest of nature. We are indeed special in the degree to which we have evolved great intelligence and the technological fruits of that intelligence, but we are not different in kind from the rest of nature. There is throughout nature a continuum of consciousness, complexity and of technology.

Many species use tools, technology, language – though in almost all cases these are much simpler than our human examples. Beavers are master dam builders, termites master mound builders, birds master nest builders. And in a very real sense, the sum of species on our planet created the very livable environment we humans enjoy – with bacteria leading the way in producing oxygen and many other components of our biosphere during the course of planetary evolution.

With respect to language, the more we learn about animal, plant and microbial communication the more we realize that there is a cacophony of language all around us – we have not heard because we couldn't understand. We are beginning to understand, however, and this increased awareness of the depth of complexity in non-human species will help create the post-modern worldview we need.

There is a growing awareness that the philosophical positions of the modern worldview are inadequate. The modern worldview evolved in part from Descartes' dualist view of mind and matter, and later into today's prevailing materialist worldview, which has generally lopped off the mind/spirit aspect of Descartes' dualism and left behind only dead matter. Today's materialists, who dominate the cultural elite in science and philosophy, believe that all things can be explained, at least in principle, by explaining the relationships between fundamentally mindless particles that are thought to comprise everything in the universe.

An increasingly popular alternative, however, is the view that mind is very much part of nature from the top to the bottom. It's all a continuum. In this view, known as panpsychism, all of nature includes mind and matter as complementary aspects in each unit of nature. Alfred North Whitehead, Henri Bergson, William James, David Ray Griffin, Christof Koch and David Chalmers are a few of the philosophers and scientists in this long tradition.

Panpsychism is just one of many possible routes to a healthy post-modernism, but it is in my view a particularly promising one because it is logically coherent, can explain the available data in many areas of science, and also leads to many interesting new paths for science and philosophy.

Ultimately, science is a process of self-discovery, whether it is inward- or outward-directed. The deep environmentalist, the deep scientist, realizes that the entire universe is our extended body and our extended mind. Wilson's biophilia hypothesis becomes simply an expanded version of self-reflection. As we seek to understand our own world and seek other worlds or even other dimensions, we will with this understanding always end up staring at ourselves in the mirror. This is not a bad thing: self-reflection is to be encouraged. It is also inevitable because even if we are not consciously self-reflective, we can't avoid interpreting literally everything about the world around us in terms of its importance to each of us. This is what it means to be a conscious being – we are necessarily self-centered.

This necessary self-centeredness doesn't, however, have to contain the negative implications this term normally conveys if we expand our sense of self. Through learning, exploration, immersion in life and nature, we expand our sense of self. There are no real limits on this process.

This process of self-expansion and self-reflection could be a powerful cure for the numerous and pressing environmental problems we face on the only habitable part of the universe we currently know: our planet Earth. Let's get to it.

Chapter 14

Paths to Immortality

Imagine you wake up in a room with no doors and no windows. You are lying on a stone slab of a bed that meets the floor seamlessly. The room appears to be carved out of a single piece of stone that looks like granite. The room is quite large, many hundreds of feet long and about twenty feet high. An eerie glow emanates from the stone, in a manner that appears to defy your understanding of light and electricity.

As you stand up and explore the room's contours, you grow increasingly alarmed about your predicament, realizing that there appears to be no way for air to circulate from outside into the room. How on earth did you get in here and, more importantly, how do you get out before your oxygen runs out? Hold that thought.

Who wouldn't want to live forever? Who would?

This is largely an academic debate for now, but perhaps not for long. We seem to be at a point in our technological and medical knowledge where some type of physical immortality may become possible in a couple of decades or so. But there are many paths to immortality, some of which are here now.

Pondering immortality raises the question: "immortality of what?" What exactly are we suggesting will become immortal? Generally, these kinds of discussions assume that we mean immortality of our bodies, brains and the minds contained therein. This combination of body, brain and mind is what we refer to as our "self." And the self, our identity, is what we are talking about when we talk about immortality.

With our dramatically-improved medical understanding of the human body, the most substantial improvement possible today may simply be extending our lives by a number of years. Extension is not immortality, but it's an important step in that direction. In *Longevity Made Simple*, two medical doctors, Richard J. Flanigan and Kate Flanigan Sawyer, discuss how practices available today can add twenty good years to our lives. These are mostly common-sense solutions, but the authors back up their recommendations with hard science, discussing which solutions really do seem to make a difference. Their top recommendations include: exercise, quitting smoking, avoiding fatty and processed foods, sleeping well, enjoying good relationships and sex, and drinking alcohol and green tea in moderation.

But let's look beyond "mere" life extension. Other thinkers have suggested we can do much better. "Biological immortality" refers to extending the life of our bodies and brains potentially indefinitely. We can never know, of course, if such an approach would lead to true immortality, but as long as we keep on keepin' on, with bodies and minds intact, this path could indeed be called "true" immortality.

Scientists at the Harvard Medical School announced recently that they had succeeded in prematurely aging lab mice – and then turning back the clock on aging – with various substances that affect cells' ability to reproduce accurately. If what they achieved with mice is replicable in humans, it would be like aging from 20 to 80 and then back again, all through the use of various medications. This is very exciting science and highly suggestive that we're onto something in terms of potential human biological life extension.

Ray Kurzweil, in his amazing book, *The Singularity Is Near*, and his more recent book, *TRANSCEND*, has suggested that medical science, aided strongly by exponential growth in computing power (Moore's Law), will in the next couple of decades provide us with ways to become biologically immortal if we wish. He argues that all we have to do "is live long enough to live forever" – that is, until 2025 or so – because ours is the first generation that will be able to take advantage of medical science to become immortal.

Aubrey de Gray agrees generally with Kurzweil's optimistic approach in *Ending Aging: The Rejuvenation Breakthroughs that Could Reverse Human Aging in Our Lifetime*. De Gray, a colorful character with an incredibly long beard and a lisp, focuses in his research on how to stay healthy far longer than is now possible. He argues that avoiding sickness and staying young is simply more fun than the alternative of traditional aging!

But these authors are certainly in the minority of scientists and futurists and the fact that Kurzweil personally takes about 250 pills a day to maintain his health, and the fact that he sells supplements online, casts a shadow on the reasonableness or practicality of his views. Most scientists in this field seem to think that anything approaching immortality will elude us for a lot longer than twenty years, and possibly forever, simply because human biology is far more complex than we realize even now. What took almost four billion years to come into being cannot be understood in full in the matter of a few decades of modern medical research. Time will tell who's right regarding biological immortality.

What about fame as immortality? There is a venerable tradition of seeking personal fame as a way to immortality of … something. This requires we think back to what constitutes our "self." If our self is indeed comprised of our bodies, brains and minds, then fame is no antidote to death. However, there is a decent argument that a self consists of something different than just a body and brain. If we instead look to our personality as the essential feature of who we are, fame may indeed lead to immortality. By "personality," I mean the sum total of what we leave behind us in terms of images, writings, things we've said to everyone we've met and thus the sum total of the impressions we leave behind in those who are still living, in a biological sense.

If we define self as personality, in this manner, then by definition our self is immortal as long as some impression of us during our biological life remains among those who are still biologically alive.

This may have been good enough for the likes of Marilyn Monroe or James Dean, but this is a thin type of immortality for most of us who rather like the biological aspects of self. Is there a middle ground?

What I call "robot immortality" offers a potential middle ground. We can't entirely dismiss the notion of fame/personality immortality. It is clear that the residue we leave in other minds and in physical artifacts like books, photos, movies, etc., is indeed part of who we are. But fame immortality doesn't allow for the continuation of an active agent (me, you), which is rightly thought to be pretty important to the idea of self!

Kurzweil and others also discuss the possibility of humans becoming part or wholly machine at some point in the not-too-distant future. There is of course a long sci-fi tradition of cyborgs, androids and robots, but Kurzweil suggests that these sci-fi speculations may soon become reality as we learn how to meld our bodies with computers. And over time, our bodies may become wholly machine – that is, we may become robots.

We are already at the point where computers can literally read minds. There are even some popular games that use electrodes on the surface of the skin to allow players to manipulate balls through mazes, etc. (though there is some controversy about how much these early-stage games are pre-programmed and how much they depend on measuring actual brain waves). Less controversially, there are now many artificial sensory devices available, such as an "eye" that actually uses one's tongue as a rudimentary retina. It is clear, then, that we are at the point where artificially interfacing between mind and environment is no longer just sci-fi.

Where do we go from here? Kurzweil speculates that we will be able to shift our consciousness over time to a robot/computer substrate that will be just as much the person it began in biological form. And since robots can be repaired or replaced as they wear out, this could be a true path to immortality – if we accept that what a robot/computer contains could rightly be called a self.

This prompts a deeper examination of what "self" is. I have suggested above that self is a combination of body, brain and mind. I've also suggested that personality, as captured in the artifacts and memories we leave as we move through the world, is part of self. But what is the essential self, the part of each of us that we will always be able to recognize as the individual in question?

This is a question that has been pondered for millennia in East and West. Buddhism is well-known for its central doctrine of "no-self." What does this mean? In brief, it means that there is no permanent self, no intrinsic self that exists independently of other beings and things.

Indeed, if we are asked to list all the things that make us who we are we see quickly that not a single item is permanent. Our bodies change over time and the molecules that comprise our bodies are entirely replaced every few years. Our personalities change, our values change, our preferences change and of course our history changes in every second that we are alive. Our names can appear to be permanent, but this is a small hook to hang a self on when we consider that it can be changed with the stroke of a pen or through a personal decision to use a different name. It seems that the Buddha may have got this one right.

But what about the soul? Isn't this the permanent essence of who we are? And isn't this why any notion of a robotic future self fails to capture what makes us human?

There is no definitive answer on this issue. But it seems very unlikely that there is an immaterial thing that is us that forever remains unchanged – the essential soul. This is the case because we must first ponder what exactly it is about a soul that is essential and unchanging? I don't accept automatically that because modern science has attempted to rue out the soul that it doesn't exist. But if our soul includes our personality and our history as a human being, as most notions of the soul do, then the soul must indeed change – or else it couldn't contain the changes that happen to us as we live our lives.

I won't be able to resolve this issue in a short essay, of course, and it is certainly not rational to rule out entirely the existence of an essential soul. We never know the full extent of what we don't know. Nevertheless, it does seem unlikely that there is an essential soul, given what we know now about the natural world, human psychology and biology.

If there is indeed no permanent self, then robotic immortality presents a real alternative. If I am a hundred years from now contained in a robot/computer substrate and there is no longer any trace of my current biological self, that Tam Hunt will have just as much right to call itself Tam Hunt as I do currently. This issue has been a standard philosophical debate for years, usually framed something like: "If doctors replaced your brain one neuron at a time with an exact artificial replica, at what point do you stop being you?" (For more permutations on this question than you probably care to ponder, see Derek Parfitt's Reasons and Persons.)

Under the ideas I've outlined here, the answer is easy: you don't stop being you. And this is because "you" are simply a constantly changing pattern of awareness or information contained in some physical substrate. And as the pattern that is you changes over time from a biological being to a robotic being, it remains you each step of the journey. In other words, it doesn't matter what one's physical substrate is because each of us is comprised of a relatively stable pattern of information/awareness/energy and this pattern can be maintained in various physical substrates. The idea of robotic immortality is highly unsatisfying to many people, however, because there is a reasonable attachment to our biological forms!

But there is yet another way that true immortality can be reached. This last path to immortality is in my view the most promising and the most genuine. There has been a long debate between Buddhism and Hinduism over the "no-self" doctrine. Hindus, particularly the Advaita Vedanta school, argue that what we normally call the self is just the "little self" and that it isn't fundamentally real. So Hindus agree with Buddhists that the little self is at least partially illusory. The real Self, however, is everything for Hindus.

There is no real separation between what we normally call our self (the little self) and the rest of the universe, the Self. There is an apparent separation, to be sure. But this is only apparent and when we delve deeper than appearances we realize that it is impossible to extricate our "self" from the universe because no matter how hard we try there remains some tendril of connection – this is what it means to exist in the universe. And if we can't separate our self from the rest of the universe, we are part and parcel of that universe. It's all just one thing: Self with a capital S.

This Self, also known as *Brahman*, is our true identity. When we wake up to our true Self, we realize that we are and always have been the entire universe. And the universe never dies. You, me, we, all of humanity, are in this view of reality immortal. And we don't even have to realize it consciously to make it true. We are immortal whether we realize it or not. But it helps for personal happiness, in the realm of appearances, to realize this truth.

The concept of Brahman/Self is particularly compelling to me because it is undeniable that all things are connected to varying degrees. And the more we learn about the physical world, the more science confirms this truth. Quantum entanglement, for example, is the latest phenomenon that confirms that things are connected in ways previously deemed impossible. And who knows what else we will discover in coming decades.

You have probably forgotten the riddle that I began this essay with. The answer to the riddle is this: "you" escape the windowless and doorless room by realizing that you are the room, you are the planet, you are the solar system, the galaxy, the universe. If you are the universe, you never die.

Chapter 15

On Lucifer

I mourn the loss of thousands of precious lives, but I will not rejoice in the death of one, not even an enemy. Returning hate for hate multiplies hate, adding deeper darkness to a night already devoid of stars. Darkness cannot drive out darkness: only light can do that. Hate cannot drive out hate: only love can do that.

Mangled quote from Martin Luther King, Jr.

This quote achieved instant fame/notoriety on the Internet in 2011 because of the powerful virality of Facebook, Twitter and other social media.

It turned out, after some Internet sleuthing by various intrepid journalists, that one Jessica Dovey, a teacher based in Japan, had posted these words on her Facebook status update, expressing her own sentiments in the first sentence and then following with an actual quote from King. Others inspired by her words copied the paragraph in full as though it were all from King. And thus it spread.

Despite the mangled nature of the King quote, did it express a wise and compassionate sentiment even with respect to the world's most notorious terrorist, a modern-day Lucifer?

This brief history is meant to be a light introduction to a heavy topic: Lucifer, the devil, Satan, evil. What do these words mean? Why is there evil? Is there evil?

Lucifer is, of course, the name used in the Christian tradition for a particular fallen angel, a powerful adversary to the God of the Old Testament. Lucifer was at God's right hand until he fell out of favor and was cast out of Heaven by God. Lucifer has been waging war on God and the good ever since. (Interestingly, Lucifer means, in Latin, "light bearer" and was originally the Latin name for the Morning Star, Venus; it was only later that Lucifer became synonymous with the devil).

Very few people take this story literally today – we are generally more sophisticated than this. But the metaphor of Lucifer is still in many ways apt. Lucifer is more generally known as Satan today – conceived as not merely a fallen angel, but the powerful counter-balance to God's goodness. Where there is light there must also be dark, so Satan, evil, is in some ways inevitable, according to many thinkers.

Satan, however, simply means "adversary" or "the accuser" in Hebrew. Satan doesn't appear as the "devil" or as the embodiment of evil in the Old Testament at all.

Long before the New Testament was written, the Greek tradition shed some light on good and evil. Plato, in his most famous work, The Republic, was anxious to make his case that Zeus, the king of the gods in folk religion and also the single God in Plato's philosophical system, could only be responsible for good and not bad:

> Then God, if he be good, is not the author of all things, as the many assert, but he is the cause of a few things only, and not of most things that occur to men. For few are the goods of human life, and many are the evils, and the good is to be attributed to God alone, of the evils the causes are to be sought elsewhere, and not in him.

These dichotomies between good and evil have continued until the present day with discussions of the "problem of evil" in theology. If there is a God, why does he/she/it allow evil? I won't delve into the many answers offered and will instead simply acknowledge that many theologians and philosophers agree that there are many things deserving of the name "evil" and that there's no easy answer as to why it persists.

Let me shift gears here and bring these philosophical and theological musings back into the real world. Osama Bin Laden was killed in early 2011 [a recent event when this essay was written] by US Navy seals in a private compound in Abottabad, Pakistan, not far from the capital of Islamabad.

Was Osama a modern-day Satan or Lucifer? Was he the epitome of evil? What Osama did, or at least encouraged (his role is not clear), was horrific – let's be clear on this. There is no justification for killing innocent civilians or encouraging such killing. Islamist fundamentalists seem to be focused on a dogmatic religious view of the world and accompanying morality that is more appropriate for the 7th Century than the 21st Century.

By the same token, there is no justification for killing innocent civilians as "collateral damage" when it is 100% certain that civilians will be killed through US military actions. The US has killed countless civilians in the ten years since 9/11, in Iraq, Afghanistan, Pakistan, Yemen and perhaps many other countries. Far more civilians have died at our hands than died at Al Qaeda's hands in 9/11 or all other attacks they've perpetrated. Far more. Various surveys of civilian casualties in Iraq alone, since the US invasion, report deaths of 100,000 (news accounts and US secret documents revealed by Wikileaks) to one million (private surveys).

Increasingly, our preferred method of violence is the unmanned drone – known aptly and chillingly as Reapers or Predators. Every week or so a new tragedy occurs as US drones or other machines of war, guided by "pilots" based in the US, kill women, children and other non-combatants. In March of this year nine Afghan boys were killed by NATO helicopter rockets while gathering firewood on a hillside. NATO (a proxy for the US) apologized for the mistake.

Even more tragically, and less predictably, a number of US Army soldiers have been indicted for actively targeting Afghan civilians and killing them in faked gunfights. Rolling Stone reported in detail on the activities of the US "kill team" in Afghanistan. Jeremy Morlock, a US enlisted soldier who has admitted to these activities on camera, was recently sentenced to life with the possibility of parole in March of this year. The kind of behavior that is condoned, if not officially approved, by US troops in Afghanistan, revealed through these reports, should shock the conscience.

How does Obama's decision to wage aggressive and illegal drone warfare in Pakistan and Afghanistan, knowing with certainty that hundreds or thousands of civilians will be killed, truly differ from Osama's role in 9/11 and other attacks on civilians?

There is a difference, but it's a very fine difference. Perhaps what could be called a "distinction without a difference."

Obama's actions have perpetuated the overly aggressive foreign policy of Bush before him. Bush, however, brought us back to a far older era when he told the world after 9/11 that "you're either with us or against us." There should be no room in the modern era for such an atavistic view of morality – just as there should be no room for the Islamist fundamentalist worldview. This approach perpetuates "evil" through its unreflective dichotomizing. It is more similar to Bin Laden's version of morality than it is different. It is more similar to the attitude of foes of the US who label us the "Great Satan" than it is different.

Good and evil are simply labels we give to what would be more accurately labeled "things we like" and "things we don't like." As more and more people agree on things we like and don't like, particular labeling of certain things as good and evil gains traction. There is nothing objective about this process.

Does this bring us to moral relativism? Yes. There is no objective morality. For those who believe in objective morality, it is generally grounded in "my holy book says" rhetoric. If one doesn't accept the holy book at issue as authoritative, the moral claim will be equally lacking in authority – unless it can be based in more generally acceptable arguments. And it becomes very difficult to accept religious morality when, for example, a holy book like the Bible includes passages such as "love your enemies and pray for those who persecute you" (Jesus, Matthew 5:44 in the New Testament) alongside far more savage sentiments (Psalm 137 in the Old Testament):

O Daughter of Babylon, doomed to destruction,

happy is he who repays you

for what you have done to us --

he who seizes your infants

and dashes them against the rocks.

This kind of dissonance is why secularists are adamant that hope for the future should be placed on secular morality and not religious morality. One doesn't have to be an atheist (I'm not an atheist) to be a secularist (I am a secularist) – all we have to do is witness the suffering caused by religious dogma over the millennia to see a brighter light in secular morality.

Secular morality generally doesn't use terms like "evil," because of obvious religious connotations. Secular morality makes arguments based on the common good. The common good is what most of us can agree are beneficial goals and outcomes, independent of any particular religious creed. Democracy, human rights, good jobs, being kind to your neighbor, are all examples of secular morality that may or may not be shared by any particular brand of religious morality. And there is nothing set in stone about secular morality: it's always changing, always debatable. The debate itself is very much part of the common good.

There is no necessary conflict between secular and religious morality – it all depends on what the commonalities are. There are various types of religious or spiritual morality that can be entirely compatible with a secular morality. I will flesh out in later essays a "process theology" view on morality that shares much with the Vedanta tradition of the East. But secular morality doesn't require any theological justification.

Violence is not a solution, as King stated so eloquently: "Darkness cannot drive out darkness: only light can do that. Hate cannot drive out hate: only love can do that." Even though King was a Christian minister his arguments did not rely on the Bible for authority. They relied as much or more on basic human decency, our secular sense of right and wrong. He reminded us, as did Jesus, that we should abandon the primordial "us versus them" mentality that gives rise to so many emotionally-driven conflicts.

We all have angels and demons within us, we all have God and Lucifer within us. By celebrating Osama's death, we give in to those demons and stifle our better angels. Only through exalting our better (secular) angels will we be able to achieve a better world for all people.

Chapter 16

Avatar, Blue Skin and the Ground of Being

A Dec. 20, 2009, *New York Times* columnist described Jim Cameron's latest blockbuster, Avatar, as a "long apologia for pantheism." This is, we learn as we read further, a bad thing. *Pantheism* is the notion that the entire universe is God.

Pantheism is generally relegated by modern theologians and scholars to an earlier, less advanced, stage of humanity, with a less well-developed notion of divinity. But the Na'vi people of Avatar's moon known as Pandora may well hold the more accurate – and ultimately more helpful – notion of divinity after all.

Theism is, since the days of Thomas Aquinas, the basis for most of Christian faith (though what defines Christian faith in the many hundreds of different Christian traditions is itself rather hard to pin down). Aquinas was a 13th Century Italian monk who wrote the authoritative text for Christianity in his era, Summa Theologica. This work remains highly influential today. The basic tenets of traditional theism hold that there is one God and the universe is His creation. God and the universe are separate. God is eternal and uncreated. The universe is created and will one day end – rather soon, according to some of the more fiery theologians.

Pantheism, to the contrary, holds that God and the universe are one: it's all the same stuff. Pantheism doesn't necessarily require that there be only one god, and the more "primitive" versions of pantheism view the world as containing a multiplicity of gods. Einstein, not exactly an intellectual scrub, subscribed to Spinoza's pantheistic God. Spinoza, a 17th Century Dutch Jew, stated that "matter and soul are the outside and inside aspects, or attributes, of one and the same thing in itself ...; that is to say, of 'Nature, which is the same as God.'" (Spinoza's *Ethics*, 1677).

As with most things in real life, there are more than two flavors possible. In this case, in between traditional theism and pantheism is *panentheism*, described by one scholar as "the god of the philosophers." Panentheism – the extra "en" being very important – holds that the universe is within God but not identical with God. So all of the universe is God, but God transcends the physical universe. Modern proponents of panentheism include the British philosopher and physicist Alfred North Whitehead, Ralph Waldo Emerson and Charles Hartshorne. And of course Hinduism has taught a version of panentheism for many thousands of years, based on the Vedas and Upanishads, which were first written about 1800 BCE. In Hinduism, Brahman is the ultimate ground of being, what some describe as God.

This takes us back to Avatar's blue-skinned *Na'vi*. Cameron's epic depicts a far-flung moon inhabited by a humanoid race that enjoys a tight bond with nature. This bond can at times be physical, due to a bio-psychic link that allows the *Na'vi* to literally connect with the global living network they describe as *Eywa* by using open nerve endings at the end of their long ponytails. *Eywa*, a global network consisting of all life on Pandora, is a clear parallel to Hinduism's Brahman. Brahman is the source of all things. It is the soil from which every other thing grows.

And the *Na'vi's* blue skin is a clear parallel to Krishna, Hinduism's Christ-like figure. Krishna is always depicted with blue skin. Krishna stars in such epics as the *Bhagavad Gita*, one of the primary books of the Hindu tradition. The third indication that Cameron intentionally mirrored Hindu teachings is the name of the movie itself. In Hinduism, an avatar is an earthly incarnation of a god, such as Krishna.

We realize, then, that Avatar does not really describe pantheism; rather, it describes a panENtheistic way of life, made very real for its people due to the actual physical connections the Na'vi enjoy with Eywa.

Avatar, as with all movies, is a metaphor. The metaphor in this case is complex and of course open to interpretation. My personal interpretation is that the Na'vi's ability to interconnect with Eywa and download the collective wisdom of all life on Pandora is a metaphor for every human's ability to connect with the ground of being and enjoy that same kind of wisdom.

Ross Douthat, the New York Times columnist who decried Avatar's alleged pantheism, apparently disapproves of Avatar's religious message, based on his conclusion that this message contradicts Christian teachings. This, however, misses the true meaning of Jesus' life and message. Interpreting exactly what Jesus' life and message really were, however, is a veritable cottage industry in this new millennium.

Two books have been helpful for me in gaining a better understanding of Jesus and situating his teachings within the broader context of universal spiritual truth: Deepak Chopra's The Third Jesus and Bart Ehrman's Jesus, Interrupted.

These books and many others demonstrate that we may accurately interpret Jesus' teachings as harmonious with the Hindu teachings of Brahman and Atman. Jesus claimed to be God, according to the Gospel of John (interestingly, the only gospel that contains this teaching). Jesus' claim was considered heretical by not only the Jewish authorities of his day, but also the Roman oppressors. For this and other crimes, he was crucified.

To a Hindu, however, the realization that each of us is God is greeted with a hearty congratulations – "welcome to reality!" Alan Watts, the British-American philosopher, stressed this point throughout his teachings. This is the case because the core teaching of Hinduism – particularly the Vedanta tradition – is that not only is Brahman the ground of being for all things, but that all things constitute a non-dual oneness. It's all just one thing. And when we realize that it's all just one thing, we realize also that we are that one thing. I am the universe, you are the universe, we are the universe. I am God, you are God, we are God.

For Jesus to say he is God is not, then, such a stretch. In fact, it becomes rather pedestrian. But it is a pedestrian truth that all of us should internalize and live, each day. Paul Tillich, a 20th Century German theologian, has written extensively on a similar interpretation of Christian faith.

When we realize that all other people are in fact just pieces of the grand oneness that is us, *Brahman*, the ground of being, it becomes a lot harder to treat each other inhumanely. And the same realization leads to a renewed reverence for the natural world – because the natural world is just another manifestation of our true identity, the entire universe. And this is, ultimately, a very Christian teaching.

Chapter 17

On Self and Soul

Imagine you are in an isolation tank. All you can sense (barely) is the lukewarm water in which you float. You hear nothing except the slightest movements of water against the side of the tank. You see nothing. You smell nothing. And you taste nothing but your own saliva.

Now imagine that a video screen is added to your isolation tank connected to a camera outside the tank that shows you an image of the world around your tank. And a microphone is added. Then, with some cool new technologies, scents are wafted to your nostrils. You begin to get an idea of what the outside world is like from the vantage point of your isolation tank.

Now imagine that your isolation tank is mobile – it is re-engineered to be small enough that you can walk around in a roughly body-shaped tank even though you remain immersed in water. Servos help move your massive limbs, which articulate your strange machine torso and limbs. The technologists add even niftier gadgets that allow you to feel the outside world from the "skin" of your isolation tank, based on contact with the outside of the tank. And a tube is added that allows food to enter your mouth from the outside and another tube for waste. You now have almost normal access to the outside world from within your isolation tank. You could remain perhaps indefinitely in this unnatural environment.

Now imagine that this scenario is real. In fact, little imagination is required. We do exist in biological isolation tanks that we call our bodies. Literally all we know about the external world comes from various sensory "windows" we have to the external world. The world we know is entirely a creation of our brains, our nervous systems, with its various perceptual abilities. We can never know what really is the cause of our perceptions. All we know directly are our perceptions.

We can only infer what reality is separate from our perceptions of reality, our individual experience. The fact that different people agree on so many things about the world outside our skins is strong evidence that we're not totally clueless about what is really out there. This is known as "intersubjective" confirmation. This confirmation helps us avoid going entirely crazy because we have other people to help us construct models of reality – even if we realize that what we know directly of those other people and their constructed worlds is also entirely constructed by our own minds.

What do we really, I mean, really know?

This is not really new ground. Take away the technological aspects of my thought experiment and you have much the same insight that Descartes famously pursued in the 17th Century, leading to his famous statement: "I think, therefore I am." He concluded, in other words, that the only thing he knew with certainty was that he existed, based on the simple fact of experience, of consciousness, of thought. This is the only fact any of us knows with certainty: there is some experience, right here, right now, and this flow of experience we can call a "self."

But what is the self beyond this flow of experience?

Descartes' logic on this particular issue is not quite impeccable. There is actually a more modest conclusion that we can draw from his approach. I cannot, if I am being entirely rigorous, conclude that "I" exist based solely on the fact of my experience. Rather, I should conclude only that my experience itself exists. The "I", the self, is an additional conceptual overlay. But definitions are important in this (and any) discussion. The self is generally thought to be a permanent or semi-permanent center of identity – and this is what I mean when I say that Descartes went a bit too far.

In the sense of a permanent identity, Descartes' insight is no support at all. Why would we conclude that there is a permanent self based on the mere fact of experience? We have very limited evidence of permanence in our lives. We have only memories going back to our toddler years, as well as the undeniable fact that all other people we know have died at some point around 80-100 years old. We could quibble over what "permanent" means, but I don't think any reasonable person would suggest that this very limited span of time should be called permanent.

So how "semi-permanent" is the sense of self? Is our direct experience good evidence for semi-permanence? I would argue that it is not because our experience changes literally in each moment, and sometimes dramatically.

The only thing my experience as a five-year-old self seems to have in common with my 40-year-old self is my name (not even that, technically, because I use a shortened version of my first name as an adult). My body, revealed through my direct experience, has changed dramatically and is literally changing in every moment. My memories and my preferences have changed dramatically. And my name could be changed as easily as asking people to use a different name (with or without resorting to any legal name change).

It seems clear that all aspects of our selves change regularly. What, then, is the argument for even a semi-permanent self?

The best argument is that there is obviously some degree of continuity moment to moment, year to year. Each of us can trace our own development backwards in time, sometimes for many generations. There is something that continues, a thread of selfhood. But this thread itself, while traceable, is itself constantly changing. There seems to be no thing, no substance, no essence, that we can point to as our self, permanent or semi-permanent.

My "self" seems to be a constantly changing pattern of experience, of awareness. And that's it. As Derek Parfitt put it: "The self is like Paris." That is, it is a generally useful term we apply for a loosely-defined collection of phenomena, the constituents of which are always changing, at different rates.

Soul?

How does this relate to more mystical or religious notions of a soul, a type of permanent self? The closer we examine the idea of the soul, the more clear it becomes that the notion of an enduring self, either in the secular sense, or in the more religious sense of the soul, is little more than an illusion because change is inescapable in the actual world. This is a difficult idea for many to accept. And I recognize fully that whether one chooses to believe in an unchanging soul, or not, is a highly personal decision.

For me, however, it seems clear that the common view of one's soul as unchanging essence is both an unnecessary concept and one that is hard to justify rationally. I can't rule it out, of course, because I can never know the full extent of what I don't know. The soul's existence nevertheless seems quite unlikely. This is one of the basic teachings of Buddhism, and some other religious and spiritual traditions. It is a truth originally derived without the aid of modern science and its knowledge of atoms, molecules and metabolism. Modern physics, chemistry and biology have done much, however, to bolster the ancient teachings in this area.

In Buddhism, this idea is known as "no-self" or *anatman*. The *atman* is the Hindu version of what we call in the West the soul. Buddha contradicted the Hindu tradition of his day, which he grew up with in 5th Century BCE India. As with Jesus growing up in the Judaic tradition, Buddha was raised in an ancient tradition and eventually found good reasons to contradict many key teachings of the ancient tradition he was raised in. Buddha, contrary to the Hindu teachings, could find no reason to believe in atman, the permanent self. To the Buddha, all things are ultimately empty of any inherent nature. All things are relational – they arise through "dependent origination," to use the common English translation of this doctrine. In Western terms, Buddha denied the reality of the soul. This is the anatman doctrine.

Was Buddha right, and does it really matter? Buddha, in his original teachings, avoided discussions of metaphysics because he thought such discussions were unfruitful and not helpful for the true goal of spiritual inquiry: liberation from the self.

Later schools of Buddhist thought failed to heed Buddha's example and many different schools have since developed detailed metaphysical views. Buddha didn't have much to say about the Hindu Brahman, but he did talk about "emptiness." As with the "vacuum" of modern physics, however, Buddha's emptiness, now part of many Buddhist schools of thought, is not really empty. It is, in fact, everything.

So for Buddha even though all things are ultimately relational with respect to their existence, he advocated a concept, which he called emptiness, that performs the same conceptual role as Brahman performs in Hinduism. Do Buddhism and Hinduism still disagree on this issue? If you asked ten Buddhists and ten Hindus this question, you would probably receive twenty different answers. I believe, however, that Buddha's emptiness is equivalent to Brahman. Buddha's real difference with Hinduism lies in his denial of the reality of the atman, the soul. And here is where I think Buddha's departure from Hinduism is helpful and valid.

What does it mean for us to accept that the self as a permanent or even semi-permanent essence is invalid? For me, it means accepting that change is pervasive, that the now is all we have, that we can enjoy the world with a lighter step and less attachment, that I am a pattern of awareness associated with a particular pattern of matter and energy. These realizations are, it seems to me, good things that outweigh any negatives that come from denying the validity of a permanent self or soul.

A related question arises when contemplating the "self": how do we draw the boundary for self, regardless of what concept of self we subscribe to? The next essay explores how a larger sense of self may lead to a rational type of spirituality, with room enough for God(s) and a ground of being. We may indeed exist in biological isolation tanks (albeit constantly changing), but we may at the same time cultivate a larger sense of self that transcends this evolutionary isolation.

Chapter 18

The Anatomy of God, Part 1

The search for the 'one', for the ultimate source of all understanding, has doubtless played a similar role in the origin of both religion and science.

Werner Heisenberg (1901-1976), Nobel Prize winner for physics

When, as a teenager, I first began engaging intellectually with the world I often perused the philosophy sections of bookstores and libraries, avidly inspecting books for pearls of wisdom. If a philosopher dared to mention spirituality or God, I would consider the book misplaced and not relevant to my philosophical questions – it should have been in the religion section, an area for individuals with weaker minds and weaker stomachs. I was, for some time, an avid atheist, embracing the modern scientific and philosophical trend that has become quite pervasive.

My how things change.

I have realized in my own personal journey that examinations of God and spirituality are part and parcel of philosophy – if we define philosophy as the broad endeavor to understand the universe and our place in it. There are many functions of philosophy, to be sure, but this is as good a definition of philosophy as I have found.

Any rational inquiry into the nature of the universe and our place in it – which includes science as a more specialized form of philosophy – must face one of the most basic questions: how does complexity arise? It seems that it must arise from simplicity – this is, at least, the phenomenon we see all around us: simpler constituents generating more complex forms through combination, separation, and emergence. What place should God have in this story of simplicity producing complexity? Can't we explain the universe in terms of merely matter, energy and space? In a word, no.

The modern trend has generally been to whittle away God's role in the world and in philosophy. Modern science, with Galileo, Newton, Descartes, etc., began this trend by defining the scientific pursuit as rational inquiry into God's work. This inquiry was, and is, all about discovering the rules that govern the world. The broadest hypothesis of modern science and of the modern era more generally was that the world is regular and rational, i.e., it operates through discernible rules. This hypothesis has generally been borne out, as evidenced by the miracles of technology all around us. By discovering the rules that govern the world, many early philosophers and scientists supposed, we explain the handiwork of God and perhaps even the mind of God.

Over time, this hypothesis became stronger and in the 19th Century many scientists and philosophers became overtly atheistic. Rather than viewing the universe as the handiwork of God, many came to view the universe as inherently without design. We may never know what caused the universe to come to be, it was thought, but we certainly could explain everything worth explaining without invoking God. Laplace, an early 19th Century French materialist scientist and philosopher stated, when asked by Napoleon what place God had in his system: "I had no need for that hypothesis."

Nietzsche crowned this trend in the 19th Century with his pronouncement that "God is dead." Even though large majorities of Americans today proclaim belief in God in some manner, the general view among the cultural elite of scientists and philosophers is that God is indeed dead and that the universe can be explained entirely through various permutations of mindless matter, which combine in complex forms like humans to produce very complex minds. The problems with this view, known generally as scientific materialism or materialist reductionism, were fleshed out in my series on "absent-minded science," which attempted to show how modern science went astray by intentionally or unintentionally excluding mind from its explanations in many different fields.

My intellectual journey took a sharp turn when I began thinking seriously about the nature of mind. I began reading in this area in my late teens and have continued to this day, over twenty years now. When I realized what I consider to be the fatal problems in the materialist worldview with respect to explaining the nature of mind and matter, I also realized that a far better explanation is found in the view that all matter has some degree of mind attached. Where there is matter there is mind and where there is mind there is matter. It's all a matter of degree, of complexity. In most cases, matter and mind are extremely rudimentary, but as matter complexifies, so mind complexifies (as a general matter). This view is known as panpsychism or panexperientialism and it turned out that this philosophical position is also a universal acid for resolving all manner of philosophical and scientific problems – and spiritual problems. (This blog is generally an exploration of the many problems the panpsychist view of the world can solve).

This is a key step in my argument in this essay, so the interested reader should, if not already convinced of the problems facing the materialist view of the world, and its "emergence" theory of mind, review parts I through IV of my series on absent-minded science.

I realized, in reading through the works of Alfred North Whitehead and David Ray Griffin, two well-known panpsychists, that the process that leads to our complex minds is unlikely to stop at our level of complexity. There may be – and probably are – many levels of complexity higher than our level. It's a matter of scale, as Whitehead and Griffin themselves discuss. This knowledge leads to some interesting possibilities when we consider spatial and temporal scales far beyond the human level, as discussed further below and in Part II of this series on the Anatomy of God.

Source and Summit

A major problem with traditional notions of God in the western tradition is that He (she, it) is invariably presented as already extremely complex, perhaps the most complex (and powerful) entity that exists. This puts the cart before the horse if God is not simply to be accepted as complex from the outset and thus to be considered outside of any rational inquiry. (As I've explained in earlier columns, there are a great many areas of human inquiry where rationality must at least in part bow to intuition and faith; spirituality is certainly one of those areas, but this is not an all or nothing kind of thing. Rationality may certainly shed some light on these issues even if intuition and faith generally win the day).

It seems that God, in a rational approach to spirituality, must be explained in an evolutionary manner. In other words, how did God become complex? It seems clear that any kind of conscious God – worthy of the name – is necessarily highly complex. We need to be clear, however, in what we mean by "God." Does God have to be conscious? David Ray Griffin writes about "twin ultimates," Ken Wilber about "Source and Summit." That is, there are two types of divinity: the ground (Source) and the sky (Summit). The Source and Summit enclose all of reality and we exist at some middle level of reality. Where exactly we exist, we'll never know because even if succeed in scaling any particular summit we can never know if there are not higher summits beyond. (Griffin would not agree with my version of the twin ultimates, but I nevertheless borrow his apt phrase here).

The Source is – no surprise – more fundamental than the Summit and is probably not conscious. The Source is the ground of being, the soil from which all things grow. The Source is far simpler than notions of God as a complex being (the Summit in the framework I'm sketching here). There are many lines of reasoning that seem to require some kind of ground, a foundation for the universe. I don't have space to explain these in detail, but here's a brief summary:

- Quantum theory suggests that our universe is comprised of a seething mass of quanta that pop in and out of existence. Rather than suggest that these particles (and all of reality with them) simply pop into existence from nothing, it is more reasonable to suggest that there is a ground of pure potentiality from which they grow

- Similarly, the prevailing view of our universe's origin, the Big Bang theory, suggests that a "primordial egg" appeared and expanded rapidly to eventually form all that we observe around us. Where did this egg come from? Rather than positing that it came from literally nothing, it is more reasonable to suggest that it came from a more basic level of reality, the ground of being, pure potentiality

- A more recent development provides additional support for a ground of being: entanglement/non-locality. This phenomenon, first raised by Einstein as an objection to quantum theory, has been well-established experimentally. Entangled particles exhibit non-local behavior because they appear to affect each other instantaneously or near instantaneously at speeds far faster than the speed of light. How does this influence work? There is a very healthy debate surrounding these issues, but it is again reasonable to suggest that this influence is mediated by the ground of being

- In process philosophy, the most sophisticated panpsychist thinking, which emphasizes the temporal nature of all actual things (process), we must have something that forms the basis for process. Whitehead called the ultimate of his system creativity and the process by which the universe is created in each moment is the creative advance. Creativity and the creative advance are analogues for the ground of being

There are other lines of reasoning, but this should suffice for now. If we accept these lines of reasoning, we realize that the mainstream ontology that consists essentially of only matter, energy and space is insufficient. We must add the ground to our list and it is in fact more fundamental than matter, energy and space.

Explaining complexity

In approaching the ground/Source from an evolutionary perspective we are, then, still confronted with explaining complexity from simplicity. The ground must have some degree of complexity built in if it can produce all the marvels of our universe, what can be labeled in this case "primordial complexity." Given this degree of complexity, is the Source, the ground of being, simply to be accepted with no further explanation? It seems that the answer is yes. The ground of being is the ultimate brute fact. There is nothing below the ground of being. There is only an above. Why is there something rather than nothing? Why is there anything at all, including our entire universe? The answer: because there is a ground of being. This is the role that the ground plays in my ontology. It is the level below which there is nothing further.

While the ground's primordial complexity cannot be denied, we can console ourselves that the ground is as simple as possible, but no simpler. That is, to have the universe we know from direct experience we must accept some degree of primordial complexity. We don't, however, have to accept the kind of complexity evident in Western notions of God – and Part II will discuss why this traditional notion of God lacks a rational basis – but we must accept some type of complexity "built in" from the beginning if we accept the ground of being as a necessary part of our ontology.

Even if we accept the ground of being as without beginning and without end (presumably), we can never rule out the possibility that the ground itself evolves. We can never say that it didn't start simple and become complex over the eons. We may in fact gain new insights in coming decades or centuries with respect to the origin of this realm beneath our feet, but for now it seems fair to state that we must at least accept the brute fact of its existence.

The ground of being has many names. In modern physics, it is the "quantum vacuum" or just the vacuum, representing pure potentiality; to Anaximander, an influential pre-Socratic philosopher it was *apeiron*; to Plato and Plotinus it was the One; to ancient Hindu philosophers and mystics it was *Brahman*; to Shaivists it was *Shiva* or *Shakti*; to some schools of Buddhist thought it was *Adibuddha* or Emptiness; to Jewish Kabbalah it was Ein Sof; for Hegel and other Idealists it was the Absolute; for Jung it was the *unus mundus*. And in Christian philosophy the ground of being is either the ground of being (Tillich) or *agennetos* (Origen).

Whatever name we prefer they all refer to the same concept: the ground from which all else grows. And this is as good a definition of God as any – but not the only relevant definition, as we'll see in the next installment in this series.

Chapter 19

The Anatomy of God, Part II

[God] has a primordial nature and a consequent nature. The consequent nature of God is conscious; and it is the realization of the actual world in the unity of his nature, and through the transformation of his wisdom.

Alfred North Whitehead, *Process and Reality* (1929)

What is the ultimate nature of reality? And how does it interact with each of us?

Part I of this series introduced the idea of "twin ultimates," the notion that there are two types of divinity worthy of our consideration. The first, the more fundamental type of divinity, may be referred to as the ground of being, the Source, God's "primordial" nature (as in the Whitehead quote above), or any of a number of other names from various philosophical, scientific or spiritual traditions. The ground of being is the metaphysical soil from which all actuality grows.

The other ultimate, the Summit, lies at the opposite end of the spectrum of being and becoming. The Summit is closer to traditional western notions of God and God is as good a name as any other for this ultimate.

This essay will explore the Summit in more detail and compare Source and Summit. As with all of my essays, I appeal both to science and spirituality in my explanations. This is the case because I don't believe there is any fundamental distinction between science, philosophy and spirituality. To be sure, there are differences in current practice and focus, but in terms of conceptual structures, if not all their methods, these endeavors should be essentially the same ("should" being the essential word here). By this I mean that the "deep science" (to use Ken Wilber's term) that meshes science, philosophy and spirituality together relies on logic, intuition, faith and facts – recognizing that all human endeavors are a mix of these tools.

The deep science that reconciles science and spirit doesn't ignore inconvenient facts, nor does it elevate reason above all other tools as the only source of legitimate knowledge. Deep science recognizes that all our attempts at understanding should be empirically based as much as possible, but it also recognizes that some sources of knowledge lie beyond empiricism and even beyond logic. Defining the contours of where facts and reason should give way to intuition and faith is an entirely personal matter. I tend to the intellectual and rational approach in my own explanations (particularly in these essays), while acknowledging that logic has limits; but I have no independent basis for preferring this prioritization. It's entirely personal.

The Summit

We are predisposed in thinking about the nature of solidity to think of the stuff around us as far more solid than it really is. Though it is commonly known now that we are each comprised of massive numbers of molecules and atoms, and what we think of as solid molecules and atoms are in fact extremely sparsely populated regions of space, this truth has not reverberated as far as it should. We are mostly empty space, and when I say mostly, I mean 99.999999% or more. We, as human beings, are mostly vast voids of emptiness, with tiny isolated specks of matter dispersed at distant intervals.

Moreover, we don't even know what matter "really is." As I wrote in an earlier essay, the mind-body problem presupposes that we've solved the "body problem" (the nature of matter) – but we haven't. Is matter really condensed energy (Heisenberg) or really fields (Einstein) or tiny vibrating strings?

Or is matter really a projection of an underlying neutral substrate, the ground, as I argued in my previous essays? This means that matter arises as quantum fluctuations from the ground of being and these quantum fluctuations constitute matter but also mind. That is, each unit of nature has dual aspects of both mind and matter. The process that produces each quantum fluctuation leads, as the hierarchy of complexity is scaled, to more complex structures like gnats, rats, bats, cats and eventually humans.

This process does not, however, have to stop at the human level. Clearly there are structures in the universe far larger than us, such as planets, stars, galaxies, superclusters, etc., and possibly infinite universes beyond our own that comprise the grandest scale of all: the multiverse (see Brian Greene's 2012 book, *The Hidden Reality*). Tradition suggests that there is no mind present in such supra-human organizations; they consist of mindless matter, as do sub-human levels of complexity. But this is an unjustified prejudice that results from basic philosophical mistakes at the beginning of the modern era. When we recognize that the better solution to the mind-body problem acknowledges that all matter has some type of mind attached, we recognize also that supra-human levels of organization may also have some type of mind attached.

Can the entire universe have a mind? Could the universe itself, with its vast swaths of empty space be akin to the structure of humans with our own vast swaths of empty space? I don't know, but I do know that the conceptual structure that best explains the human level of mind does not in any way preclude the possibility of a universal mind. Let me explain in more detail.

Mind at its most basic level consists of a subject, an object and a link between the two. Consciousness necessarily implies "consciousness of." That is, each subject must have at least one object to be a subject. And there must be some causal link between subject and object to have any such relation. At the human level, we call this causal link perception and we can explain it in purely physical terms as the transmission of information about the world around us through our senses into our internal theater, which is transformed into a picture of the world unique to each of us.

This process is not, however, limited to humans. What we call perception can legitimately be applied to an electron. The electron perceives its environment insofar as it responds to physical forces, such as gravity and electromagnetism. Why is this not normally called perception? Because "perception" implies the presence of a mind. But in the panpsychist view of the universe there is no qualitative difference between an electron's reception of information from its environment and a human's perception of information from her environment. Each has some type of mind, which consists of the same process: a subject receiving/perceiving information from its environment.

Freeman Dyson, the Princeton physicist, stated succinctly: "[M]ind is already inherent in every electron, and the processes of human consciousness differ only in degree but not in kind from the processes of choice between quantum states which we call "chance" when made by electrons." Dyson recognized also that the process that creates mind need not stop at the human level, stating in his 1979 book, *Infinite in All Directions*: "I do not make any clear distinction between mind and God. God is what mind becomes when it has passed beyond the scale of our comprehension."

God is mind at the level beyond the human level. Universal mind surely deserves the name of God. This is the Summit in the system I am describing here. It is made conceptually possible due to the recognition that causality itself, which is the link between subject and object, has no limitation to the human level. Does universal consciousness operate at the same timeframe as humans? I don't know. Perhaps this universal consciousness, if it exists, operates at a vastly slower pace. Perhaps it cares not a whit about humans or other life on other far-flung planets. But perhaps it does.

Unconscious Source, conscious Summit

It seems that the Source is itself unconscious. The Summit must, however, be conscious given the framework I've sketched here.

The *Rig Veda*, the oldest Hindu texts, supports the notion of the Source (*Brahman*) as unconscious:

Neither death nor immortality was there then [in the very beginning],

No sign of night or day.

That One breathed, windless, by its own energy:

Nought else existed then

...

In the beginning this [One] evolved,

Became desire, first seed of mind.

Wise seers, searching within their hearts,

Found the bond of Being in Not-being.

I think of the Source as pure potentiality. It is only when matter/mind bubbles up into actuality from the depths of pure potentiality that consciousness arises. Reality consists, then, in a spectrum from pure potentiality to complete actuality: GoB to God. Ground of Being to actuality to God. This conceptual structure allows us to respect Occam's Razor – explanations should be as simple as possible – while also explaining how complexity and consciousness arise from simplicity and non-conscious processes.

A consistent vision of science and spirituality

Ken Wilber has spent decades attempting a "marriage of sense and soul" (this is the title of one of his books): reconciling science and spirituality. I don't agree with all of the details of his system of thought, but as mentioned I do agree with his "deep science" as key to this reconciliation. Deep science requires that we take seriously the experiences reported by both scientists – who focus on the natural world – and spiritual explorers of all stripes – those who focus on the inner world of human experience. Wilber's *Quantum Questions* details the thoughts of many prominent physicists in the 20th Century with respect to ultimate questions like those I'm addressing here.

Beyond the purely intellectual understanding of the Source and Summit, we should, as thinking and feeling beings, ponder what good this understanding achieves? The highest good it can achieve is a different type of knowledge than purely intellectual understanding, what can be described as *gnosis*. I use this Greek term, typically associated with the Gnostic sects of early Christianity and pre-Christianity, because it best typifies what West and East share in terms of a deeply emotional and spiritual understanding of the nature of God. Other terms for gnosis include *satori*, *Samadhi*, *moksha*, *nirvana*, enlightenment, or simply "awakening."

Erwin Schrodinger, one of Wilber's inspirations, and perhaps the most spiritually attuned of the major 20th Century physicists, is worth quoting at length on gnosis.

From "The I That Is God":

I – I in the widest meaning of the word, that is to say, every conscious mind that has ever said or felt 'I' – am the person who controls the motion of the atoms according to the Laws of Nature...the insight is not new. The earliest records, to my knowledge, date back some 2500 years or more. From the early great Upanishads the recognition Atman = Brahman (the personal self equals the omnipresent)... was in Indian thought considered to represent the quintessence of deepest insight into the happenings of the world... Again, the mystics of many centuries, independently, yet in perfect harmony with each other (somewhat like the particles in an ideal gas) have described, each of them, the unique experience of his or her life in terms that can be condensed in the phrase: *Deus factus sum* (I have become God).

Looking and thinking in that manner you may suddenly come to see, in a flash, the profound rightness of the basic conviction in the Vedanta.... [I]nconceivable as it seems to ordinary reason, you – and all other conscious beings as such – are all in all. Hence this life of yours which you are living is not merely a piece of the entire existence, but is, in a certain sense, the whole...This, as we know, is what the Brahmins express in that sacred, mystic formula which is yet really so simple and clear: *Tat tvam asi*, this is you... 'I am in the east and in the west, I am below and above, I am this whole world.'

Chapter 20

Buddha, Evolved

We find ourselves alive. And struggling to make sense of why we are alive, how to live, and where we go when this life comes to an end, if anywhere.

These are the big questions that spirituality and religion seek to address; they'll never be answered definitively, this much we know to be true. There are, however, many answers available and it is up to each of us to figure out which answers are the most satisfying.

This essay will focus primarily on Buddhism's answers to these questions largely because I have had the good fortune to be a member of an informal group of academics convening at UC Santa Barbara (where I teach part-time) each month for the last two years to discuss the interaction of Buddhism and modern science. I will also present some thoughts on how Buddhism could, and should, evolve to become more relevant and widespread in the modern world.

I am not a Buddhist, but I have read widely in Buddhism for some time. I have also dabbled in meditation, the key praxis (practice) of Buddhism, though I am very much a baby when it comes to realizing the benefits of a regular meditation practice. I feel much less a baby when it comes to the philosophy and intellectual coherence of Buddhism – and how Buddhist views mesh (or not) with modern science.

Buddhism is appealing to many people today because of its emphasis on practical spirituality, on living a better life through insight and regular meditation practice, and the compassion that these activities naturally engender. Buddhism is also appealing to many trained in Western science because Buddhism is far less about metaphysics, heaven or hell, spirits, God, than it is about how to live a better life in the present moment.

The key features of Buddhism, from my perspective, are the emphases on compassion and meditation. Compassion arises naturally from the understanding that all people and all things are mutually interdependent (the doctrine of "dependent origination") and that all people are struggling with the same set of basic problems: the pains of birth, illness, death, relationships, and an ongoing search for meaning.

Alan Watts, a bubbling brook of wisdom through his books and audio recordings, described meditation as "the discovery that the point of life is always arrived at in the immediate moment." Meditation is the path to realizing the essential truths of Buddhism, though meditation is of course not exclusive to Buddhism. The essential truths of Buddhism relate to the impermanence of all things (the doctrine of "emptiness," the flip-side of dependent origination), including our own selves, and the cessation of suffering that arises from this realization. Meditation is practice. It is through consistent practice, not only through seated meditation, but through every action we pursue, that we can realize the essential truths.

An emphasis on compassion is also not exclusive to Buddhism – most religions urge compassion toward others. Buddhism goes further, however, at least in its Mahayana form, in stressing compassion for all creatures and the *Bodhisattva* ideal, in which realized persons – Bodhisattvas – refuse to exit the wheel of life and death until all other beings are also liberated.

Another appealing feature: Buddhism generally lacks the more savage aspects we find in the Abrahamic religions. There are no rules regarding who gets stoned, or who gets burned to death, for adultery or wearing two types of cloth (read Leviticus to get a sense of how extreme the Old Testament view of the world was). There were no conquests by Buddhist rulers wielding swords to convert people to Buddhism. Rather, Buddhism's success has come almost entirely through the power of its ideas.

A final feature of Buddhism that I'll mention is its (general) non-exclusiveness. Most strands of Buddhism don't claim to be the sole path to enlightenment. To the contrary, many schools of Christian thought do indeed claim that Jesus is the only path to salvation. This is a big turnoff to a lot of people who take a more modern view of spirituality, recognizing that no one religion/spiritual system/person has a lock on the truth.

It is for these reasons that I am personally sympathetic with much that Buddhists teach, even though I do not call myself a Buddhist. My views, sketched in two in-progress books, appropriate some ideas from Buddhism, but also from Vedanta Hinduism, and much from the process philosophy school of Alfred North Whitehead, John Cobb, Jr., and David Ray Griffin. I would, however, expect the world to become a much better place if Buddhism's key teachings, compassion and meditation, were adopted more widely.

Buddhism today

Only 0.7 percent of Americans self-identify as Buddhists, a little more than Muslims or Hindus, but much less than the 78% of Americans who identify as Christians. The fastest-growing "religion," however, is no religion. That is, people are increasingly rejecting organized religion in favor of the "spiritual but not religious" approach to the big questions. Fully one-third of Americans under thirty are non-religious ("unaffiliated), compared to only one-tenth of those over 65. Clearly, transformation is afoot.

Figure 1. *Pew Research Center's findings on religious affiliation.*

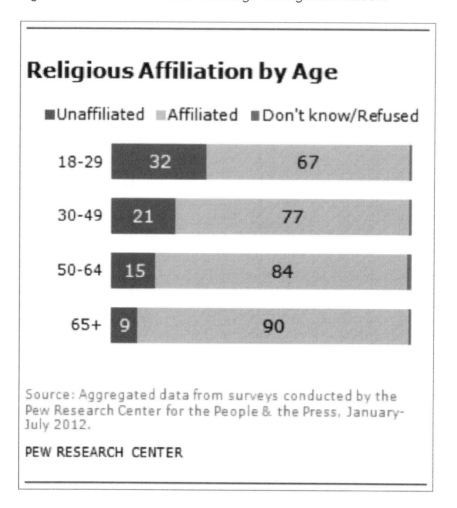

The key teachings of Buddhism are well-suited to the spiritual but not religious crowd. But my feeling is that these ideas could be a lot more appealing – and this is the key point of this essay – if modern Buddhism is willing to evolve further to reflect more scientifically-sound ideas about the nature of reality. There is clearly a large opening for Buddhism's key teachings to find a wider audience as the radical generational shift away from organized religion continues.

Buddha changing

Buddhism, as is the case with all religions, has evolved steadily since the Buddha first taught his insights. For example, I friended the Dalai Lama a few months ago on Facebook. I appreciate his regular status updates and posts, such as:

> *By implementing the practice of love and compassion, we will naturally live a non-violent way of life. Helping others and not harming them is the work of non-violence. We need to develop love, compassion and forgiveness to develop inner peace and that naturally gives rise to non-violent conduct.*

Who could imagine even a few years ago that Tibetan Buddhism's leader would be using social media to spread his message? Change has, however, been a constant in Buddhism, as with all religions or social movements more generally.

Buddhism's oldest sect is known as Theravada and is today found primarily in Sri Lanka and southern India. Many found Theravada's focus on personal liberation too narrow and urged a broader focus on the liberation (awakening) of all beings. This led to what is known now as the Mahayana ("great vehicle") schools of Buddhism, which stress the Bodhisattva ideal of universal liberation. Tibetan Buddhism is generally viewed as a type of Mahayana. Zen Buddhism is also Mahayana but is the product of many centuries of Chinese and Japanese Buddhist thinkers. There are hundreds of other schools of thought in Buddhism, resulting from changing views, personality conflicts, changing times, etc.

I think it's time for Buddhism to be further modernized, specifically by re-interpreting the doctrines of karma and reincarnation. Karma is generally framed as a system of moral accounting where individual actions have repercussions that have both short and long-term reach. Wrong actions may lead, in some schools of thought, to reincarnation in a lower plane of being or as a lesser type of creature – a fly, for example. Conversely, right living will lead to reincarnation in a higher plane or better personal situation (or caste, which is the historical milieu of Buddhism in India, still extant today). Karma is thought to operate independently of the Western notion of physical cause and effect, as a parallel system of spiritual cause and effect.

This notion of karma is problematic for the obvious reason that modern science finds no support for this idea of a parallel system of cause and effect. Modern science seeks to explain all things through four fundamental interactions: gravity, electromagnetism and the strong and weak nuclear forces. This may not be a complete list, particularly because quantum entanglement seems to operate outside of these four interactions. But even if we add quantum entanglement as a new force there is still no room for karma as a parallel system of cause and effect in the Western scientific tradition.

Moreover, there is a fundamental tension between the idea of karma and the far more compelling Buddhist idea of "no self." No self, or *anatman*, refers to the fact that if no things have any permanent existence, the self also has no permanent existence. It's always changing and much of our unhappiness comes from grasping at a notion of a permanent self. Yet the idea of karma as attaching to individuals, even to the point where actions may affect how each of us is re-born, seems to go the opposite direction from the teaching of no self.

One reconciliation of this apparent tension rests on the idea that karma can attach to a non-permanent self, what one Buddhist scholar, Matthew Kapstein, has called a "continuant," in distinction to a "soul," which is thought to have some kind of permanent existence. Just as a candle's flame is constantly changing, there is some continuity between the flame of one candle and flames on other candles that are lit from the first flame. The pattern of the flame remains somewhat stable and certainly recognizable as a flame. This is what a person is: a pattern that remains somewhat stable and recognizable.

This is also a rationale for reincarnation, a concept common to almost all Buddhist and Hindu schools of thought. The doctrine of reincarnation holds that at least some aspects of personality will continue between each incarnation, and the way in which this continuation occurs is guided by the karma of each individual. However, this concept again bumps up against modern science because the evidence for reincarnation is not very strong. Ian Stevenson, a now-deceased scholar at Duke University, and his successor at Duke, Jim Tucker, gathered data on reincarnation for decades. Stevenson's book, *Children Who Remember Previous Lives*, is probably the best summary of this data.

I didn't find this evidence convincing with respect to the reality of reincarnation, if reincarnation is viewed strictly as the recycling of a personality into a new body. There is, however, good data, including Stevenson's and Tucker's data, suggesting that some kinds of information may somehow be passed from the dead to the living, or between one person to another person. This itself is a very strange anomaly from the perspective of modern science, which may require profound changes to modern science. However, suggesting that some types of information may be recycled between lives or between individuals more generally, independent of the known physical forces, is a far more parsimonious suggestion than the traditional Buddhist view that personalities may pass wholesale from body to body.

I am personally open to the idea that modern science needs to evolve, and possibly radically, as well as Buddhism – more than open, as I'm actually a strong advocate that science needs to evolve. The process philosophy views of Alfred North Whitehead and his followers are a richer and more comprehensive basis for an accurate and satisfying worldview than the overly-materialist views of mainstream science today. I've described various ways in which I think modern science should be re-thought in a serious of ten columns here (beginning with "Absent-minded Science"), as well as in my in-progress books.

That said, I don't see any compelling reason why modern science should evolve to accommodate traditionalist views of karma and reincarnation. Rather, I think that Buddhism should evolve and re-interpret the doctrines of karma and reincarnation. Who "gives" in the face of irreconcilable differences? In this case, I think it is Buddhism that should give, though modern science may also need to give some back.

Karma is just a name for the truism that actions have consequences. We can stick to a pretty traditional scientific view of reality and accept that any actions you or I take will have personal repercussions and repercussions on others. The difference between this notion of karma and traditional notions of karma is that there is no parallel system of cause and effect based on a hidden spiritual reality. There is, in the view I'm advocating here, one reality and it operates seamlessly through a single set of laws of cause and effect. Western science clearly doesn't have these laws all figured out yet (see my above comments about quantum entanglement), but we've made a good start. And they aren't really "laws of nature" *per se*, but, instead, habits of nature, to use Whitehead's phrase.

As we learn more about the physical world, we also learn more about the spiritual world because they are the same world. There is no parallel reality. A single "deep science" should include physical and spiritual understandings, to use Ken Wilber's apt phrase.

Reconciling reincarnation is trickier than karma because of the evidence I've already mentioned regarding the apparent transmission of some kinds of information in ways that our current scientific notions say simply can't happen. For example: Stevenson writes in *Children Who Remember Previous Lives* about 14 cases selected from hundreds he'd collected, including those from nine different cultures (in order to counter the view that cases of reincarnation only happen in Hindu or Buddhist cultures): "In every case, the subject made statements about the life he claimed to remember while he was still a young child; in every case one or several adults corroborated that he had made such statements at that age."

Stevenson and Tucker are clearly convinced that their evidence supports a traditional view of reincarnation as the passage of personalities between physical vessels. I was not convinced, as already mentioned, that this is necessarily the case. The accounts are always partial and problematic in various ways. And the idea of an incorporeal entity of some sort literally passing between bodies is riddled with logical problems that I've addressed here.

I'm always open to new evidence and I can't say personally that the idea of reincarnation is clearly wrong. But I haven't found the evidence so far convincing for the recycling of personality. It seems that the best reconciliation of reincarnation with modern science may be to reject the traditional view of reincarnation and continue to examine the evidence for transmission of some kind of information between minds and bodies that is not an entire personality.

A fine balance

Some modern Buddhists have suggested going much further than I am advocating here. Stephen Batchelor, for example, in *Buddhism Without Beliefs*, states "Buddha was not a mystic." Batchelor generally rejects suggestions that the Buddha had anything to say about a deeper reality. Batchelor advocates an agnostic approach to karma and reincarnation: we simply don't know if these doctrines are accurate or not, and they're not crucial anyway. I agree with Batchelor with respect to karma and reincarnation, but I disagree that Buddha rejected all types of mysticism.

Entire sutras have been written on the Buddha's enlightenment experience, which was profoundly mystical, if we are to accept the teachings of the sutras at all. The *Avatamsaka Sutra*, for example, goes into great and exhaustive (and repetitive) detail about this experience.

Moreover, we have little good information about what Buddha "really" taught because it was an oral tradition only for centuries after the Buddha's death. The idea that early texts accurately captured all of what the historical Buddha taught is not very credible.

Moreover, the Pew surveys indicate that about two-thirds of the "unaffiliated" believe in some kind of God. Buddhism is traditionally viewed as being atheistic or agnostic on the issue of God. My views on this important matter have changed much over the years, as I've described here. I am now comfortable labeling myself a theist, but my God is not a traditional god. It's certainly not an angry dude on a cloud hurling lightning bolts at naughty humans. Rather, my process philosophy view of God is summed up well by the American physicist Freeman Dyson: "God is what mind becomes when it passes beyond the scale of human comprehension."

Being a theist, atheist or agnostic is not, however, key to living a better life today, through compassion and meditation; so debates over the existence or nature of God aren't essential to the key points of this essay.

More generally, understanding mind is the key to reconciling science and spirituality, as well as achieving a fine balance between the teachings of Buddhism and the understandings of modern science. We are now undergoing a renaissance in our understanding of mind and the brain, and our philosophies, religions and cultures will surely change as a new understanding of the mind emerges from the current tumult. I'm an advocate of the panpsychist school of thought, in which all material things have some mind associated and vice versa. Where there is mind there is matter, and where there is matter there is mind. I'm very encouraged by some recent high-profile "coming out" statements on panpsychism, including in particular, Christof Koch's recent book, *Confessions of a Romantic Reductionist.*

I'll close with a quote from Batchelor, with which I wholeheartedly agree:

An agnostic Buddhist vision of a culture of awakening will inevitably challenge many of the time-honored roles of religious Buddhism. No longer will it see the role of Buddhism as providing pseudoscientific authority on subjects such as cosmology, biology, and consciousness as it did in prescientific Asian cultures. Nor will it see its role as offering consoling assurances of a better afterlife by living in accord with the worldview of karma and rebirth. Rather than the pessimistic Indian doctrine of temporal degeneration, it will emphasize the freedom and responsibility to create a more awakened and compassionate society on this earth.

Chapter 21

Nature, Version 2012

2012 was my year of backpacking. Returning from Europe earlier in the year, from my fourth trip to Europe in five years, and flying over the Sierra Nevada mountains, I realized that I should stay a bit closer to home for a while. I needed to explore the wealth of the West before gallivanting off to more far-flung locations.

What do we learn from nature? Well, let's see…

I went on four backpacking trips in 2012, three to Yosemite National Park and one to Zion National Park in Utah. Two of my trips were with friends and two were solo. I enjoy hiking and camping by myself, and sometimes seek it out actively, but generally speaking, as with most activities, it's more fun to share experiences with others.

Another major inspiration for my trips was my re-kindled interest in photography. I've dabbled for years (who hasn't nowadays) in photography, but started getting a little more serious after getting a new Nikon.

Yosemite and Zion are so beautiful that they sometimes seem to be overlooked, the way an obviously beautiful woman may be overlooked by hipster types seeking a less accessible kind of beauty. I'm still awed by the beauty of these parks and shall continue to seek them out for years to come before their beauty wears thin with me.

My first trip to Yosemite, in August, was a warm-up trip. I hadn't been to Yosemite in decades and had never really explored it well. I felt, upon gazing upon Yosemite from the famous Tunnel View, just as LaFayette Bunnell did – the first Westerner to gaze upon this seemingly preternatural beauty:

> None but those who have visited this most wonderful valley, can even imagine the feelings with which I looked upon the view that was there presented. The grandeur of the scene was but softened by the haze that hung over the valley—light as gossamer—and by the clouds which partially dimmed the higher cliffs and mountains. This obscurity of vision but increased the awe with which I beheld it, and as I looked, a peculiar exalted sensation seemed to fill my whole being, and I found my eyes in tears with emotion.

On this first trip I scouted out a couple of locations for more serious hiking and backpacking, and camped out near Nevada Fall. I got my first blisters in years and realized that Vaseline would have been really helpful to stop my thighs from chafing, as would chapstick for my lips.

My second trip was more of an adventure. I convinced two of my friends to join me on a hike up Tenaya Canyon – the one area marked on the map as "strongly discouraged" – to Cloud's Rest – the highest point in the Valley area. I discovered after visiting this area in real life that Google Earth can be a bit deceptive regarding actual terrain… What was supposed to be a day and a half up-and-back overnighter ended up becoming two and a half days and required hitch hiking to get back to civilization. The trip was epic, we survived, and my friend Diana swore to never join me again on a backpacking trip if I was the planner.

Trip number three, in November, took us out-of-state, to my first love: Zion. While Yosemite's gray granite beauty suggests permanence and solidity, Zion's red rock sandstone and water-carved canyons suggests a more fragile beauty. Late fall light only enhanced this feeling and I realized from this trip that cold weather should be a bonus, not a deterrent, to backpacking.

Adventure beckoned again, with my friend Cameron reprising his role in our Yosemite adventure and my long-time Heterosexual Life Partner (as a mutual friend of ours designated him) Justin also joining us this time. I planned the Zion adventure too, and got as much flack from my buddies as I had for the Yosemite planning. But my brand of adventure requires some seat-of-the-pants navigation, or it wouldn't be adventure.

We hiked up about five thousand feet, past Angel's Landing, to Horse Pasture Plateau and the West Rim. The view isn't quite as breath taking as that first glimpse of Yosemite Valley, but it's a close second.

We found a secret down-rappel location from the West Rim and discovered that we could indeed rappel down into Phantom Valley – if we had a different route back out of the valley, or two ropes. We had only one rope and didn't have the time to hike out of the valley to the west. So we rappelled and scrambled down as far as we could with one rope, chalked it up as a scouting expedition and vowed to return in the spring.

We camped out on Horse Pasture Plateau, with the three of us sharing my two-person tent. Staggering head to feet to head did the trick. The extra warmth was worth the cramped conditions. We woke at dawn and got warm without anything hot because someone, who shall remain un-named, had left the gas valve on the stove open the night before.

We broke for lunch at the trailhead for Angel's Landing and took a quick, but scary, jaunt out to the end of the Landing. I swear this is the most dangerous public park trail in the country. Sheer cliffs, sometimes on both sides, are frequent and one little slip could – and does about once a year – literally end what would otherwise have been a really good day, for good.

Epic adventure number two: completed.

Having acquired a taste for winter, I decided to tackle Yosemite in the cold months, and to photograph her beauty in a very different mood. I couldn't convince anyone to join me on this trip, so solo I went. I bought snowshoes and some good cold weather gear. I even bought real hiking boots, dispensing with my customary running shoes.

My target this time was Mount Starr King. The name alone required that I visit it. This peak is south of Half Dome and a bit higher, at 9,092 feet. It has an accompanying lake: Starr King Lake. My plan was to hike up the John Muir Trail to Little Yosemite Valley and then strike cross country, in snow shoes, to Starr King Lake, camp out at the lake in the snow and attempt to climb Mount Starr King.

None of that happened.

Well, most of none of that happened. I did hike up the John Muir Trail to Little Yosemite Valley, but that's about as far as I got. I actually went a couple of miles further, to Moraine Fall, and camped out there. There wasn't any snow to speak of even in Little Yosemite Valley and I forgot a pretty key fact: streams and rivers get a lot bigger in winter from rain and snow melt. So I couldn't cross over the stream for a long while and yet again Google Earth fooled me into thinking the slopes up to Starr King Lake are more gentle than they are in real life.

After hiking almost six hours with a full backpack, I decided to abandon my original plan, make camp, and scramble around some of the Moraine Dome area. Setting up camp I realized that my water bottle had leaked all over my sleeping bag. This was unfortunate since it was about forty-five degrees in early afternoon and I was anticipating a very cold night. Somehow, not only had the water leaked only on my sleeping bag, but it had leaked into the hood of my sleeping bag, probably the worst place it could have leaked. I set up my tent and left my sleeping bag on a rock to dry in the sun while I did some rock scrambling on the slopes around the campsite.

I returned two hours later, with evening already falling around four-thirty and a still-very-wet sleeping bag. Luckily, I had brought plenty of fire-starting stuff. Well, not luckily, because I had actually planned ahead.

Unfortunately, none of it worked to get a fire going. My wax cotton tinders were not strong enough to get the damp kindling going. And my limited tissue paper supply didn't do the trick either. Finally, my backup heating candle ("18 minutes to heat a cup of tea") couldn't get the damp wood to cooperate either. I finally gave up and resigned myself to enjoying the three wicks of the heating candle as my evening's entertainment and warmth. I tried to dry my sleeping bag with the candle and succeeded mostly in just burning holes in the nylon.

This didn't stay fun very long, so I ate a delicious veggie chili and avocado dinner and went to bed at six. There's not much to do when camping alone, without a fire, in the middle of winter. I did stay up a couple of hours in my tent, enjoying some hot green tea and listening to audiobooks on my iPhone.

I was a good camper and bear-proofed my food supplies by hoisting them into a tree. I also kept a large knife right next to me in my tent just in case any wild animals got some wild ideas about invading my tent at night.

A bear kept pawing around my camp all night and on a few occasions pushed his jaw up against my tent. But he didn't actually attack me.

All right, I'm lying: there was no bear other than in my fearful imagination. But it's amazing what a bad night's sleep, cold, and ancestral fear of the wild can do to a person. The wind did push the rain fly up against my head a few times, enough to wake me, and I swear I saw a large bear muzzle silhouetted by the new moon outside my tent when I looked up in dismay. But no bear actually attacked me or my food, and there were no bear prints outside in the morning. I didn't have to use my large knife to do any bear slayin'.

So why camp solo in winter, get scared to death, and not achieve much of what I set out to achieve? Well... I'd do it again because we get soft in the cocoon provided by civilization. It's good to be reminded of how much we have going for us. I'm so soft I can't even sleep well with a thin sleeping pad and sleeping bag. I need a double pillow top mattress nowadays. Soft, I tell you.

It's good to be reminded that there are natural creatures that could harm us if we gave them the chance. It's good to challenge ourselves; to re-discover the beauty in nature; and to share it with others. I'd do it again, sleeping in a wet sleeping bag in Yosemite in winter, anytime. But I'd bring a better sleeping pad next time. My old back needs some creature comforts.

Chapter 22

Seeking the Divine

"Spiritual but not religious" has become cliché because it's true – we are increasingly rejecting organized religion in favor of a more authentic and individualized spirituality. The fastest-growing religious movement seems to be that of no religion.

There are many reasons for this transformation, including the growth of alternative explanations about the "big questions," often provided by modern science, as well as a rejection of the overly restrictive or outdated rules that many traditional religions impose. Reading Leviticus today, for example, with its sentences of death for adultery or homosexuality, or prohibitions against wearing clothing of wool and linen together, is a surreal experience. "We're supposed to believe this?" many of us ask ourselves. Similarly outdated, brutal and simply strange rules exist in most of today's religions.

What ideas should fill the gap in our psyches, if we reject, as many of us are now doing, organized religion? How do we honor our need to find meaning and purpose in our lives, if we are suspicious of the answers offered by organized religion, and also want to apply reason as much as faith in developing our spiritual views?

I am fortunate to have enjoyed a profoundly mystical experience in my early twenties. This experience seared itself into my heart and mind one night as I lay on my brother's couch in Seattle. I had spent the evening with my brother and my father, talking with each other and with friends. We ended the evening out by returning to my brother's apartment, where we were staying, and all went to bed, me to the couch.

Upon closing my eyes to sleep I quickly found myself overcome by waves of joy and comfort, each one more powerful than the last. Lying on the couch, with eyes still closed, I felt engulfed by love. I saw a bright white light and felt myself drawn to it. Pure ecstasy is the closest description I can give. This kind of white light vision seems to have been experienced by many others throughout human history. Upon seeing and feeling the white light, I felt a deep oneness with all of nature, my fellow human beings, and a dissolution of the ego. Seeing God is as good a description of this experience as any – and many who have enjoyed experiences like mine describe it this way.

Here's the catch: I was high on marijuana when the vision occurred to me. For many years I discounted this experience as drug-induced and thus "merely" an interesting psychological phenomenon that had happened to me. I was at that time an opinionated atheist, after having been raised an agnostic and after having some time in my childhood in a 60s-style commune where "God talk" was common. I had developed a healthy skepticism toward religion and spirituality, due in part to the break-up of the commune (which occurred after revelations about the sexual and financial improprieties of its founder), combined with my growing knowledge about organized religion and its many downsides.

I was, from a fairly young age drawn to Eastern mysticism and read voraciously through some of the Buddhist and Taoist oeuvre, at the same time that I read many Western philosophers, including Bertrand Russell, a well-known atheist who was also active in the anti-war movements of his era.

I was attracted to Buddhism because it seemed to make sense to me and it didn't require belief in a deity. It is more of a psychology and philosophy of life than a religion. It's mostly a way of managing emotions and negative thinking, and ultimately a way to find lasting peace. Buddhism doesn't necessarily exclude God, in most of its many sometimes disparate schools. But it generally doesn't highlight the role of any kind of personal God and Buddha apparently chose to stay quiet on this topic in his direct teachings.

I found many aspects of the Buddhist approach appealing and it allowed me to develop my spiritual views further while at the same time I continued to reject the concept of God in my life or in the universe more generally.

Things change – and I continued to think, read, discuss, and experience. For what it's worth, I also smoked pot a number of times after that particular powerful occasion and experienced nothing as remotely as profound as that first time. I have now, based on the initial impetus of my early mystical experiences and my later purely intellectual investigations, arrived at a place where I can say that I believe in God. I've transformed from an agnostic to an atheist to a theist. My many years of thinking about the nature of mind was key to this transformation. This has been a long but steady process of independent study, growing more serious over time. I view mind, defined simply as subjectivity, as ubiquitous. As matter complexifies, so mind complexifies. Recognizing this feature of reality has allowed me to construct an edifice of ideas that is intellectually rigorous and spiritually satisfying. This notion, that all matter has some degree of mind, is known as panpsychism and it can be viewed as a "transcendental acid" for eating through difficult, even intractable problems in many different fields.

As I've written in previous columns, mine is by no means a traditional notion of God and it may not be a personal God at all (a God that relates to us directly as individuals). But it is God nonetheless. I feel quite confident in the notion of God as Source, the ground of being from which all of reality grows. God as Summit, a conscious entity, regardless of whether it has any role in our lives, is not as clear to me. I haven't personally felt a conscious God speaking to me, but I can't rule it out as a possibility. I do find it unlikely, nevertheless, that any higher intelligence worthy of the name God would take an active role in our lives, as many traditions claim. And the workings of consciousness for such higher-level entities may be so slow compared to our own as to preclude any real interaction - like our timescale compared to that of a bacterium.

The ground of being, however – Brahman, Source, or whatever name you prefer – has been established in my life as a very real entity, through experience, insight and meditation (I should meditate more than I do…). Through contemplation and meditation, it seems, we can remind ourselves of our identity with the Source. It is through both my own experiences and the many lines of reasoning discussed in my columns that I know the ground of being is real and that it is the source from which we all spring, from which all things spring, including God as Summit.

I do my best (not always succeeding) to re-establish this mystical connection on an on-going basis, intellectually and viscerally, in my heart and bones. It is through this connection to God as Source, that I find a perpetual and infinite source of happiness, meaning, and wholeness.

But this is my own path and it is certainly not for everyone. I don't call myself a Buddhist, even though I'm attracted to many features of Buddhism. And there are some aspects of Buddhism that I reject, or at least view with suspicion (karma and reincarnation, for example). Many schools of Buddhism reject the notion of a ground of being or Brahman, which I find fundamental and compelling. I'm very attracted to Vedanta Hinduism (which is based on knowing Brahman and our identity with Brahman) and Taoism, but I don't label myself as part of these traditions either. Rather, I generally reject labels, and this is my broader point: a lot of people are now choosing to reject all religious labels. We are, instead, choosing our own paths.

Yogananda, an Indian mystic in the Kriya Yoga tradition, said it well: "Everything else can wait, but your search for God cannot wait." In this search for authentic spirituality, experience seems to precede reason for most people. Words and concepts only go so far. For others, experience without a rational basis for spiritual views is not enough. For yet others, reason alone may well be enough to accept God and the ground of being as real, even without the profound direct experience of God as Source or as Summit.

We're all different, and this is, perhaps the most important insight we can take from the trend away from organized religion toward a more authentic spirituality. As that pretty smart guy, the Buddha, reportedly said in his last teachings: "Be a light unto yourself." Don't take anything on faith or on authority. Explore, challenge, read, think, discuss. Experience.

Chapter 23

A Mini-Discourse On Spiritual Method

We don't know much. That's the one thing we do know as we survey this universe of ours, and the human milieu that is such a small part of it.

But what of spirit, the soul, the *psyche*, human well-being? What do we know about that? Again: not much. So here we find a unifying factor between science and spirit: a common ignorance about ultimate answers. This suggests, perhaps, a common method for learning, first, the more complete contours of our ignorance and, second, pursuing a productive path to reduce our ignorance.

Descartes, one of the founders of modern science and philosophy, made his mark in part through his approach to knowledge in his Discourse on Method (full name Discourse on the Method of Rightly Conducting One's Reason and of Seeking Truth in the Sciences). In his Discourse, he introduced his most famous statement: I think, therefore I am. What he meant with this foundation for his intellectual edifice was that he knew nothing with any certainty except this one thing: there is thinking here, and we can conclude from the very act of thinking that there is a thinker.

Descartes' first step was the ultimate in intellectual modesty. It is ironic, therefore, that he immediately deduced as his second step, away from the certainty of his knowledge of self, that God must also exist. I won't go into the details here, but will say only that I found his logic very dubious in making this secondary conclusion. (I have written on my views of the Ultimate here and here).

We may still emulate Descartes's humility, however, for spiritual method, as well as for scientific method. Science today, particularly in its more popularized forms, all too often states as fact things that are more correctly labeled conjecture or inference. Karl Popper correctly noted that all of science is a series of conjectures and refutations. There is no proof. Bateson made it even more clear: "Science probes, it does not prove."

In terms of spiritual method, the historical Buddha, Siddhartha Gautama, stated in his final sermon that we should all be a light unto ourselves. That is, we should always forge our own path and not follow any particular set of views on authority or faith alone. We should test statements, test methods, and find our own path.

Based on his own teachings, if the Buddha were alive today, it is highly unlikely that he would wholeheartedly embrace Buddhism. Why? Because human knowledge has improved since the Buddha's time and because we have also become more humble in our approach to knowledge.

Our worldly knowledge has undeniably improved vastly since the time of the Buddha. Modern science has only been around for a few hundred years, kicking off a vast accretion of empirical knowledge that only began in earnest more than two thousand years after Buddha died. Our knowledge of the cosmos, while still extremely limited, is vastly different than it was even a hundred years ago. Until about eighty years ago we didn't even know there were other galaxies in our universe. We now know that there are billions of other galaxies, mini universes in their own right, floating alongside our own Milky Way; some near but most incredibly far from us. Medical knowledge has vastly improved, as has average human life span. More generally, technology is the real proof in the pudding for the improvement of human knowledge. As one example, we now have access to the sum of knowledge of entire civilizations in the palm of our hand. Literally.

If our knowledge of the world around us has grown so much, isn't it reasonable to think our knowledge of the realm of spirit has also grown?

Evolutionary spirituality

There is an interesting debate between those traditions that believe final and complete knowledge has already been achieved by an individual or individuals, and those who believe that knowledge is always improving, evolving, accreting. For the first group, it is our task as spiritual seekers today to follow those teachers (whatever tradition it is that resonates) and to emulate their example in order to achieve their level of knowledge and spiritual attainment. There is no going beyond, there is no improving our collective knowledge of spiritual matters if all has been previously revealed by Christ, Muhammad, Buddha, as the case may be.

For the second group, all is process, improvement, including our knowledge of spirit. There is no endpoint or final knowledge and we can all, each of us, advance our collective knowledge and attainment. Empirically, we can see that the second group is probably closer to the truth.

All spiritual traditions evolve, through insight, dialogue, schisms, conflicts, etc. Looking first to our own history in the West, the Christian movement today is generally acknowledged to have four or five major denominations: Catholicism, Protestantism, Eastern Orthodox, Oriental Orthodox and Anglican. And there are dozens of sub-denominations within these major schools. These numerous denominations exist because each generation produced thinkers who didn't agree entirely with previous thinkers – and, accordingly, they created their own denominations with the support of those they inspired. This process continues today, with Mormonism, a very recent branch of Christianity, gaining influence.

In the eastern traditions, we see very similar evolutionary changes. Taking Buddhism as our example, we have the following major denominations: Theravada (Hinayana), Mahayana, and Tibetan Buddhism. Tibetan Buddhism is, however, often considered a Mahayana denomination even though it has become so prominent it's often given its own category. There are dozens of other denominations in the Mahayana grouping, including Zen, Pure Land, Nichiren, Hua Yen, Tendai and others. Again, these different schools of thought arose because new thinkers were dissatisfied at some level with the teachings handed down to them by previous thinkers.

There is a fairly new term for the idea that there is no endpoint or final knowledge: "evolutionary spirituality." It is not just that this view of spirituality attempts to take evolutionary theory's insights into account (in the Darwinian sense); rather, evolutionary spirituality recognizes that all is process, all is change, all things are evolving – including our knowledge of the universe and ourselves. If all is process, the future is unknown and necessarily so.

Carter Phipps' *Evolutionaries: Unlocking the Spiritual and Cultural Potential of Science's Greatest Idea* is a wonderful book on this movement. Michael Murphy, founder of the Esalen Institute in Big Sur, has coined the term "evolutionary panentheism" for the modern movement that views all things as process and sees the universe we live in as an emanation of God or ground of being. (The link contains an excellent short article summarizing Murphy's ideas). This phrase is a mouthful, but it's a great title for what is a comprehensive view of the universe and our place in it, shaped by many great thinkers, old and new, including Hegel, Schelling, Sri Aurobindo, Henry James and Alfred North Whitehead.

So what's the big deal?

The difference in these approaches comes down to one's views of omniscience or at least the potential for omniscience. Can we or any being ever know everything? And what does it mean to know everything? This is a tough question with no certain answers. However, it seems to me that there are logical limits that transcend any current empirical limitations to what can be known. Is the universe deterministic or not? If it is, we may be able to know the future with certainty, at least in theory. And the past, as an extrapolation from present conditions. (Let's set aside for now discussions about deterministic chaos). If the universe is not deterministic, however, we can't know the future with any certainty.

A big problem with the idea of a deterministic universe is that this view eliminates the possibility of free will. This is the case because if the future is entirely determined from present conditions and the laws of physics, and was equally determined from the Big Bang or whatever starting point we choose, then there is no room for human agency, for actions that aren't determined by prior forces. There is no free will in a determined universe – despite the best efforts of compatibilists old and new.

If we, instead, recognize our immediate and deep-seated intuitions about the validity of our own free will, our own ability to make real decisions, we must reject the idea of a deterministic universe. We must recognize that the universe is wide open and that time, and the universe itself, is a process of creative unfolding. *And we are part of that creative unfolding.*

This second view is not just wishful thinking. The essay just linked to describes the work of Nobel-prize winning physicist Ilya Prigogine's efforts to show that the universe is indeterministic and ultimately creative and free. Similarly, Alfred North Whitehead and other process thinkers have suggested that free will, agency, is built into the fabric of the universe at every level in some form. It is highly rudimentary in the vast majority of the universe, but where matter complexifies into biological forms, so free will and consciousness complexify.

The friendly disagreement between the evolutionary views of spirituality and the non-evolutionary views comes down to different models of reality. There are an infinite number of possible models of reality, but there seems to be two particular (simple) models or metaphors of reality that are relevant to the themes I've raised in this essay: is the universe a perpetual cycle of suffering/dissatisfaction or is the universe an upward spiral, always improving, creative and free?

Buddhism, in particular, has sometimes been criticized for its seemingly gloomy view of the universe. "Life is suffering" is often presented as the first Noble Truth, a foundation of almost all Buddhist schools of thought. Some modern translations prefer to translate the Pali word (the Buddha's tongue) *dukkha* as "dissatisfaction" or "frustration" rather than "suffering." (See my recent column endorsing key Buddhist ideas, but suggesting ways in which Buddhism could evolve further).

Indeed, much of life is frustrating. And yet, in our modern era, *it seems that many people, in ever increasing numbers, can reasonably expect to live a life that is generally satisfying, despite frustrations of various types.* And we are on a civilizational trajectory (barring catastrophic events) to bring the majority of humanity to this new position over the coming decades and centuries.

However, even in this brighter future where the basic needs of all, or most of, humanity are met, human life will inevitably involve dissatisfaction and frustration, and suffering too. We can't yet avoid illness, pain or death. And even if we could conceivably avoid these inevitable features of life in the future, due to the marvels of technology, we will always suffer in various ways due to jealousy, rivalry, bias, unfairness, heartbreak, etc.

Maybe, just maybe, we will, as we progress in both our scientific and our spiritual knowledge, achieve societies in which people not only have their physical needs met without great striving, but also reach a state where we can en masse truly focus on unleashing our own creativity, our own search for beauty in all aspects of life. If this kind of future is possible, the prevailing Buddhist and Christian notion of escaping this human level of existence becomes far less pressing and a new objective becomes more relevant: a co-evolution of higher spirituality in our present realm. While we can recognize, as logically possible, the potential for different realms of existence (Nirvana in Buddhism, heaven in Christianity, etc.), the yearning for these other realms becomes less important. And we can focus on creating heaven on earth, nirvana in our time.

But I am personally torn on these ideas. We can never know, under the principles I have suggested here, what is the true shape of the universe, the fate of the universe, our own fate. So the debate will surely go on.

What is the shape of the universe?

A final thought: it does seem that the Eastern spiritual tradition lacks any substantial thinking on how things *came to be* as they are in our universe, as is the case too with the western Christian tradition, which is in most of its forms highly opposed to evolutionary thinking – the study of how things (any things) change. There is a general attitude in both traditions toward trying to understand how things are, and to live our lives accordingly, rather than to understand how things came to be and how they might change in the future. The difference is the same as the difference between viewing a snapshot versus a movie. Which is more revealing?

I would suggest that understanding how things came to be as they are now is a major step in living a better life and achieving more complete spiritual understanding. Just as a doctor wouldn't dream of prescribing medication without at least trying to understand how the patient became ill, we should, as spiritual seekers, do our best to understand how we came to be in our current condition – and this requires that we also do our best to understand how the universe as a whole came to be, because we are an inextricable part of the universe.

In the last analysis, we may certainly pursue a productive spiritual path, whatever path that entails, without a full understanding of how we came to be in our current predicament. Indeed, a key point of my essay is that we will never have such a complete understanding. But, by the same token, we should always continue our search for better answers because any spiritual path we follow will have an implicit model of the universe – and how our universe came to be – within it. If the model of the universe implicit in our preferred spiritual practice is lacking, it may have negative repercussions on our spiritual practice.

Part III

On Matters Scientific

In addressing the big questions of life, the universe and everything, it seems to me that the fields of cognitive psychology, philosophy of mind, evolutionary biology, physics and cosmology are pretty crucial. These are the key fields I've sought to understand in relation to the spiritual themes also tackled herein, and I offer in this chapter some tidbits of what I've gleaned from my studies.

Chapter 24

On Relativity

Neutrinos, the most ghostly particles we know of, are hitting far above their weight class. Evidence obtained in 2011 from the European physics mecca known as CERN, and an affiliated group in Lyon, suggested that neutrinos, tiny subatomic particles with almost no mass, travel slightly faster than the speed of light. If this evidence is replicated by other teams it will definitively up-end one of the pillars of modern physics: Einstein's theory of special relativity [since writing this essay, the accepted view is that these results were mistaken].

Special relativity is a theory about the nature of space and time and is today widely considered to have replaced earlier more naïve notions of space and time advocated by Newton and many others.

Explaining special relativity is generally viewed as a very difficult task. The essentials can, however, be explained rather simply. A basic assumption that Einstein used in crafting his theory was that the speed of light, apparently the fastest speed possible in our universe, is constant for all observers. This assumption was based on experimental evidence from the 1882 Michelson-Morley experiment, and other sources, that the speed of light seemed to be constant no matter how fast or in what direction the observer was moving.

This is a highly counter-intuitive notion because in our regular life all things seem to change speed as the observer's speed changes. For example, a train passing by as I sit at a station has a certain speed in relation to me, let's say 100 miles an hour. But if I am in a car next to the train driving at 60 miles an hour in the same direction as the train, the train is now traveling at 40 miles an hour in relation to me in the car. Speeds are generally entirely relative.

The speed of light was, for Einstein, different than all other speeds. It was absolute and constant no matter how fast the observer was moving. Speeds are by definition measured in units of distance divided by time – such as miles an hour or kilometers per second. If we accept that the speed of light (186,000 miles per second) is constant, we see quickly that space and time must become malleable and not constant. That is, the "miles" or "seconds" in the speed of light must change if the figure of 186,000 is to remain constant for different observers, as Einstein postulated. This is the essence of the theory of special relativity: space and time are malleable but the speed of light is absolute and constant.

Let's take an example. If I were to measure the speed of light in a lab, with very accurate equipment, I would get the answer of 186,000 miles per second. And if I measure the speed of light from nearby stars from the point of view of our planet as it moves in orbit around the Sun toward those nearby stars, I will get the same answer. What happened? Why isn't the speed faster because we are, with our entire planet, moving toward the source of light?

Well, according to special relativity, time and space shifted such that the speed of light remained constant. More specifically, the faster objects travel the slower time proceeds from the perspective of an observed in that reference frame, a phenomenon known as "time dilation." And as objects travel faster they become shorter in the direction of motion as space itself contracts ("length contraction"). These are necessary consequences of the assumption that the speed of light is constant for all observers: time and space become malleable.

Relativity theory does not, then, hold that all things are relative. Whereas previous theories like Newton's subscribed to notions of absolute space and absolute time, Einstein flipped orthodoxy on its head and suggested instead, based on the best empirical evidence at the time, that the speed of light is in fact absolute and everything else is relative.

A slow revolution is underway, however, that may demonstrate Einstein's assumptions, and thus his theories, to be wrong – or at least incomplete.

Alain Aspect and his colleagues in France showed, starting in the 1980s, that "entangled" quantum particles can communicate either instantaneously or near instantaneously. This now well-established experimental phenomenon – known as "non-locality" or "entanglement" – showed that Einstein's assumption that the speed of light is constant for all observers and is a cosmic speed limit is wrong in at least some circumstances. The phenomenon is called non-locality because it seems to violate the even more well-established principle that every action must have some proximate cause, not a distant cause without any apparent mechanism

Since the original Aspect experiments, many other experiments have been conducted, with increasing rigor and accuracy. In 2008, a Swiss team led by physicist Daniel Salart, confirmed entanglement and faster-than-light effects over a distance of 18 kilometers, in an experimental setup that makes alternative interpretations difficult. Salart calculates that the apparent information transfer between entangled particles is at least 10,000 times the speed of light.

Even if we can't ever use entanglement, and the apparent faster-than-light information transfer, to influence distant events (through "signals" in the technical sense), the Aspect and Salart experiments seem to have already up-ended Einstein's interpretation of relativity theory by demonstrating that the universe itself does allow causal influence to travel faster than the speed of light.

At the least, it is clear the speed of light limitation that forms one of two key assumptions in special relativity has been falsified. And without the relativity of simultaneity or the faster than light prohibition, there is no Einstein/Minkowski interpretation of the theory of relativity. Rather, we have substantial evidence for an earlier version of relativity advocated by one of Einstein's mentors, the Dutch Nobelist Hendrik Lorentz.

This conclusion is far from the mainstream at this time, however, in part because the Aspect and Salart experiments themselves are still being debated in terms of their correct interpretation and because of the many decades of entrenched acceptance of the validity of Einstein's theories of relativity. The new neutrino evidence will surely add much heat to this fire.

Given the Aspect and Salart experiments, the more recent neutrino evidence (which may turn out to be inaccurate), and the very basic philosophical problems with relativity theory, it seems to me that we are in the middle of a slow shift away from the Einstein interpretation of relativity and the consensus will eventually shift back toward a Lorentzian approach. Arrhenius, the Swedish physicist who wrote the Nobel Prize award letter given to Einstein in 1922, may have been correct when he stated in that letter that relativity theory "pertains essentially to epistemology."

While still very much a minority position, we find some support for this view in the writings of physicists and philosophers of physics. Lee Smolin, a well-known physicist at the Perimeter Institute in Canada, stated in an email to me in 2009: "I would say that this point of view [the Lorentzian interpretation] is taken as a logical possibility by a number of thoughtful theorists, although the number who advocate it is fewer." Smolin is not himself an advocate of the Lorentzian view.

J. S. Bell, the colorful Irish physicist who formulated the Bell inequalities, which formed the theoretical basis for Aspect's non-locality experiments, was a supporter of the Lorentzian view. He stated in a 1986 interview with physicist Paul Davies:

[T]he pre-Einstein position of Lorentz and Poincare, Larmor and Fitzgerald was perfectly coherent, and is not inconsistent with relativity theory. The idea that there is an aether ... is a perfectly coherent point of view. The reason I want to go back to the idea of an aether here is because ... the suggestion that [in nonlocality experiments] behind the scenes something is going faster than light. Now if all Lorentz frames are equivalent, that also means that things can go backward in time ... [This] introduces great problems, paradoxes of causality, and so on. And so it is precisely to avoid these that I want to say there is a real causal sequence which is defined in the aether.

Yuri Balashov, a philosopher at the University of Georgia, stated in a 2000 paper in the Journal of Philosophy:

[T]he idea of restoring absolute simultaneity [the basis for the Lorentzian interpretation of relativity theory] no longer has a distinctively pseudo-scientific flavor it has had until very recently. It is a well-known fact that one could accept all the empirical consequences of SR (including length contraction, time dilation, and so on) and yet insist that there is a privileged inertial reference frame, in which meter sticks really have the length they have and time intervals between events refer to the real time.

A last point I'll mention is that the holy grail of modern physics, the unification of relativity theory (the physics of the large-scale) and quantum mechanics (the physics of the small-scale), may be much easier if we recognize that Einstein's relativity theories are lacking. David Bohm, an American physicist who made contributions in many areas of physics, including quantum theory, stated with respect to unification in his book, *Wholeness and the Implicate Order:*

[R]elativity theory requires continuity, strict causality (or determinism) and locality. On the other hand, quantum theory requires non-continuity, non-causality and non-locality. So the basic concepts of relativity and quantum theory directly contradict each other. It is therefore hardly surprising that these two theories have never been unified in a consistent way. Rather, it seems mostly likely that such a unification is not actually possible. What is very probably needed instead is a qualitatively new theory, from which both relativity and quantum theory are to be derived as abstractions, approximations and limiting cases.

Einstein's special relativity will always remain an interesting and very useful theory advocating a particular epistemological point of view. But it will, under the view I'm promoting here, not be our best theory of space and time.

I won't, however, be at all surprised if the recent neutrino evidence will be found to be inaccurate [as it indeed was]. But even if this data is invalidated, we already have enough data from numerous entanglement experiments to state that special relativity has been falsified. This truth simply hasn't sunk in to the physics community yet, for a variety of reasons that seem to relate more to sociology, psychology and politics than science as it is ideally practiced.

(For brevity and simplicity I have kept the discussion to special relativity and not touched on general relativity, which is an extension of special relativity to all frames of reference regardless of motion. When it comes to unification, however, the discussion must focus on general relativity because this is our current theory of gravity, as opposed to special relativity, which does not incorporate gravity).

Chapter 25

On Time and Free Will

In any attempt to bridge the domains of experience belonging to the spiritual and physical sides of our nature, time occupies the key position.

Arthur Stanley Eddington, 1928

Everything is determined, the beginning as well as the end, by forces over which we have no control. It is determined for insects as well as for the stars. Human beings, vegetables, or cosmic dust, we all dance to a mysterious tune, intoned in the distance by an invisible piper.

Albert Einstein

Even very smart people can get things wrong. After all, Einstein showed with his theories of relativity that Newton, another very smart guy, didn't have the whole picture on the nature of space or time. But nor did Einstein, it seems, as I'll describe. It is becoming increasingly clear that Einstein was off-base about the nature of time and determinism.

What is time? For Einstein and most physicists since, time is considered an additional dimension, akin to a spatial dimension – sometimes described as "the spatialization of time." We arrive at a four-dimensional universe in which time is reversible and there is no real difference between past, present and future. Past, present and future are all just different coordinates in an unchanging and eternal "block universe."

Einstein made this view explicit in a 1955 letter to a friend: the appearance of past, present and future as distinct features of our experience is a "stubbornly persistent illusion." Sometimes developments that seem like advances can actually be a setback.

Einstein's views on time have become prevalent in science and philosophy, but what is far less prevalent is the understanding that in a world where time is an illusion and the universe is deterministic, there is no room for free will.

Free will is an active area of interest in psychology and philosophy. There is an increasing, and disturbing, trend toward a kind of hard-nosed acceptance that we don't have free will. The attitude is something like: "Science is increasingly showing us that we are not that important. Copernicus showed us that we're not at the center of the universe, Darwin showed us that we're just another animal, and physics has shown us that there is nothing special about consciousness and that we suffer from an illusion of free will because past, present and future all exist at the same time."

This attitude, while increasingly pervasive, goes too far in my view. Much of it is, of course, correct: we are not at the center of the universe and we have evolved just as all other creatures have evolved on this blue/green planet of ours. But we are also the leading edge of that creative process, with our highly complex consciousness and associated attributes. Even though many things are indeed beyond our conscious control, it is not the case that we are conscious automatons in a deterministic world. New physical ideas support this view and we are now seeing the dissemination of these ideas slowly but surely, steadily eroding Einsteinian determinism.

Do you really believe you have no free will? Does a physicist who subscribes to Einstein's "tenseless" theory of time really believe she has no free will? I believe the answer is "no" in both cases. Even those who deny free will certainly act as though they do have free will. And let's not forget that our criminal justice system, not to mention our entire system of morality and ethics, rests on the notion that we do have free will.

Doesn't common sense demand some kind of reconciliation with our innate sense of free will and physical conceptions of time?

Ilya Prigogine (1917-2003), a Belgian physicist and Nobel Prize winner, worked for decades to show why Einstein was wrong about his views on time and determinism. Prigogine states in his 1996 book, *The End of Certainty*, which summed up his life work on the nature of time: "The spatialization of time is incompatible with both the evolving universe, which we observe around us, and our own human experience."

Indeed, our own human experience is tensed through and through. All we know with any certainty is the fact of our own experience now, now, now. All we know is the now. The past is remembered and the future imagined. Only the now is real.

How, then, do we reconcile the obvious facts of our experience with the strange physics of tenseless time, with Einstein's "block universe" in which past, present and future are all said to exist concurrently?

It is becoming increasingly apparent that we reconcile these competing views by bowing to common sense and embracing new ideas in the area of physics known as thermodynamics – Prigogine's life-long area of focus. Prigogine describes at length in his work how thermodynamics demonstrates the necessity of an arrow of time. There is no block universe. Prigogine writes: "Nature itself ... distinguishes between past and future. There is an arrow of time." He also states that we need to reformulate the "laws of physics in accordance with the open, evolving universe in which man lives." Hear hear.

Prigogine's work is of the highest rigor and provides at least a partial solution to the problems of time and free will. He shows that classical mechanics and the prevailing versions of quantum mechanics can't describe much of the universe accurately because they consist of time-reversible equations. Irreversibility must be included in the equations in order to accurately model our universe.

Prigogine concludes: "We see that human creativity and innovation can be understood as the amplification of laws of nature already present in physics or chemistry…. Nature is indeed related to the creation of unpredictable novelty, where the possible is richer than the real."

Why did Einstein believe time was an illusion?

I'm going to get a bit more detailed at this point and explain how Einstein arrived at the notion of the block universe, of tenseless time. It's based on an assumption that is not necessarily true and that I believe is not true.

Einstein developed his theory of special relativity in 1905 by starting with the idea that "time" can best be defined by using light as a tool for establishing the simultaneity of distant events. He further assumed that the speed of light is constant in all directions, regardless of the speed of the observer. I've written previously about how strange this assumption is, because nothing else in the universe behaves this way. It has nonetheless become the prevailing view of the nature of light, space and time.

The problem of establishing simultaneity between distant events was a major inspiration for Einstein's special theory of relativity. Establishing whether one event is simultaneous with an event elsewhere was a thorny problem in Einstein's era – and remains so today. In late 19th Century Switzerland (where Einstein lived at the time), the problem of synchronizing the country's many town clocks became an obsession among physicists, including Einstein, in large part because of the growing network of trains and train schedules.

Einstein proposed, in his 1905 paper on special relativity, that rather than making an assertion about whether a given event was "really" simultaneous with other events elsewhere, the problem could be resolved by postulate. Einstein's postulate was to assume that light travels at a uniform speed at all times for all observers no matter their own speed. Light could be used to synchronize distant clocks under this assumption. With distant synchronized clocks, events occurring at those clocks may be judged as simultaneous or not by noting the readings of the clocks at each location at the time of the events and then adjusting for the speed of light. Einstein wrote in his 1916 popular book on his relativity theories (emphasis in original):

> There is only one demand to be made of the definition of simultaneity, namely, that in every real case it must supply us with an empirical decision as to whether or not the conception that has to be defined is fulfilled. That my definition satisfies this demand is indisputable. That light requires the same time to traverse [paths of equal distance, regardless of motion] is in reality neither a supposition nor a hypothesis about the physical nature of light, but a stipulation [postulate] which I can make of my own free will in order to arrive at a definition of simultaneity.

In other words, to arrive at a way of determining simultaneity, Einstein stipulated (postulated) that the speed of light is constant for all observers, regardless of their own motion. So rather than treat the speed of light like any other speed, which does depend on the speed of the observer, light is to be considered the exception to this otherwise universal rule.

Einstein is certainly correct when he stated that he may stipulate what he wishes, but there is, however, more than one demand to be made of a definition of simultaneity: that it help us arrive at an accurate understanding of nature and not conflict with undeniable aspects of human experience, such as the flow of time and evolution of the universe.

There are other interpretations of relativity that don't require assuming a constant speed of light for any observer – Hendrik Lorentz's, for example, a Dutch Nobel Prize winner who was a mentor to Einstein. Under Lorentz's theory, the speed of light acts like any other speed in that it changes with respect to the speed of the observer. Lorentz's theory explains empirical observations just as Einstein's theory does because both theories use the same mathematical framework known as the Lorentz transformations. Thus we need not lose the accuracy of the mathematical formalisms of special relativity even if we reject Einstein's assumptions.

Another well-known Einstein saying, with respect to Niels Bohr's "Copenhagen interpretation" of quantum mechanics, is that "God does not play dice with the universe." Indeed, he does not. But nor is the universe deterministic, as Einstein believed. Rather, God has given to his creation the ability to choose, the ability to exert free will, at every level of nature, as I have described in a number of columns. Thus, what is thought of as chance is better described as choice. Choice, not chance. This panpsychist expansion of Prigogine's work brings us full circle.

Reconciling relativity and quantum theory?

Determinism is a common theme in relativity theory (the physics of the very large scale) and quantum mechanics (the very small scale), which conflict in many ways. Resolving the nature of time, free will, and determinism, may well lead us to a reconciliation of these two pillars of modern physics. This reconciliation remains the biggest challenge in modern physics.

There are more than two choices, however, when it comes to the famous debate between Einstein's determinism and Bohr's complementarity and indeterminism. Bohr's view is that the act of measurement and choosing what to measure has a real role in determining the results of measurement. This has given rise to all manner of suggestions that humans literally create their own physical world around them. This goes too far in my view.

There is a third choice: the view that all aspects of the universe enjoy at least a rudimentary free will. In this view, all entities "measure" themselves through their ongoing and necessary interaction with the universe around them. This conclusion follows from the extension of at least a rudimentary consciousness to all matter.

This position seems very strange to most people encountering it for the first time, but it has support from good sources. The well-known British-American physicist Freeman Dyson, with Princeton's Institute for Advanced Studies for many years, stated in 1979 (as mentioned in previous essays): "[T]he processes of human consciousness differ only in degree but not in kind from the processes of choice between quantum states which we call 'chance' when made by electrons." David Bohm, a highly influential American physicist, wrote similarly in 1987: "Even the electron is informed with a certain level of mind."

The rudimentary free will that exists in subatomic particles like electrons compounds upward until it reaches the rarefied heights that we humans enjoy. We are not different in kind from the rest of the universe, in terms of free will or consciousness. We human beings, the result of almost four billion years of evolution, are instead different only in degree. The difference seems to be a difference in kind because the gap is very large. But the spectrum of free will is surely grand and we happen to enjoy a rarefied position at its most advanced terminus.

Under the views on time that I've sketched here, we realize that choice, free will, pervades our universe. Each moment is creative and free for each and every entity in our universe. At lower levels of complexity, habit dominates and the exercise of free will is quite regular – which is why our statistical laws of mechanics work quite well in most situations (with some key exceptions, as Prigogine describes). But as choice complexifies, outcomes become less certain – as befits a creative and evolving universe.

I'll end with another Prigogine nugget: "[T]he more we know about our universe, the more difficult it becomes to believe in determinism."

Chapter 26

The Higgs Field as the New Ether

The Higgs boson has been found!

The Higgs boson has not been found!

What the heck is the Higgs boson, has it really been found, and why should we care?

The Higgs boson is a key particle in the Standard Model of particle physics, which currently stands as our best theory of the very small. The problem is that the theory predicts the presence of the Higgs boson as a necessary ingredient for imparting mass to particles that have mass; and it hadn't been found after decades of searching.

Particles like electrons and protons have mass. Particles like photons, the quantum of light, don't have mass. Photons are a type of boson, which are essentially energy particles, as opposed to fermions, which are matter particles. The Higgs boson imparts mass to massive particles like electrons and protons. Or so the theory goes.

Dennis Overbye in the *New York Times* provides a good analogy: the Higgs field that produces the Higgs boson, is like molasses. As massive particles travel through the field they are slowed down like a spoon pushed through molasses. Without the Higgs field, particles would all travel at the speed of light and have no mass.

So what did the European science team at the Large Hadron Collider, a multi-billion dollar project completed in 2008, find exactly? Well, UC Santa Barbara physicist Joe Incandela, elected spokesman for one of the LHC teams, announced that after going through literally trillions of data points, they had uncovered strong evidence of something Higgs-like. This is far from a confident assertion that the Higgs boson has been found, as many outlets erroneously reported. There is still plenty of room for doubt and interpretation.

For many, however, despite the ongoing uncertainties, which will be reduced with additional experiments, the new findings represent an amazing vindication of the power of the human mind and of international collaboration. I agree with these claims but I find the Higgs field discussion very interesting from another perspective: the Higgs field has brought back the notion of an ether.

The ether is generally described, along with things like phlogiston, as one of science's big screw-ups. We know now, the story goes, that there is no ether. Einstein dispelled this myth, right? Wrong.

Frank Wilczek, a Nobel Prize-winning physicist at MIT, writes in his 2008 book *The Lightness of Being: Mass, Ether and the Unification of Forces*:

> No presently known form of matter has the right properties [to play the role of the ether]. So we don't really know what this new material ether is. We know its name: the Higgs condensate [or Higgs field], after Peter Higgs, a Scots physicist who pioneered some of these ideas. The simplest possibility ... is that it's made from one new particle, the so-called Higgs particle. But the [ether] could be a mixture of several materials. ... [T]here are good reasons to suspect that a whole new world of particles is ripe for discovery, and that several of them chip in to the cosmic superconductor, a.k.a the Higgs condensate.

As the title of Wilczek's book suggests: he argues from many lines of evidence that there is in fact an ether that undergirds space, which he calls alternately the ether, the Grid or the "cosmic superconductor."

In a little-known tale of 20th Century physics, Einstein himself regretted his 1905 dismissal of the ether as "superfluous," in his seminal paper on special relativity. Einstein's own thinking evolved to the point that he realized that some type of (relativistic) ether was theoretically necessary after all. Einstein called this his "new ether," but changed his terminology over time, as we shall see below.

In 1916, Einstein published his general theory of relativity, which asserted a very different conception of space and time than that put forth in 1905. In general relativity, space has no independent existence; rather, it is a consequence of the various fields that are ontologically fundamental. Shortly after his momentous general relativity paper was published, he exchanged letters with Hendrik Lorentz, the Nobel Prize-winning physicist and one of Einstein's mentors, on the topic of the ether. Lorentz argued throughout his career that some notion of the ether was necessary for a valid description of reality. Einstein conceded eventually that indeed a non-material ether was necessary to explain inertia and acceleration. Einstein first described his "new ether" in a 1916 letter to Lorentz:

> I agree with you that the general theory of relativity is closer to the ether hypothesis than the special theory. This new ether theory, however, would not violate the principle of relativity, because the state of this ... ether would not be that of a rigid body in an independent state of motion, but every state of motion would be a function of position determined by material processes.

Einstein also wrote in a 1919 letter to Lorentz:

> It would have been more correct if I had limited myself, in my earlier publications, to emphasizing only the non-existence of an ether velocity, instead of arguing the total non-existence of the ether, for I can see that with the word ether we say nothing else than that space has to be viewed as a carrier of physical qualities.

From 1916 to 1918, Einstein was in the thick of discussions with a number of colleagues about the nature of space and the ether, with respect to general relativity. As Walter Isaacson recounts in his wonderful biography of Einstein, Einstein's thinking changed dramatically during this period. In 1918, he published a response to critics of special and general relativity. In this dialogue, Einstein writes that the "diseased man" of physics, the "aether," is in fact alive and well, but that it is a relativistic ether in that no motion may be ascribed to it.

In 1920, Einstein became more emphatic regarding the ether, recognizing explicitly that the ether was a necessary medium by which acceleration and rotation may be judged, independently of any particular frame of reference:

> To deny ether is ultimately to assume that empty space has no physical qualities whatever. The fundamental facts of mechanics do not harmonize with this view... Besides observable objects, another thing, which is not perceptible, must be looked upon as real, to enable acceleration or rotation to be looked upon as something real ... The conception of the ether has again acquired an intelligible content, although this content differs widely from that of the ether of the mechanical wave theory of light ... According to the general theory of relativity, space is endowed with physical qualities; in this sense, there exists an ether. Space without ether is unthinkable; for in such space there not only would be no propagation of light, but also no possibility of existence for standards of space and time (measuring- rods and clocks), nor therefore any spacetime intervals in the physical sense.

Again, Einstein stressed that this new ether was relativistic. Einstein struggled with these ideas for much of his career. As a realist, Einstein argued during the middle and latter parts of his career that physics must attempt to describe what is truly real and not avoid discussion of concepts that cannot be directly detected – such as the ether – even if they seem to be logically necessary due to indirect evidence. So for Einstein, even though the ether was considered undetectable, he deduced its existence because of its effects on observable matter through inertia, acceleration and rotation.

We are, of course, now at the point where we are starting to find direct evidence of a sort for the ether in the form of the Higgs field.

Einstein labored mightily in the 1920s and 1930s to develop a unified field theory that would re-cast all things, including space, as a manifestation of the "total field," a synonym for his "new ether." Einstein stated in his 1938 book, The Evolution of Physics: "This word ether has changed its meaning many times in the development of science. ... Its story, by no means finished, is continued by the relativity theory."

Back to the present day, Lawrence Krauss, a well-known physicist and science popularizer, wrote recently of the Higgs field announcements in a way that strongly supports a revival of the ether concept:

> The brash notion predicts an invisible field (the Higgs field) that permeates all of space and suggests that the properties of matter, and the forces that govern our existence, derive from their interaction with what otherwise seems like empty space. Had the magnitude or nature of the Higgs field been different, the properties of the universe would have been different, and we wouldn't be here to wonder why. Moreover, a Higgs field validates the notion that seemingly empty space may contain the seeds of our existence.

In sum, the recent evidence regarding the Higgs boson lend support to Einstein's "new ether" concept and, more generally, to the idea that there is a ground of being that undergirds our reality: the "seeds of our existence," as Krauss states. This ground of being is apparently not directly detectable but we can infer its presence through many lines of reasoning, including discoveries like the Higgs field, if this data is supported by future experiments.

On a related note, recent evidence of dark energy, a mysterious repulsive energy emanating from ostensibly empty space and thought to be responsible for the accelerating expansion of the universe, may mesh nicely with the "Higgs field as ether" notion. More on this in future essays.

It's an exciting time to be a physicist – or simply someone who follows physics closely, like me. Actually, it's a very interesting time to be alive, no matter what one's interests are...

Chapter 27

On Ends and Endings

I like big butts and I cannot lie.

Sir Mixalot, *Baby Got Back* (1992)

Have you thought much about the evolution of the human butt? Neither had I until recently.

Survival of the Prettiest, by Nancy Etcoff, a psychologist at Harvard Medical School, is a great summary of the current science on human evolution and standards of beauty. The main surprise is that many aspects of beauty are not entirely in the eye of the beholder. In other words, many aspects of human beauty are common to all cultures and all times. Contrary to popular wisdom, preferences by men for women's features such as large eyes, small chins, good skin, long lush hair, and an hourglass figure are common to all cultures studied so far. Similarly, preferences by women for men's features such as a solid jaw, broad shoulders, good skin and nice hair also seem to be common to all cultures.

Preference for a certain butt type is not, however, one of these universal features. Some do like big butts! And some like small butts. Our culture generally prizes a relatively small taut butt as the ideal, but there is quite a lot of variation in preferences even in our culture. Compare Kate Moss to Beyoncé and we get a feel for the variety in judgments about this particular aspect of beauty (forgive me if I focus on female body parts in this essay).

Taken to an extreme, these preferences can seem pretty bizarre to us 21st Century Americans – as can many beauty habits in various cultures around the world. The Hottentots, for example, were and are known for having enormous behinds. This fact became well-known in England in the early 19th Century due to an unfortunate episode wherein the "Hottentot Venus," Sara Baartman, a Khoi tribeswoman from South Africa, was displayed to the public in the nude at various venues in England over a period of about five years. Of particular fascination to anatomists and other scientists at the time, as well as the general public, was the accompanying enlarged *labia minora*, which apparently hung down quite a ways and confused early European explorers as to the nature of the body part on display. Google for further juicy details if you're interested.

I've studied biology since my early teens and have always found questions about evolution fascinating. But it wasn't until recently that I began thinking deeply about "sexual selection," a term Darwin invented to distinguish the power of mating competition and choice from the environmental forces that define "natural selection." This topic isn't just a titillating aside to discussions about natural selection and evolution. Sexual selection is, in fact, central to evolution.

For example, an interesting debate is taking place among biologists with respect to the evolution of human hairlessness – or relative hairlessness. Racial differences in hairiness, and individual differences, are obviously quite pronounced. So too is taste for hairlessness or not – though the clear trend in all cultures today is toward women being hairless except for the hair on their head. Female taste for hair on men is a bit more varied, with some women in various cultures still preferring a good coat of chest hair, etc., but the more common trend seems to be toward relative hairlessness of men too. Why is there such variety in human hair/fur? One increasingly accepted answer: because we prefer less hair. In other words, we are, with each generation, expressing our sexual preferences for less hairy humans and, accordingly, each new generation is being born with less and less body hair. This is known as "sexual selection."

Sexual selection is the evolutionary force resulting from competition for mates and – crucially – mate choice. The prototypical example is the peacock's tail. Why is it so large and beautiful? Simply put: because peahens love a large and colorful tail in their guy. Darwin highlighted this force of nature in his second major work on evolution, *The Descent of Man, and Selection in Relation to Sex*, first published in 1871, twelve years after *On the Origin of Species*.

Geoffrey Miller, an evolutionary psychologist at UCLA, describes the checkered history of the theory of sexual selection in his entertaining and insightful book, *The Mating Mind*: "It was one thing for a generalized Nature to replace God as the creative force. It was much more radical [with sexual selection theory] to replace an omniscient Creator with the pebble-sized brains of lower animals lusting after one another. Sexual selection was not only atheism, but indecent atheism." (One doesn't have to be an atheist, of course, to believe in evolution, as I've written about in previous columns).

Human evolution has most likely been far more subject to sexual selection in our recent history than to other forces of evolution. The best evidence for this is the broad variety of tastes in many aspects of beauty that we see around the world – separate from the universal human tastes I described above. Why do Nordic Europeans look so different than Chinese, and why do they both look so different than sub-Saharan Africans? There are many reasons for these differences, but sexual selection has surely had a large role in these largely cosmetic changes (the genetic differences in the various types of humans are extremely small, but since we are so visually-oriented we tend to exaggerate the differences). In other words: mate choice has probably had a large role in shaping many of our modern-day features, such as butts and other obvious physical features such as hair, eyes, breasts, etc.

Miller concurs, and writes about the human butt: "Women's breasts and buttocks did not evolve because hominid men happened to develop some arbitrary fixation on hemispheres as Platonic ideals of beauty. They evolved as reliable indicators of youth, health, fertility, symmetry and adequate fat reserve."

I agree that there are many utilitarian indicators in particular aspects of human evolution, including the shape of secondary sexual characteristics like breasts and butts. But one thing Miller passes over, and most evolutionary biologists also pass over, is the purely aesthetic aspect of sexual selection that Darwin himself stressed. Many features that evolved through sexual selection evolved, it seems when we consider the body of evidence, purely because the opposite sex liked those features, independent of any utilitarian benefits to those features.

When we consider that various birds of paradise in very similar climates have evolved quite different plumage in a relatively short period of time – but equally ornate – it is hard to find any reason as to why such differences would have evolved other than that the female taste for this plumage differed in certain ways in different areas.

Darwin agreed with my point here, even though the modern trend among biologists is to discount the role of aesthetics in sexual selection. Darwin mentioned in many passages in The Descent of Man the "choice" exerted by birds and other creatures in sexual selection. He was very clear that he was attributing mind and aesthetic powers to non-human creatures. Here's one example: "On the whole, birds appear to be the most aesthetic of all animals, excepting of course man, and have nearly the same taste for the beautiful as we have."

The future of human evolution

Turning our gaze from the past toward the future of evolution, where are we going as a species? The quick thinking is that we aren't evolving physically very much anymore because we're so pampered, in a relative sense. That is, with modern medicine, technology and supportive social structures, we face far less environmental pressures than we have for the vast majority of our history. But this quick thinking is very likely wrong. There is plenty of room for debate, but it's becoming clear that human physical evolution is speeding up in the modern era, not slowing down. Some biologists have suggested rates of evolution in humans at up to 10,000 times the historical average. Why?

Well, there seems to be a positive feedback process in evolution: as consciousness becomes more complex, as it has in humans in particular in recent millennia, that consciousness exerts more pressure back on the evolutionary process that produced it. It's a positive feedback loop, and like all such loops, it speeds up over time.

The more interesting aspect of modern evolution is not, however, biological evolution but cultural and technological evolution. We are now at the point that cultural and technological evolution are far more powerful forces than traditional evolutionary forces. Our technology is at the point that we will soon be shaping ourselves and our progeny in increasingly important ways. In other words, technological evolution is now at the point that it can take over much of the role that biological evolution has played for billions of years. We can select the gender of our children now, and can also select specific traits within limits. In coming years, this trend will become far more pronounced. This increasing power to shape our own evolution is part of the same evolutionary process that has always been present, but it has taken a huge jump in rapidity with the advent of modern technology, made possible by another similar jump a few million years ago: the rapid growth of the human brain. Evolution does seem to occur in leaps and bounds, with long periods of stasis in between (an idea known as "punctuated equilibrium").

Armed with modern technology, we'll soon be able to design the perfect butt for each of our tastes. And every other body part with it...

The deep span of evolution

The more important trend in evolution does not, alas, concern our body parts. Rather, it concerns the far longer span of future history and the ongoing evolution of consciousness. Where are we going when we look toward the very distant future? Where does it all end? Does it have to end?

Pierre Teilhard de Chardin, an influential French anthropologist and philosopher who was also a Jesuit priest, defined the "modern man" as one who sees evolutionary trajectories all around, not static points or objects in time. Teilhard's vision was one of an evolutionary spirituality, an integration of evolutionary theory with spirituality. His primary work is the visionary book, *The Human Phenomenon*, written in 1940 but published in English for the first time in 1955 under the title *The Phenomenon of Man*.

Teilhard also described "the Omega Point," a synonym for God, or "the Summit" that I've discussed in previous essays. But the Omega Point is different than traditional notions of God because Omega evolves. Omega is here now and is the sum total of all conscious beings that already exist. Just as the cells in our body create a unity (us) out of the plurality (the trillions of cells in our bodies), we collectively create, under Teilhard's thinking, a far higher-level entity through our combination. Part of this process is the ongoing creation of the "noösphere," the realm of thought swirling already over our heads with our radio and TV waves, and now incarnating as the Internet, in all its glory and transformational power.

For Teilhard, there was an end point to this process of God's – and our – evolution. Once the energy breathed into creation at the beginning of our universe has been exhausted through the ongoing interiorization of matter (another way of describing the complexification of consciousness), and the achievement of perfect consciousness in Omega's final form, then it all ends.

This idea is particularly relevant in the year of our Lord 2012. There are various cultural threads suggesting that we're at an end point to history. Teilhard himself said nothing about 2012, to my knowledge, and it seems clear that the end of history he envisioned will take place far in the future. However, the end of the Mayan calendar, Terrence McKenna's Timewave Zero model, some Christian apocalyptic models, and some other ideas popular among the Burning Man set and New Age types suggest that we're in for a rough ride this year.

I'm part of the Burning Man set (I've been three times and will be going again this year, with ticket already in hand – my condolences to everyone who failed to win in the lottery this year), but I view 2012 as a time of major transformation, not doom and gloom. Just as death can be viewed as an ending or as a transformation, I think we're in for major transformation at this point in our history. My feeling is that Teilhard got this idea wrong: there is no end point to evolution, at least not for the reasons he supposed. I can respect and admire his edifice of thought but still reject the notion of an end-point to evolution.

Nor do I think there's anything special about 2012 – except for the cultural significance we collectively give it, kind of like the power of financial markets or currency more generally. Rather, I think we're in a time of rapid change and turmoil that has been building for millennia, and that will ultimately lead to something even better than we have today. There may be some real speed bumps in the road ahead, but the road does seem to me to be winding its way upward to a beautiful house on a hill. With a great view.

We can, in this vision of the future, look forward not only to the perfect butt but also to helping God itself evolve – because we are part and parcel of God – as we all unfold forward in a never-ending process of improvement and creative exploration.

Chapter 28

iParasitism

As I write I am surrounded by my iFamily: tapping on the keyboard of my MacBook Pro with my iPad next to me on my couch and my iPhone in my pocket. Across from me is my Apple TV, which allows me to stream Internet, music and video to my TV. And I'll soon purchase an iMac desktop computer to replace my increasingly wobbly desktop PC in my office.

I spent an hour or two while watching TV tonight updating my software with iOS 5 and the latest version of the Mac Lion operating system. Who needs real people when I have my iFamily of electronic gadgets to keep me busy? I have truly been iParasitized.

Are we inevitably all becoming iParasitized, or at least eParasitized (as in some form of electronic media parasitization)? It seems we are – and those who are not will eventually die off and leave the rest of us parasite hosts to keep up the good fight. Or will they?

It's not all bad. Far from it. In fact, we are, as a consequence of eParasitism, more and more interconnected with those we love, as well as with some of those we hate, such as our bosses.

More profoundly, this latest form of parasitism is only beginning. Surely Steve Jobs, a towering figure in US history and worthy of all the plaudits that went his way after his death, envisioned far greater integration of Apple products into our lives. And where Apple goes everyone else now seems to follow.

Isn't it clear that by, let's say, 2020, the iPhone 10, or whatever they call it then, will connect directly to our brain in some manner and will probably include a display that shines directly onto our retina, or least on an eyepiece attached to our head like sunglasses. Maybe it will be the iphone 10BC (for "brain connect").

Siri, Apple's new electronic "personal assistant," is an exciting advance. But it's just the tip of the iceberg. With the dawn of useful Artificial Intelligence (AI) like Siri, and the increasing ease with which electronics can read brain waves (increasingly without invasive electrodes) it seems we are indeed just a few short years from integrating electronics wordlessly and wirelessly into our very brains.

We are quickly becoming cyborgs.

I remember little more than a decade ago when I scoffed at the idea of owning a cell phone. Why get a cell phone? I found out why before too long and never looked back. Then I scoffed at those weirdos who wore wireless earphones, until I realized how useful they can be. I won't scoff at the first people who wear a brain-reading iPhone. I'll probably be one of them.

More broadly, electronics and other artificial components will increasingly become part of us, and probably in a much more invasive manner than a brain-reading iPhone. Artificial hips, knees, and organs are becoming more and more common. Amazingly, we can now grow new organs with stem cells from actual patients over an inert scaffolding from a dead donor. This type of organ transplant is becoming increasingly common and scientists are working on growing functional hearts and lungs, building on existing successes with tracheas, bladders and other simpler organs. Are these organs artificial? They're not electronic, but they surely should qualify as part of the "cyborgization" of humanity.

Perhaps the "bioelectronics revolution" is what this cyborgization will be known as when it starts to kick in seriously.

Beyond fixing medical ailments, the justifiable focus of most medical research in this era, a small number of scientists are working on rejuvenation techniques that will surely involve a mix of replacing failing organs, turning back the clock on existing cells, tissues, and organs, and also incorporating artificial components where appropriate. An advantage of electronic or mechanical components is that they're far easier to fix or replace than biological components.

The writing is also on the wall when it comes to including artificial intelligence in robots and having these become far more useful personal assistants than Siri version 1.0. Similarly, our homes, cars and offices will almost certainly become wired (wirelessly) with the same artificial intelligence that we keep in our pocket, allowing us to control our environments in many ways with a voice command and, soon, our minds alone.

The cyborgization of humanity seems all but assured, at least for those who can afford it, and then perhaps for the majority as costs come down. Most of those who don't like such ideas will, again, die off and those who remain will be those who don't mind the merging of man with machine. Or will neo-Luddites, modern-day Amish groups, spring up pervasively, announcing a line in the sand of cyborgization that they will not cross?

We can't say, of course, how long this process will take and I suspect it will be many decades, if not centuries, before it gets well under way (despite the claims of smart people like Kurzweil). It seems to me that even though so many people have embraced the personal electronics revolution around the world, once we really start messing with mother nature with increasingly intrusive procedures that seriously blur the line between man and machine, there's bound to be a backlash.

I'm personally quite torn about the seemingly inevitable march of bioelectronics and cyborgization. As mentioned, I've recently embraced the most recent manifestations of this trend and I can see myself continuing to embrace future developments for a while. But when this march starts to truly blur the lines between the human organism and bioelectronics creations, I may start to balk. And I think a lot of others will too. It will certainly be interesting to see how these events unfold and I won't be surprised if we do have many communities who decide cyborgization is not for them.

Legislation will probably be passed in some countries to prevent certain invasive technologies, as has been the case with human cloning in recent years. The lesson we've learned, however, from attempts to postpone such developments is that they're only slowed down, never stopped. And eventually they become accepted as normal.

The next few decades promise to be interesting times. Kurzweil is one of a few thinkers who have pondered the deeper aspects, including spiritual aspects, of this transformation of humanity – at least a little. Before he became famous for his ideas on the Singularity he wrote a book called The Age of Spiritual Machines. Kurzweil describes his view that mankind will lose none of our spiritual capacity even as we move away from our strictly biological origins. But his understanding of spirituality seems rather limited in his book and his discussion isn't particularly convincing.

Francis Fukuyaman, best-known as a student of foreign policy, wrote a 2003 book, *Our Posthuman Future: Consequences of the Biotechnology Revolution*, in which he sketches out some policy recommendations to mitigate the negative effects of our pending cyborgization. He appeals primarily to outmoded philosophical ideas such as an essential quality that makes us human, an idea going back to Aristotle, Plato, and of course long before. As much as I like some of the Greek philosophers' ideas I don't find much support at all in modern science or philosophy for any notion of an unchanging human essence.

Rather, it seems that "humanity," as with almost everything in the universe, is a term we use to describe a constellation of always-changing features. When does an embryo become a human? I won't go down that rabbit hole. When does a human stop being a human? That's perhaps an even harder question. When did the first human appear? Will humans ever evolve to a point where we don't call ourselves humans anymore? This is, of course, what many thinkers are starting to suggest with the potential of the bioelectronics revolution to make us more than human, to transcend our humanity.

There is really just one question, though, that will determine the course of this profound transformation we're currently undergoing as individuals and as a species: Are we happier with our ever-increasing electronic and biomedical interventions?

Judging by the exponential success of smart phones and iPads there is a huge demand for this kind of iParasitism. I can personally attest to the enjoyments of instant electronic communication made possibly by my electronic toys, and the immense wealth of information at my fingertips at almost any moment.

I do, of course, feel a burden sometimes: the degree to which I feel like I need my electronic connections and those times when I reject them purely because I do feel addicted (try going a weekend or a week without your cell phone sometime – it's hard!).

It is obvious but worth stating that as the benefits are outweighed by the downsides of our bioelectronics wizardry, we may start to see a wide-scale rejection of further cyborgization. But that threshold will be different for each individual, community and country, so all I can say now is that we're in for an interesting ride in the coming decades.

My iFamily and I will be there to witness it.

Chapter 29

I Controlled a Huge Freakin' Laser With My Mind:

The Science of Remote Causation

I contrive no hypotheses.

Isaac Newton, in discussing gravity in his *Principia Mathematica*

Isaac Newton, perhaps the greatest scientist who ever lived, did of course make many hypotheses about gravity. In fact, he developed an incredibly profound general theory of gravity that united such seemingly different phenomena as a falling apple and the circling of the planets around the Sun. His theory of gravity stood firm for over two centuries before Einstein argued convincingly that Newton's theory was incomplete (Einstein's general theory of relativity renders Newton's theory a "limiting case").

What Newton refused to do, however, was speculate about exactly how gravity works its magic. Gravity just is, and Newton apparently recognized that his era's scientific knowledge was not sufficient to go beyond the equations that formed his theory of gravity. He contrived no hypotheses as to the mechanism behind gravity, but he recognized fully that it seemed to be some kind of "action at a distance" that operates quite differently than through direct contact, which is how the world around us operates more generally.

Cause and effect is what physics is all about, and science more generally. What causes what? Even though we can never make definitive statements about what caused what, we can probe correlations and make reasonable inferences about cause and effect.

The most familiar form of causation is the direct contact of push and pull. A billiard ball bounces directly away from the cue ball due to the direct contact of ball upon ball. The energy from the pool cue is transferred by the pool player's arm to the cue ball and then to the second ball.

But even this extremely simple form of cause and effect is not as simple as matter pushing matter. Rather, the electromagnetic force that hold the molecules of the balls together is the intermediary for these actions. Electromagnetism is in fact the most important force at our scale of reality: it holds all molecules together and it allows us to see, hear, touch, etc. Due to electromagnetism, the billiard balls don't actually touch; rather, the electromagnetic forces generated by the molecules in each ball repel each other.

Gravity keeps us, as well as apples, on terra firma, and of course plays a very large role in the universe outside of the scale of human life more generally. But it is electromagnetism that forms the basis for life and much of our existence as earth-bound organisms, due to its attractive/repulsive qualities at the molecular level.

What's behind the various forces of nature?

Electromagnetism – the combination of electricity and magnetism, which we know now are different aspects of a single force – was described comprehensively by Maxwell and others in the 19th Century. These scientists developed what are now known as "Maxwell's equations," even though their modern form wasn't actually Maxwell's work. While we can describe electromagnetism quite well mathematically, and predict its workings based on these equations, there is still no consensus as to what electromagnetism actually is.

The photon is a massless particle that carries the electromagnetic force. Einstein stated around 1955, shortly before his death: "A full fifty years of deliberate brooding have not brought me any closer to the question: What is the [photon]? Today every clod thinks he knows it, but he deceives himself." Einstein had for decades tried unsuccessfully to develop various field theories of electromagnetism and the other forces, but still couldn't say what the photon really is. For Einstein, in his later work, fields were fundamental. Despite significant development of field theory since Einstein's era, we're not much closer today in understanding what the photon really is.

Similarly, we still don't know the mechanism for gravity with any certainty. Einstein's general relativity suggests that matter and energy literally curve space, and gravity simply reflects the easiest path for matter and energy to follow as it moves through curved space. It's a two-way street, then, with matter/energy curving space and curved space causing matter/energy to change its trajectory.

However, the Standard Model of particle physics, based on the other pillar of modern physics – quantum mechanics – suggests that gravity works through the exchange of "gravitons" (boson particles) between massive bodies. The Higgs Boson is yet another way in which today's physics attempts to explain gravity, which made big news in 2012 due to evidence suggesting it had actually been found by the Large Hadron Collider.

Reconciling these different models, general relativity and quantum theory, is the objective of theories of *quantum gravity*, none of which are yet widely accepted. String theory is the most popular approach to quantum gravity, though it has yet to lead to any experimental verification, and it suggests, through its "brane cosmology" approach, additional ideas on gravity that go beyond both the quantum mechanical and general relativity notions of gravity.

So who's counting? How many forces are there?

Anyway, my point is to show that our physical understanding of cause and effect is still pretty nascent and always evolving. While there is a broad consensus that there are only four fundamental forces or interactions – gravity, electromagnetism, and the strong and weak nuclear force – there are also serious efforts underway to explain key observations through additional forces.

For example, dark energy, which is thought to comprise the majority of the matter/energy in the universe (about 70%), would itself constitute a new force. Specifically, dark energy is posited as the force behind the accelerating expansion of our universe, and also of the very early inflationary period that saw our universe expand from minute dimensions to a sizeable fraction of its current size in literally millionths of a second.

Yet another possible new force or interaction is suggested by the strong evidence for quantum entanglement, which appears to operate far faster than the speed of light. In 2008, a Swiss team led by Daniel Salart showed that entanglement operates at least 10,000 times the speed of light. What's behind this effect? No one really knows yet, but apparently it is not one of the traditional four forces.

So even without getting very exotic in our survey of different physical theories (which is certainly a relative notion given the extremely broad array of theories in physics today!), we can make a good argument that there should be at least six fundamental forces. A seventh force is compound interest. Einstein declared that "the most powerful force in the universe is compound interest." Okay, that's a joke...

Action at a distance

Now here's where I'm going with all of this discussion about cause and effect, and forces of nature: while action at a distance, mediated by fields or force particles like the photon or graviton, is very much part of our mainstream physical and cosmological theories, action at a distance when it comes to human causation is far too often dismissed as impossible or as wacky "woo woo" science. And while action at a distance is recognized widely in physics, we still don't know much about the actual mechanisms behind such action at a distance, for example, with respect to gravity or quantum entanglement.

In fleshing out a more complete understanding of the physical world, and the role of mind in the physical world, we are gathering substantial evidence that the human mind may have a broader causal role than has been assumed. It seems clear that human minds can directly impact more than just our immediate bodies. Dean Radin's excellent book, *Entangled Minds*, surveys the field of what is known often as parapsychology, or ESP.

The data in this field are certainly debatable and the effects are clearly subtle, if they are indeed real. If they weren't subtle there would be far less controversy surrounding them. However, there is one area of parapsychology that I've found pretty convincing, and I've now been personally involved with research in this area – I'm referring to work with random number generators (RNGs) and the influence of mass celebrations on the output of electronic RNGs.

This is a really interesting area of research but it takes a little background to explain it. Traditional RNGs include dice, coins, shuffled cards or any physical device used to produce a random outcome. Modern RNGs, however, are small electronic devices that produce zeros and ones (bits) randomly – hence the name. They're traditionally used in cryptography, gambling, and other areas, by producing true randomness and thus foiling attempts to algorithmically discover passwords or predict outcomes. However, there is a more recent tradition of using RNGs to probe the impact of minds on matter, and the evidence produced is increasingly convincing that there is a causal link between mind and matter.

Probably the best way to explain this area of science further is to explain the experiments that I've been involved with recently. I'm a visiting scholar in psychology at UC Santa Barbara (under Professor Jonathan Schooler) and I'm also a regular Burning Man attendee (a "Burner" in the parlance of this sub-culture). I've met some very interesting people by being a regular at this massive celebration in the Nevada desert. About 50,000 people attend each year, celebrating music, art, and collaborative creation.

A few years ago I met Cassandra Vieten, the executive director of research at the Institute of Noetic Sciences, in Petaluma, California. IONS focuses on frontier science, which includes working toward a better understanding of the relationship between mind and matter. IONS was founded by Edgar Mitchell, the sixth man to walk on the moon. Mitchell was so inspired by a profound spiritual experience as he hurtled back to Earth that he wanted to re-direct some scientific attention to phenomena that are too often denied as impossible by mainstream science. IONS was the result.

Cassi, Schooler (another Burner) and I were chatting at the Burn in 2010, about the research that IONS does, and we decided it would be awesome and fun to do some RNG experiments at Burning Man. Many past experiments have shown a correlation between mass celebrations, like New Year's Eve in Times Square, and a deviation from randomness in RNGs. The reasonable inference from these correlations is that there is a causal link between the mass focus on a single event and whatever mechanisms produce the random events in the RNG.

The twist in our idea was that we decided to add a huge freakin' laser to our experiment, connecting the output of the RNG to a laser in order to show visually any deviation from randomness. This would, we hypothesized, create a positive feedback loop and the effect would be enhanced.

We turned this idle talk into reality last year by completing our first experiment on the Playa, which is where the Burning Man event is held each year. It worked! We obtained strong evidence of a correlation between the collective focus of thousands of minds on the burning of the Man (which happens on Saturday night every year) and the burning of the Temple, another major structure that is integral to the Burning Man celebration (on Sunday night), and the output of our RNGs.

Figure 1 shows the key result of our experiment: a strong spike in deviations from randomness during the burning of the Man, with a p value of 0.004. (A p value of 0.05, which means a one in twenty odds of the result occurring due entirely to chance, is considered standard in most areas of science; a value of 0.004 is far more significant and means that the odds of our results occurring entirely due to chance were four in one thousand).

Figure 1. *Peaking of deviations from randomness during the burning of the Man in 2010.*

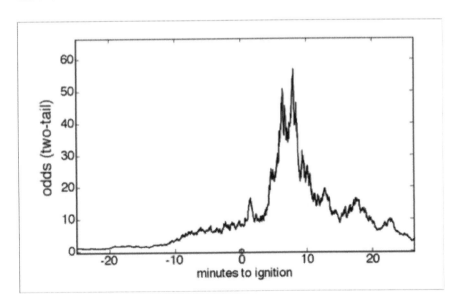

Unfortunately, our huge freakin' laser wasn't very huge and it didn't function very well due to various technical problems. So we're going back this year, in August, to repeat the experiment and use a really big laser, in collaboration with other more experienced laser technicians. We're going to use a 30 watt laser rather than the 1 watt laser we used last year. A 30 watt laser is easily visible across the whole Playa, so the positive feedback loop should be substantial. Yes, it's huge!

But what does it all mean?

At the end of the day, what does all this mean? Who cares if there's a tiny impact from mass celebrations on the output of zeros and ones from a little electronic device? Well, first, we think it's just really cool and intriguing that this stuff works at all. It's denied as impossible by many scientists today. Personally, I think the really powerful result of this research is to show that we could in theory, if we can amplify what are obviously very subtle effects, use just our minds to influence macroscopic events in the world around us.

There is an ironic convergence of traditional science and this frontier science, when we consider that "mind reading" using electromagnetic technologies is advancing quickly. Using various types of brain imaging, we can now tell what words subjects are thinking (from a pre-selected list only, at this point), and monkeys have used the power of their minds, implanted with electrodes, to control mechanical arms.

It may be the case that using electromagnetism alone will be the more fruitful path to manipulating macro events with thoughts alone. However, understanding that there may be other ways for mind to influence matter is really important for a more complete physical understanding of the universe, and it may give rise to more options for helping physically disabled persons to transcend their disabilities, allow us to create interesting new forms of entertainment, and perhaps help in many other human endeavors.

Figure 2. *Our t-shirt design for our first RNG experiment at Burning Man.*

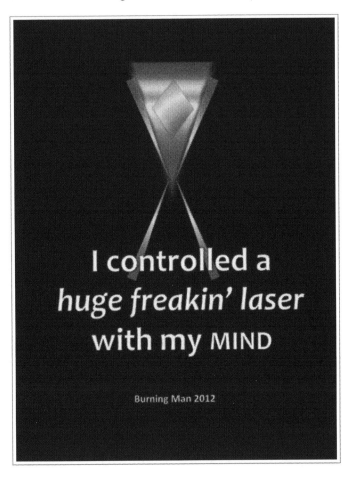

Part IV

Interviews of Various Flavors

It's no fun to talk to yourself all the time. And one of the many marvels of modern technology is that it's so relatively easy to reach out to practitioners in all fields. I've not been shy in reaching out to experts in the fields that interest me, including for the purposes of this book, experts in philosophy, physics, biology, cosmology and various types of spirituality. No debates have been ended, only extended. And the learning process marches on.

Chapter 30

Evolutionary Enlightenment:

A Conversation With Andrew Cohen

I was struck recently when perusing the religion section of my local book store by how many versions of the Bible are now available. About three sections of shelves, with five shelves each, displayed the numerous different translations, annotated versions, and other variations of the Bible, both Christian and Jewish. Clearly, the Bible has evolved!

Bart Ehrman, a professor at University of North Carolina, Chapel Hill, has written many books in the last decade on Biblical scholarship. He has demonstrated in books like Misquoting Jesus and Lost Scriptures how the Bible came about through a limited selection of books among many hundreds available from early Christian groups; and through translation after translation, from the original Greek to hundreds of languages today. This history suggests strongly, as Erhman argues, that even the earliest editions of the Bible were subject to all sorts of human foibles, as well as transcription and translation errors and emendations. Things change. Things evolve.

What about spirituality more generally? Views on spirituality obviously evolve, with sect after sect splitting away in schism after schism, leading to the many hundreds of Christian, Hindu, Jewish, Buddhist, Islamic, etc., sects we see in the world today.

But does God evolve? Andrew Cohen, a spiritual teacher based in Massachusetts thinks the answer is a resounding "yes." Andrew is the author of a number of books, including most recently Evolutionary Enlightenment: A New Path to Spiritual Awakening. I interviewed Andrew for my column, via email. This will be the first in an occasional series of interviews with thought leaders in many different fields.

How did you arrive at your own synthesis of spiritual teachings?

I experienced my own transformation through the grace of H.W.L. Poonja, the great master of Advaita Vedanta who I met in Lucknow, India, twenty-five years ago. He had been a disciple of one of the most respected and revered nondual realizers of the twentieth century, Ramana Maharshi. Poonjaji, as he was affectionately called, revealed to me the ultimate truth that the deepest part of each and every one of us, which he called the Self, exists prior to all things. Before time and space, I AM. Before the universe was born, there is infinite freedom. Through awakening to that deepest part of myself, which the Buddha called "the deathless" or "the unborn," I let go of the belief that I was unfree. That meeting changed my life forever and after only three weeks he asked me to become a teacher in my own right.

His philosophy was what I have come to call "traditional enlightenment," and it was based on the perennial mystical insight that from the perspective of that deepest Self, the world is an illusion and time and space are only relatively real. This insight liberated my soul, but after I had been teaching for only a short time, I came to understand that the traditional approach only gives us half the picture. In telling us that the world isn't real, it allows us to let go of our attachment to it, and in that letting go, experience spiritual liberation. But what if we are not convinced that the world is unreal? What are we to do then? This was my predicament as a young teacher. As touched as I had been by awakening to the unborn Self beyond time and space, I had never been able to accept the assertion that the world was an illusion. Not only did I believe that the world was real but I also came to give much greater value to Spirit's power to affect change in the world than its power to liberate us from it. For this reason, I began to give more importance to spiritual actions than spiritual experiences.

As a teacher I was, and still am, looking for ways to make deep sense out of life and the human experience. The reality that was gradually revealing itself to me was that life was a vast universal process rather than merely a personal adventure. This emerging intuition began to crystallize about fifteen years ago, when I discovered, through the work I was doing with my students in creating our award-winning magazine *EnlightenNext*, the liberating perspective of an evolutionary worldview. From cosmologist Brian Swimme I learned how to see the human experience in the context of an evolving cosmos. Reading Christian theologian Pierre Teilhard de Chardin and the great Indian mystic Sri Aurobindo made it apparent to me that that process is a spiritual unfolding. Through my growing friendship with the great contemporary philosopher Ken Wilber, I came to appreciate the power of Integral Philosophy as a lens through which to see the multidimensional complexity of reality. Spiral Dynamics wizard Don Beck introduced me to the work of Clare Graves, which helped me understand how human culture has evolved through progressive stages. Slowly but surely, these powerful truths, and many others, have seeped deeply into the core of my being. Over the years, the profound enlightenment that I received from my teacher and these new big ideas have fused and become one in the most miraculous way.

How is Evolutionary Enlightenment different than traditional Vedanta or Buddhist teachings?

It's very different. As I explained, the goal of traditional enlightenment, to put it simply, is about transcending the world and experiencing freedom from it. The goal of the new Evolutionary Enlightenment is about creating the future. It is based upon the recognition that highly developed human consciousness and cognition is the leading edge of the developmental process that began almost 14 billion years ago. The energy and intelligence that created the universe is perceiving its own creation through your very own heart and mind. Where we're all going depends on the choices you make and the actions you take. That's why Evolutionary Enlightenment is not about transcending the world; it's about creating the future.

Do we have to believe in a guiding intelligence behind evolution, as you suggest, to accept the teachings of Evolutionary Enlightenment?

We don't have to believe in anything to accept the teachings of Evolutionary Enlightenment. All we need to do is look into the truth of our own experience and what science has revealed to us. 13.7 billion years of cosmic evolution has given rise to 3.8 billion years of biological evolution, which has given rise to tens of thousands of years of cultural evolution. We're on a moving train. We're all part of a process that's going somewhere. We don't have to believe in a guiding intelligence but we can feel the drive of an evolutionary impulse, as I like to call it, as a tangibly felt energetic presence in our own experience at different levels. At the lowest level, the sexual drive can be recognized as an evolutionary impulse. At a much higher level, the uniquely human compulsion towards innovation can be recognized as an evolutionary impulse. And finally, at the highest level, the spiritual impulse, which is a compulsion towards higher consciousness, can be recognized as an evolutionary impulse. Something miraculous is going on here and it's trying to happen in and through all of us in every moment.

Is the fundamental duality of nature you describe (manifest/unmanifest) a sharp split or more of a continuum from pure potentiality to complete actuality?

It's a continuum, as you say, from pure potentiality to complete actuality. From an absolute perspective, there is only One – no distinctions, no difference between the manifest and the unmanifest. But once we step down one billionth of a millimeter from that absolute position, all distinctions appear and suddenly the manifest and the unmanifest become opposites, parallel realities that are a complete paradox.

How can that which is changeless (you assert that the ground of being is changeless) form the basis of an evolutionary approach to spirituality?

Isn't that the biggest mystery of all: how did something come from nothing? But it did. Absolute zero is the foundation of everything that is. The evolving universe and all of manifestation emerged and continues to arise from infinite emptiness. That is a mystery that I believe we will never truly be able to grasp with the mind.

You state that evolution is driven by God, as an intelligent and creative force, so how do you approach the problem of evil, which has bedeviled (all puns intended) theologians through the millennia?

Using the word God is always tricky as it's a very charged term that means different things to different people. I like to use that word to represent the idea of an absolute principle. In an evolutionary context, we could choose to describe that absolute principle as "the energy and intelligence that initially created and is continuing to create the universe." In the way that I understand it, that driving force is more an impulse than it is a divine being. In that impulse, there is no predetermined plan at work. It is a directionality, a momentum, a reaching towards.

The whole question of evil is obviously a very big one. What I think is important to understand is that the very notion of good and evil only arises at the leading edge of the evolutionary process. Only after human culture emerged on our small planet around 50,000 years ago did the capacity to make moral distinctions emerge. That means that within a 14 billion year developmental process, the kind of question we are talking about has only very recently emerged in our universe. There is no creator God or divine being, separate from the evolutionary process as a whole, who gives rise to what we could choose to call "evil." In fact, it is the evolution of human consciousness itself that makes it possible for us to make the distinctions between good and evil in the first place. And it is in our ability to make these distinctions that the higher, spiritually inspired aspiration for a world free from evil and aggression arises. I believe, as do other evolutionary thinkers, that our own highly developed human consciousness is not separate from that same energy and intelligence that created the universe. So therefore, we could say that as you and I aspire for a world that's free from evil and aggression, it is actually none other than the creator of the universe, as us, that is desiring that very same possibility.

You cite Aurobindo and Teilhard de Chardin as strong influences in your thought, and you have elsewhere cited Alfred North Whitehead as an influence. All of these thinkers were panpsychists. Would you describe yourself as a panpsychist?

My understanding of panpsychism is that it states that consciousness goes all the way up and all the way down the great chain of being from matter to life to mind. It's my sense that some form of interiority goes all the way down but I personally believe that what we could call consciousness only enters into the stream of existence when life emerges.

You gently criticize the notion of "be here now," advocated by a great many spiritual teachers, in favor of a future-oriented spirituality. But isn't it true that we only ever exist in the now and if we don't embrace this truth we can never be happy now? The process philosophy view of the world holds that we do impact the present through our choices in every moment, as well as the future.

Yes, I agree that if we don't embrace the present moment we won't be able to be happy. That being said, "Be here Now" and the "Power of Now" mysticism point us towards the mystery of the eternal present, the timeless, infinite ground of all Being as the source of spiritual freedom. But in the new Evolutionary Enlightenment that I teach, I point towards a different source of spiritual emancipation, which is what I call the Evolutionary Impulse, that miraculous energy and intelligence that took that leap from nothing to something and created and is still creating the entire universe. The evolutionary impulse within each and every one of us is always reaching toward the future. So for one who has awakened to that impulse, embracing the present moment means that the future is existing as an ever-present living potential, right now. With this awareness of the future, your consciousness expands and there's a sense of being intensely awake. Why? Because your conscious, living relationship with the future begins to enlighten your relationship to the present moment—enlighten it with conscience and purpose. So yes, there is a tremendous care about now, about this moment, because of your awareness of the future. So that means that your active, participatory relationship with the present moment becomes an expression of your care for the future. It's my conviction that this kind of evolutionary orientation to mysticism is much more culturally relevant to the time and the world we are living in.

Perhaps my favorite western teacher of Eastern spirituality, Alan Watts, stressed in his teachings the full identity of our self with the universe in its totality, with Brahman. A generic term I use for this spiritual knowledge is gnosis. You fully acknowledge this timeless truth but seem to place more emphasis on personal evolution and by doing so helping God itself evolve. Can you explain the reasons for your focus on personal and universal evolution rather than working to understand that we are, each of us, the All, the universe, God, Brahman, in each and every moment?

Yes. It is true that from the perspective of absolute nonduality, we are all always one with the universe and its totality, with *Brahman*. That being said, in post-traditional evolutionary mysticism, we choose to give more significance to the all-important fact that our universe, in its totality, is going somewhere, is evolving. That introduces a new dimension to mystical insight: the realization that God or *Brahman* is also evolving. And then there is even one more step to this enlightening truth, which is the recognition that as we human beings consciously choose to evolve, God or *Brahman* evolves, in, through, and as us. That is why, in the new evolutionary mysticism, our own personal conscious evolution is of the greatest significance.

I very much like the idea of co-creating God, through our own evolution and the evolution of the rest of the universe, which you focus on in your work. Do you feel that there is a conscious God in the universe? As we help God (whether conscious or better thought of as a non-conscious principle) evolve through own evolution, will that mutual feedback loop between us and God become more pronounced?

God and the universe is only as conscious as we are, in our best and highest moments. Moments of mystical insight reveal our potential to see through the eyes of Spirit. In evolutionary mysticism, there is no God or Spirit that is in any way separate from the creative process itself. The evolving universe gains the capacity for consciousness through giving rise to life, and through life, higher and higher capacities for interiority. As life forms become more and more conscious, the universe simultaneously awakens to itself and becomes Self-aware. With the attainment of mystical insight, the creative process awakens to itself through us, as Spirit in action. So the answer to your question is yes.

Are your own views still evolving? If so, what is the single biggest area of doubt you personally have when it comes to spiritual matters?

My own views are constantly evolving and I'm always exploring dimensions of Evolutionary Enlightenment that need further scrutiny and development. That being said, I do feel confident that my teaching has now reached a fundamental degree of integrity and wholeness as a developmental path. That has taken twenty-five years! My single biggest area of doubt is whether enough human beings will attain a higher level of consciousness and cognition soon enough to prevent our collective ship from sinking.

I enjoyed your book and let me end with a more personal question: how do you personally find the balance between being human and being something of a guru to many people?

That's a good question! The truth is I don't experience the need to find any "balance" between being a human being and being a spiritual mentor. In the front office of the Sivananda Ashram in Rishikesh, India, there is a sign on the wall. It reads, "Teaching means Being." Ever since I became a teacher overnight twenty-five years ago, my experience has been that it is more natural than anything else for me to be the teacher that I've become. I know this is hard to believe, but for me being a teacher is my natural state. In that there is no fear, self-consciousness, or doubt. At times when I'm not in my teaching role, however, I find myself worrying about things that don't really matter. For example, I'm an aspiring jazz drummer, I practice every day and play in a band that performs regularly in clubs. On busy days or when I'm travelling and don't have enough time to practice, I worry that I won't be able to become the drummer that I want to be . . . When I teach, concerns like these fade into oblivion, so the answer is that I find my balance and liberation through being who I really am.

Chapter 31

Sex At Dawn:

A Conversation With Christopher Ryan

The ideas are familiar to most of us: men are from Mars and women from Venus; men and women have different mating strategies where men focus on physical beauty and child-bearing hips and women on deep pockets and faithfulness; men cheat because they want to spread their seed far and wide, whereas women should focus on a good guy and making sure her kids survive to spread her genes.

Christopher Ryan and Cacilda Jethá, authors of the 2010 book, *Sex At Dawn: The Prehistoric Origins of Modern Sexuality*, say this is all wrong. They attack this "standard narrative" of evolutionary psychology and sexuality, which has become quite pervasive, as based more on moralizing and religious indoctrination than real science.

The book is a fascinating read, whether you agree with the arguments or not. It's been very well-received by the public and also by professionals, for the most part. Though Ryan and Jethá take a number of contemporary anthropologists and psychologists to task for creating and spreading the standard narrative, their book has won widespread acclaim by sex therapists and many other professionals. It has also won its share of critiques, partly because it attempts to straddle the line between academic evolutionary theory/anthropology and a more popular style of cultural analysis.

Regardless, it's a fun read. And the audiobook version is also very good.

I had the pleasure of interviewing Ryan, who lives in Barcelona, via email, as part of my ongoing series of interviews with experts in various fields.

What's your background and how did you get interested in the evolution of human sexuality?

My background is chaotic—or well-rounded—depending on your perspective. After getting a B.A. in English in 1984, I hitchhiked from New York to Alaska, where I worked two summers in the commercial salmon industry. My experiences there convinced me to abandon my plans for graduate school (I was slated to pursue a Ph.D. in literature at Oxford). Instead, I spent the next fifteen years or so backpacking around the world, intentionally opening myself to whatever came my way. I ended up having all sorts of adventures, and made money doing strange things like teaching English to prostitutes in Bangkok, managing commercial real estate in Manhattan's Diamond District, and translating from Ebonics to English for a Spanish film festival.. Meanwhile, I was moving around, paying close attention to the similarities and differences in the cultures I experienced. Eventually, I decided to get a doctorate in research psychology, as that would enable me to formalize some of what I'd learned in my wayward youth.

What's your main point(s) in your book?

The main point is to explain that human beings evolved in a socio-sexual context very different from what we are led to believe, and that this misinformed view has huge repercussions in terms of marital stability, self-understanding, sexual shame, and so on.

Have you and your co-author been happy with the popular and/or professional reaction to your book?

Definitely. When you write a book these days, especially as first-time authors with no platform to speak of (no TV show or Harvard professorship), you're very lucky to get it published at all. To have our book win professional awards, become a bestseller, and actually touch people's lives is an incredible gift, for which we'll always be very grateful.

You describe and strongly critique "the standard narrative" of evolutionary psychology. Could you summarize the standard narrative and your critique here?

What we call the Standard Narrative of human sexual evolution assumes that human beings evolved in nuclear family units founded on a "deal" in which a man traded his "investment" of goods and services (meat, shelter, status, protection, etc.) for the sexual fidelity of his mate. Her fidelity functioned as a form of paternity assurance, so he could be certain his investment wasn't wasted on someone else's DNA. As you can see, this is essentially a very economic view of human sexuality in which individualistic, capitalistic assumptions about human nature are deeply integrated. We call this tendency to project contemporary social mores into prehistory, "Flintstonization."

Our critique basically says: Wait a minute! All four of the most relevant sources of information point toward a very different sort of sexual life for our ancestors—one of a casual, friendly promiscuity among close-knit nomadic groups. Primatology shows us that our closest primate relatives, the chimps and bonobos, both mate promiscuously, in what biologists call "mulit-male/multi-female mating.". Anthropology provides many examples of societies in which paternity certainty is either a non-issue or even avoided through rituals in which people must have sex with someone other than their habitual partner(s). Contemporary research into psycho-sexuality paints a XXX picture of our species very different from these prehistoric nuclear family-based tales. Finally, our own anatomy is clearly not that of a monogamous (or polygynous) primate. So this idea that we are an essentially monogamous (or polygynous) species has very weak scientific support. The Standard Narrative is a moralistic argument masquerading as science.

One of the many arguments in your book that I found extremely interesting and also fairly compelling is the idea that we have our sexual history literally stamped on our bodies. You discuss how our genitalia in relation to our body size, and related features, demonstrate our close kinship with bonobos in terms of our natural sexual behavior. And bonobos are famously randy creatures, and not at all monogamous. This was a pretty key argument in your critique of the standard narrative, along with the other strands you discussed above. Do you personally think, however, that the evidence is strong enough at this point in the development of our knowledge to be able to state with much certainty what the actual sexual behavior of our species was during prehistory? Or is it more that you believe strongly that the evidence for the standard narrative is far weaker than its proponents believe?

Always acknowledging that there is a wide range of individual difference in any human behavior, I think we can confidently say that long-term sexual monogamy was not typical of our ancestors' behavior. As we say in the book, if it were, men and women would be the same size, we'd have sex only when women were ovulating, men's penises and testicles would be a fraction of their actual size, human intercourse wouldn't involve repeated thrusting, women's reproductive systems would function differently, and so on. Archeologists commonly say that behavior doesn't leave fossil evidence, but when it comes to sexual behavior, it does, to some extent. Our living bodies very much reflect our ancestors' sexual behavior.

One thing I felt was missing in your book was an acknowledgement that monogamy, even if not either normal or pervasive during the vast majority of our species' history, does still work for a lot of people, and has become "natural" due to its cultural pervasiveness (we do a lot of things now, of course, that were never done during prehistory, like conducting email interviews, etc.). Was this intentional or am I being unfair to your book?

I don't think cultural pervasiveness makes something natural, though it can make it feel that way. No matter how natural it may feel to drink a 20oz Coke with our chili dogs, our bodies aren't fooled into responding to this onslaught of toxins and corn syrup as they do to a diet more typical of our ancestors. Having said that, our book is certainly not meant as a critique of monogamy. My parents, for example, celebrated their 50th anniversary two months after the book was published! In the modern world, monogamy can be the best available option for many people, but that doesn't make it natural or easy. I often say that monogamy is like vegetarianism; it can be a smart, ethical, healthy choice to make. But deciding to be a vegetarian doesn't make bacon suddenly stop smelling good. Long-term sexual monogamy is difficult for most people for the same reason bacon smells good to vegetarians, Jews, and Muslims: it conflicts with the evolved appetites of our species.

What is the most accurate critique of your book, in your view, from your colleagues?

I can't say. I'm not even sure who my "colleagues" would be, as I'm not an academician or a clinician. There have been some stylistic complaints from people who think serious ideas can only be discussed in serious tones. Others have criticized us for "cherry picking" evidence that supports our thesis, which seems both a fair critique and yet somewhat non-sensical. We make an argument and present evidence supporting it. Others do the same. We certainly discuss the counter-argument in some detail, but the bulk of our book is going to be devoted to our position. Given our strong critique of conventional sex therapy and couples counseling, we were surprised and gratified when Sex at Dawn won prestigious awards from two associations of professional therapists and sex researchers (the Society for the Scientific Study of Sexuality, and the Society of Sex Therapists and Researchers).

Have you thought much about the role of social media like Facebook in the broader framework of your ideas on human sexuality?

A little. We certainly crave community as a species, and Facebook appears to be appealing to that hunger (without really satisfying it). The same could be said of most dating sites, by the way. I'm afraid social media is to our hunger for community what junk food is to our nutritional hunger—an illusion of sustenance that leaves us full, but still empty.

You and Cacilda chose not to discuss how we should respond to, in terms of changing our own behaviors, your new insights and arguments. Are you planning a follow-up work that focuses more on solutions for modern living in a more polyamorous world? If not, what is the general outline of your views on how we should shift personally with this new insight into human nature?

No, we don't offer any solutions because we don't have any! There are very few "should"s in our book. We don't see ourselves as qualified to give advice to anyone. People have to find their own paths through life. We have enough trouble finding our own...

Turning toward the political and social implications of your book, it seems to me, if we are indeed akin to tall hairless bonobos, that this has radical implications for how our societies are structured and, particularly, on the conservative political worldview, which views the monogamous family unit as the basis for modern and traditional societies. If the ideas in your book catch on, as they seem to be, how do you see social structures changing over time in the western world? For example, do you see open marriages or openly polyamorous groups becoming far more common?

I think these things are already happening at an accelerating rate. The acceptance of same sex marriage in the United States has been incredibly swift, for example. I think the approval rate has jumped over 10% in less than a decade, which is unprecedented. We've seen questions concerning different ways to configure our intimate lives thrust into the spotlight by the repeated scandals around infidelity among public figures, a process that serves to desensitize people to the notion that conventional marriage may not be the best situation for many. In the end, authenticity is a nobler goal than adhering to some arbitrary ideal that even the most judgmental, vehement political and religious leaders aren't living up to in their own lives. If there's any advice offered in our book, it's just that: aim for honesty over conformity. To paraphrase St. Augustine—a well-known sexual hypocrite—"Love, and do as you please." In other words, be true to yourself and open to others' truths. Without all the shame and deceit around sexuality (which we hope a more accurate understanding of human sexuality will allow), it'll be a lot easier to develop relationships that allow greater happiness and, perhaps counter-intuitively, greater long-term stability in marriages.

In terms of solutions, I guess I find it hard to accept that you don't have additional ideas on how we should respond to the ideas you raise. Can you share how you and Cacilda cope with the knowledge that we aren't made for monogamy?

Cacilda and I don't talk about our private life publicly, other than to give our stock answer: "Our relationship is informed by our research." We made this decision partly just to honor the discretion essential to any intimate relationship (including ours) and partly because what's going on between us is irrelevant to the issues we raise in our book. The book is about science, not relationship advice.

Believe me, publishers pushed very hard for us to write a "Five Steps to Perfect Sex" type book. No thanks. How can I give you advice? I don't know anything about you. Are you straight? Gay? Bi? Something else? Married? Kids? How old are you? Are you healthy? Is your partner? How strong is your libido? Do you feel oriented toward novelty or safety? What's your STI status? Relationship history?... Shouldn't someone know AT LEAST this much about you before they start offering you advice? Books that purport to give advice to utter strangers about how to live their intimate lives strike me as supremely arrogant, at best.

You live in Barcelona, Spain. Europe is well-known in the U.S. and around the world for being pretty sexually liberal, particularly compared to middle America. Do you think, as a good starting point, we should or could try to emulate the more relaxed European attitude toward sex and fidelity here in the U.S.?

No doubt. In my experience, there's a cultural maturity in Europe that can sometimes feel kind of smug and tired, but when it comes to sex, there's a much more accepting sense that sex is part of life that needn't be a huge issue. American society often seems adolescent about issues like sex, violence, drugs, corruption. We're fascinated, titillated, and embarrassed by these things. It would be a step in the right direction if we grew up a bit in our approach to these parts of life.

In Holland, there's an expression that translates to, "One must tolerate to control." If you pretend teen-agers don't have sex, for example, you end up with widespread ignorance, high teen pregnancy and STI rates, and abortion rates many times higher than in places like Holland where life is accepted as it is. Denial doesn't work as public policy. It's amazing to me how resistant some political and religious ideologies are to this simple truth.

Turning to the non-sexual aspects of your book, I was very intrigued by your discussion about the effects of agriculture on humanity. You describe it as a "catastrophe" because of the relatively immediate effects on life expectancy (worse), disease (worse), quality of life (worse for most people), etc. This was news to me because, of course, agriculture and the increasing efficiency of harnessing energy from our environment is framed as progress and good for humanity in almost everything else we read. In terms of the present day and our ongoing technological revolutions, do you think technology is still taking us backwards, or should we learn how to harness technology to somehow allow us to enjoy the benefits in life that we enjoyed before the agricultural catastrophe?

I fear technology is taking us ever further away from the sort of life we evolved to live, which is—not coincidentally—the sort of life that generates the most health and happiness for us. Facebook "friends" are a poor replacement for real friends. A flurry of texts back and forth are nothing like a conversation. A digitized thunderstorm soundtrack playing on a sound-system isn't quite the same as lying in a tent with rain pattering a few feet from your sleeping bag... On the other hand, the tent and sleeping bag are also examples of technology, so one cannot demonize technology in general. But still, I think it's clear that as a species, we are moving further and further from anything resembling a life that would come naturally to us.

I was also very taken with the evidence you present that men and women aren't that different when it comes to sex. Women find novelty almost as much of a turn-on as men do. And you present some pretty humorous findings regarding women finding various sexual situations more of a turn-on than men do, who are apparently more traditional. How do these findings help level the sexes further in terms of power and gender roles in modern societies, if at all?

I think the take-away from that section of our book is that women's libido tends to be both very strong and yet more easily ignored or hidden than men's. Women are much better at keeping their sexual appetites under wraps, both because of biological traits and lessons learned through many centuries of brutal repression. Men need to understand that the scarcity of women willing to participate in friendly sex isn't biological. It's an artificially-created scarcity they worsen every time they disrespect a woman for being openly sexy or allow her to feel threatened in any way. Respected, high-status women who know that they and their children will be respected and cared for are far more likely to be the kind of women most men claim they want in their lives.

What is your next writing project? Are you planning any kind of follow up to Sex at Dawn?

I'm working on a book now called *Civilized to Death*, to be published by Simon and Schuster in 2013. It'll be a comprehensive look at many of the less obvious points of conflict between our evolved tendencies and the cultural demands we face.

Chapter 32

Darwin's Unfinished Business:

A Conversation With Simon G. Powell

All things flow

Heraclitus, circa 400 BCE

All things do indeed flow, change, evolve. The modern debate about evolution is simply a continuation of this age-old idea – how do things flow, change, evolve? And why?

The modern debate about evolution, both in its mainstream scientific version, and the cultural debate between evolution and creationism or Intelligent Design, can quickly become horrendously complex and disputatious. Many people who are not trained in biology, or come to the debate because of strong religious views, are quickly turned off because of these features.

The big picture of this debate is fairly simple, however, and can be summarized with two questions: 1) is life in all its glory here because of a creator or due to unconscious natural processes? 2) if life has come about due to unconscious natural processes, how do these processes work?

There is a third question that arises naturally, but is often left out of the debate: 3) is there a middle ground between the notion of a supernatural creator of all life and the notion of unconscious natural processes behind evolution?

What follows is a dialogue with Simon G. Powell, a British writer, musician and film-maker, and author of a new book, *Darwin's Unfinished Business: The Self-Organizing Intelligence of Nature*, which attempts to explore these questions, arguing for a pervasive "natural intelligence" that is both the process and backdrop of evolution.

What's your main point in your new book?

The main gist of the book is that our interpretations and appraisals of biological evolution are poor and misguided—in as much as they fail to capture what life actually is, and what kind of process evolution actually is. I make the case that evolution is a naturally intelligent process that weaves together naturally intelligent systems of bio-logic. I suggest this because evolution is an information-gaining process whereby life learns to make more and more sense of the larger environment in which it is embedded. Hence my repeated use of the term 'natural intelligence' in the book. This is not simply a case of words, but rather the call for a new relationship with Nature based upon a new attitude towards life. How we view the significance of life will determine how we live life. If we think evolving life is a sort of accident, or that the genetic code was a sort of lucky creative break, or that we are consciously pondering around inside a vast accident, this will invariably affect our cultural behaviour. That we are now compromising the integrity of the biosphere shows that our concepts and ideas about life on earth need to be overhauled sharpish.

What's your personal and academic background and how did you get inspired to write this book?

My academic career only got as far as a psychology degree from University College London. My primary inspiration for all my work derives from a deep love of Nature and certain profound psilocybin experiences, along with the conviction that our current paradigms of life are misguided and having unhealthy biospherical consequences. I always felt that people like Richard Dawkins were right, but not right enough, that they were missing something very important. I have since realized that they are rather blind to context, that context is everything. Nothing makes sense without a context. DNA is meaningless unless it is embedded within a sensible context that both fostered its arising and gave it meaning. And when you begin to think about environmental contexts, along with the role of such contexts in making interesting things happen, then you can start to divine intelligence. It is not that this contextual intelligence is 'outside' of Nature—rather it is Nature.

You say that biology needs to go beyond natural selection, but how exactly do we need to go beyond this key mechanism for evolutionary change?

We need to expand our view of natural selection and see that it is the intelligent characteristics of the whole system of Nature that foster and nourish the learning process evinced by biological evolution. In other words, you need intelligence in one form to generate intelligence in another form. Life is smart because the environment is smartly configured. What we call 'natural selection' is the continuous step-wise methodology of what I call 'natural intelligence'. Life and its surroundings are different aspects of one interconnected system whose inherent intelligence is feeding back on itself.

You focus on "natural intelligence," which you argue is evident through the biological achievements we see all around us, such as an octopus' ability to change its skin color to camouflage itself, the chimp's ability to use simple tools, or the design of the amazingly complex and adaptable human brain. But when you describe these as examples of natural intelligence, how is this different than saying that evolution is good at solving problems that the environment presents?

If you ask biologists whether evolution is an intelligent process, you will get frowns and often scorn. So whilst orthodoxy might concur that evolution is 'good at solving problems', this initial appraisal is shallow and is not taken further. And it is precisely the use of the word 'intelligence' that causes uproar. This is why I see the Intelligent Design (ID) movement as barking up the wrong tree. They are right to call into question our appraisals of life, but they infer a supernatural intelligence rather than seeing evolution itself as having intelligent characteristics. Also, it is not simply overt behavior that is naturally intelligent (like your aforementioned examples) but the bio-logic that underlies all that. In other words, life consists of multiple layers and networks of intelligence, all embedded within, and upon, one another. Any other view of life simply doesn't cut it.

Your point about evolution displaying intelligence, defined most simply as problem solving, seems to me to a point that most biologists could get behind, especially because you also state that intelligence doesn't require consciousness. But later you add that this intelligent process is an indication of a purpose behind evolution and the universe more generally. This is a far more controversial claim. Could you elaborate?

Yes, the notion that evolution is the operation of an unconscious intelligence might be more acceptable to some as opposed to it being a conscious intelligence. After all, biological evolution functions in the living moment and is not like conscious human intelligence that can plan and look way ahead. But just because biological evolution is an unconscious intelligence does not make evolution purposeless. One can talk of the natural purpose and natural intent of Nature. This natural intent is embedded in the laws of Nature and the forces of Nature, which ensure that that life happens and that life gets more and more adept at making sense of the larger environment. This gives evolution a direction. One can then see life as fulfilling a function or 'cosmic imperative' as Nobel Prize winning biologist Christian De Duve calls it. As far as I can see, this natural function, or inherent purpose, pertains to self-knowing. Which means that Nature is in the business of knowing itself, or waking up to itself. All this may start out unconscious, but it is becoming conscious through evolved cortices. Moreover, this awesome process can't be stopped.

You state that in evolution we "need something smart to get something smart," but isn't the point of evolutionary theory to show how complexity can arise from simplicity? Isn't suggesting that all of the amazing biological solutions we see around us could only arise from what is already complex in many ways antithetical to the goal of naturalistic explanations, of explaining how complexity arises from simplicity?

This idea that something is coming from nothing, or that the complexity of life comes from something very basic, is misguided and shows how we are curiously blind to intelligent contextual forces. The best way I know of highlighting this it to think about genetic algorithms. These are simulations of evolution that are run on computers. Such genetic algorithms are informative in many ways. Not only do they provide evidence that evolution can be modeled and can happen (which may be annoying to anti-evolutionists), they also highlight that smart things can only arise from something else that is smart. Indeed, genetic algorithms, just like all computer programs, reflect human intelligence. To be sure about it, human intelligence is evident in the hardware of the computer system as well as the software. Once human intelligence has organized and configured the simulation, then evolution can occur and highly complex things can emerge. But it is a big mistake to see these complex things as coming from nothing. Intelligence in one form (clever computer software and clever hardware) is needed to provoke intelligence in another form (highly evolved virtual entities/programs). It may look like smart complexity is arising from great simplicity, but this ignores the smart contextual environment running the show. The same unsung principle applies in the real world. You need intelligence in one form (unconscious) to beget intelligence in another form (conscious). That is why I see the ultimate source of natural intelligence as lying in the specific forces and specific laws of Nature, along with the specific Lego-like building blocks of Nature. It's intelligence all the way up and all the way down.

If the source of natural intelligence is the "specific laws and forces of Nature," and it's all about this context when we are examining how nature's wonders have evolved, is it fair to describe your views as a type of pantheism? That is, you urge us to look at the broader context of evolution and suggest that intelligence can't evolve from something which isn't in some way already intelligent, and, if so, isn't there some kind of design going on here?

I suggest in the book that the laws and forces of Nature represent natural intelligence in its primary expression, and that this primary expression gives rise to secondary and tertiary expressions like evolving life and the emergence of consciousness. I guess this is a kind of pantheism, similar perhaps to Einstein's take on everything. The problem with these 'isms' though, is that once a concept gets labeled, we may stop thinking about it. But, yes, I have, on at least two occasions, called myself a psilocybinetic pantheist. Or something like that. As for the 'design' question, it seems to be buck-passing if we opt for a supernatural designer. It seems to me that Nature must be both designer and designed. Mind is like that. Mind can think of designs and then explore those designs within itself and is therefore both creator and created. You know Nikola Tesla could apparently invent things solely in his mind. He could build things bit by bit within his imagination, test the designs, and then disassemble them—all done within his creative mind. Tesla's mind was both creator and the created—all in one.

You criticize Intelligent Design proponents and Creationists as begging the question of complexity and order in evolution by simply pointing to a supernatural designer as the source of life, but isn't your argument regarding Natural Intelligence fairly viewed as a naturalized version of this argument? That is, isn't all of Nature substituted in your arguments for a supernatural Designer? Doesn't your argument still beg the question of where this initial complexity, this "sensibleness," as you describe it, came from in the first place?

But Nature is not supernatural is it? Nature is what we know to be real. In any case, it boils down to how something can always have existed without a prior cause. Even modern reductionistic physicists talk of 'quantum foam' or curiously potent quantum systems from which the entire Universe sprang. So whatever scenario you opt for, it will always require a certain definite timeless something, or some timeless uncaused potential. It seems silly to me to see this timeless principle as being devoid of intelligence and intent given its fantastically creative potential. Thus, there has always been a meaningful something. But it changes itself over time—it converts itself from one form into another. That is what we are part of. It is not supernatural. It is real and it is what scientists study. That is why I talk a lot about the need to reinterpret the findings of science. Because all the data can be reinterpreted. One can, in fact, see the whole system of Nature as evincing intelligence. One does not need to invoke supernatural designers, or whatever. The 'will to design' is naturally inherent in the whole system. So one can see all of reality, the entire reality flow, as a natural unfolding intent.

Similarly, you suggest that there may be an underlying purpose to the evolutionary process, and you also suggest that the evolution of advanced minds like our own may somehow have been planned. How can purpose and planning be part of an unconscious, albeit intelligent (as you have defined it), process? Where is the line between purpose, planning and conscious agency, i.e., design? In general usage, terms like purpose and planning require a conscious agent.

I think natural intelligence goes through cycles of consciousness and unconsciousness. I see the Cosmos, or Nature, as a kind of vast unconscious that is becoming conscious via the evolution of advanced nervous systems (wherever they should arise). Maybe one can think of the original singularity that birthed the Universe as embodying conscious will/intelligence, the resulting expanding Universe as a rebirth process, and that the Universe will return to a singularity state in the future by way of evolving networks of conscious intelligence. From one to one via a vast period of diversity. Or akin to immense cycles of sleep and awakening described in ancient Hindu creation myths. Of course, none of this is provable in the conventional sense. But getting back to the notion of unconscious intelligence, this is a very interesting concept. I came across experiments recently that showed how we can spot patterns unconsciously. Card sequences (with a subtle underlying pattern) were shown to subjects. Even though subjects could not consciously divine a pattern, they would guess correctly. This showed that unconscious intelligence was at play. Similarly, we can learn to swing or to ride a bicycle without consciously knowing all the complex equations required. And then there are the clever robots of the artificial intelligence (AI) community. Their intelligence is not deemed to be conscious. Of course, AI intelligence derives from conscious human intelligence and is really a reflection of human intelligence. Again, this supports the notion that, in the natural world, the intelligence of Nature reverberates through different forms and expressions.

The Anthropic Principle holds that our universe is far too finely tuned, in terms of the many constants and laws of nature, to be accidental; it may, instead, be one of an infinite number of universes that have an infinite combination of constants and we just happen to live in the one with the right types of laws and constants. It is because of this good luck that we exist and can reflect on our good luck. Or we may live in a designed universe, as the Strong Anthropic Principle suggests. How do your views on natural intelligence mesh with the Anthropic Principle?

Well, that is buck-pushing again. Buck-pushing is rife and has become a sort of professional hobby for many academics. It shows how keen we are to avoid the invocation of intelligence and purpose within the reality process. Invoking an infinity of Universes really just makes the Universe bigger and then you have even more stuff to explain! Also, the term 'anthropic' means man (as far as I know). As I say in the book, the natural intelligence paradigm is not anthropocentric, rather it is 'mindocentric'. What is important is consciousness, in whatever species it should arise. Consciousness is the highly evolved means by which natural intelligence comes to know itself. In other words, we are the means by which this intentional 'thing' we keep talking about wakes up. Indeed, we are it. We just don't know it yet.

I find a lot of what your write here and in your book appealing and representative of real progress in evolutionary theory. But I'm still hung up on your use of terms like "purpose," "design," and "intent" in discussing the evolutionary process, while you also suggest that consciousness itself (generally considered to be a necessary precursor for purpose, design and intent) evolved very late in the history of the universe, at least here in our corner of the universe. Wouldn't your message be more effective if you suggested that the universe itself, in its full context of laws and regularities, has allowed evolution to happen until recently in a blind process, but that this process has now led to the awakening of the entire cosmos due to the evolution of advanced consciousness in beings like us?

The problem with the term 'blind' (and bear in mind the importance of words) is that it is pejorative. Like the term 'selfish'. Pejorative words like this seem to be quite fashionable in evolutionary science these days, but they can be misleading and their usage likely tells us more about our attitudes than it does the 'truth' at hand. Think of a genetic algorithm that evolves, say, an ultra-smart AI program. The evolution process inside the computer running the genetic algorithm is 'blind' in as much as it is autonomous and just goes ahead on its own. But it would be a mistake to think of it as no more than a 'blind' process. An evolution process transpiring inside a computer system is actually a direct reflection of the human intelligence that set it all up and intended upon a specific kind of information flow. That is why I keep talking about intelligence in one form begetting intelligence in another form. In other words, with genetic algorithms running on computers, it is clear that there is 'purpose', 'design' and 'intent' in terms of the specific way that these computations unfold. The same applies to the whole system of Nature. It is what it is, and it does what it does, because intentionality is built into it. Or rather, the Universe is intentionality writ large. But it is an unconscious intentionality, just like a clever computation lacks consciousness (at least to begin with...). 'Blind' is both a right and a wrong appraisal of the Universe—if you get my drift. Unconsciously intelligent is much closer to the mark in my opinion. At least that is what I am banging on about in the book. We have this longstanding idea that intelligence can sort of come out of nothing. This is incorrect. Intelligence of one kind is needed to drive the emergence of other forms of intelligence.

I like your use of the term "mindocentric" in describing your views. As you know, I've written some on the need to incorporate mind and agency far more into evolutionary theory than is currently the fashion. Does this mesh with your ideas: that evolutionary theory needs to more explicitly acknowledge the role of mind in nature? In other words, shouldn't "agentic selection" be placed in parallel with natural (non-agentic) selection? More generally, do you find a panpsychist approach to evolution (the view that all matter has at least some rudimentary mind associated with it, and as matter complexifies so mind complexifies) helpful in any way?

Well, as I alluded, I am thinking that consciousness only arises when nervous systems evolve a certain level of complexity and that when they do this new potential emerges—just like laser light emerges when laser systems come into being (a metaphor I use in the book). On the other hand, I often muse that the coherency of the whole system of Nature might well have a conscious aspect to it. That would be akin to what Aldous Huxley called Mind at Large. But it is so vast that it would surely be beyond our ken. As for the role of mind in evolution, for sure it is important in sexual selection. As to whether it has a role in other aspects of evolution, I do not know. Then again, never underestimate the power of unconscious intelligence! How much of our behaviour is at the behest of smart unconscious processes? If life is a kind of flowing unconscious intelligence (instigated by an even larger field of unconscious intelligence) then who knows all its ins and outs? As I say at the start of my Manna film: "DNA moves in mysterious ways". Back to the Anthropic Principle and what you describe in your book as the "multi-Universe" theory, which Daniel Dennett suggests as the basis for the finely tuned laws of nature we see around us. You strongly criticize Dennett for suggesting infinite universes in order to escape further explanation for our finely tuned laws. This gets to the issue of brute facts. If we accept that there have to be some brute facts in order to have anything at all, let alone to have a system of thought explaining the universe around us, how do we decide what those brute facts are? Shouldn't they be as simple as possible?

Brute facts are axioms, principles that are taken as given and a priori. It is curious how we generally accept them tacitly and do not ponder much over them. But even if these axioms seem simple—and the fundamental laws of physics are usually portrayed as simple—this may not be the case. I mean, we may find them simple once we have worked them out. But when you compare the existence of a definite specific law with its non-existence, it is a bit like comparing one with zero. The difference between one and zero is actually massive! So this implies that what we call simple laws may actually be compressed embodiments of immense amounts of information that just seem simple to us at this stage of their ongoing expression. Indeed, when, with hindsight, you think of the unbelievable creative potential of the Universe at the very beginning of time, you can see that such a creative potential was embodied in a seemingly simple system. But maybe not so simple!

Shifting gears a little, you discuss life as the opposite of entropy, as dissipating heat through this process. Isn't the presence of life and the very likely "en-lifing" of the universe over ensuing eons now showing that entropy as a law of the universe is in fact wrong? Isn't the actual tendency over appropriate time scales for the universe to become more orderly as life spreads?

It is often thought that life contravenes entropy. Which is to say that the evolution of biological complexity seems to go against the general tendency of the Universe to run down. But this is a mistake. Actually, life depends upon entropy. Entropy means that there is a robust and reliable current, or flow, to energy. Thus, river water will always flow downhill. Life is like a watermill that can tap in to that flow and then divert it into delicate metabolic cycles and such. So life is not contrary to entropy but rather an active extension of it that enables a move back against the general current of Nature, a bit like learning to swim against a tide, or using a system of sails to sail into the wind. Moreover, it seems likely that life and conscious intelligence will continue to spread and thus the cosmos might eventually become saturated with it. In any case, it is clear that those depressing sentiments you sometimes hear in response to entropy are misguided. You need a sensible flow of energy if you want to make interesting things happen. As James Lovelock once pointed out, if you want to use a torch to see in the dark, you need to use up some batteries. So, by evolving life and consciousness, the Universe is running up as well as down!

Last, you are a musician and film-maker, which is an unusual set of skills to combine with writing books on evolutionary theory. How do you fit these parts of your life together? What's your basic motivation in all of your work? Is there a consistent theme?

We live in an ultra-fantastic Universe. Mother Nature is an ultra-fantastic genetic engineer and an exquisite weaver of DNA. Our existence as a conscious witness to all this biospherical and cosmic majesty is equally as fantastic. That's what drives me and what goes through all that I do—whether writing books, making films, or making music. Having had a number of deeply inspirational experiences I feel obliged to give back using all and any means necessary. It can be a tough job—but someone's got to do it!

Actually, one last last question: do you have anything else you want to add in closing?

Darwin's Unfinished Business is available everywhere that books are sold. And my website is: www.simongpowell.com

Chapter 33

The Extravagant Universe:

A Conversation with Robert Kirshner

What is the shape of the universe? What is its ultimate fate, our ultimate fate? Do we face an ultimate crunch as the universe folds back in upon itself, a "big whimper" as the universe continues to expand into nothingness, or some kind of cosmic perpetual bounce of bang, crunch, bang, crunch? These are some of the big questions addressed in the still relatively young field of cosmology.

It was only a few decades ago that we realized that we inhabit just one enormous galaxy among billions of other galaxies in the observable universe. Our sense of scale has consistently been enlarged over the centuries, adding to the wonder of being alive at this exciting time.

The 2011 Nobel Prize for Physics was awarded to Saul Perlmutter, at Lawrence Berkeley National Laboratory, Brian Schmidt, at Australian National University, and Adam Riess, at Johns Hopkins University, for their work suggesting that the universe is not only expanding but is actually accelerating in this expansion. "Dark energy" is the common explanation for this accelerating expansion, though exactly what this strange form of energy consists of is still very much up for debate.

Robert Kirshner, Clowes Professor of Science at Harvard, was the Ph.D advisor to both Schmidt and Riess and has been involved intimately with this work since its inception. Kirshner was part of the "High-Z" team led by Schmidt, and Perlmutter was chief of the Supernova Cosmology Project (SCP) at Lawrence Berkeley. These two rival teams eventually came to very similar conclusions with different data, providing fairly compelling (but not unassailable) evidence that they're onto something real with this accelerating expansion thing.

I've been a long-time observer of cosmology and physics more generally, reading avidly in this field since my teen years. I was privileged to interview Kirshner recently about his book, *The Extravagant Universe*, which describes in accessible terms the interesting history of his and the SCP team's work on supernovae detection and the race to be first to announce rigorous results.

What inspired you to go into physics as a career? Was there any particular person or problem involved?

When I was a kid, my mother and father let my big brother and me do things related to science, even when they were risky. My mother was kind of busy with five kids plus her own interests in community theater, so she didn't supervise us very closely. My father had worked for the Signal Corps and had liberated a significant store of electronics parts at the end of WW II. He travelled a lot in his job at the MITRE Corporation, so he didn't supervise us either. In October, 1957, we watched Sputnik orbiting overhead and picked up its radio transmissions on an old military receiver. I remember wondering exactly how it stayed up.

We flew model airplanes, ignited home-built rockets, and built transmitters as amateur operators. For an 8th grade science project I built a 40,000 volt Tesla coil from the plans in Popular Science. You could hold a fluorescent bulb in your hand near this thing and it would light up. Or you could catch a wasp in a set of alligator clips and zap it with the high voltage. I might have injured myself with all this freedom, but fortunately that didn't happen.

When I got to Harvard, I took a freshman seminar in Astronomy. That was great -- Alan Maxwell was the instructor, and Joe Taylor (who won the Nobel Prize for his work testing General Relativity) was one of the teaching assistants. I always felt I was below average in my college classes, but now I know the average was very, very high. Richard Gott, now a Professor at Princeton, Bill Press who was the youngest professor tenured at Harvard until Larry Summers, Ned Wright, a distinguished professor at UCLA were all a year ahead of me and we took many of the same classes.

How gratifying was it to have been part of the team that won the Nobel Prize in 2011?

It was pretty clear to me that there was going to be a Nobel Prize for the discovery of cosmic acceleration. Both Brian Schmidt ('93) and Adam Riess ('96) did their Ph.D. work with me, using supernovae to measure cosmic distances, which is exactly what was needed. When the High-Z Team got going, I had Peter Garnavich as my postdoc, Saurabh Jha as a beginning student, and Pete Challis as a staff member supported on my grants. We went all-in on the High-Z project. Others on the team included Chris Smith (at Cerro Tololo) who had also been my Ph.D. student and Bruno Leibundgut (at the European Southern Observatory). And, hedging all bets, I also had Pilar Ruiz-Lapuente (Barcelona) as a postdoc and later Tom Matheson who were on the competing team.

Based on the Shaw Prize to Saul Perlmutter, Brian and Adam, and then the Gruber Prize where Brian and Adam convinced the Grubers to give their prize to all of us, any rational person could see how a Nobel Prize would be awarded. Either they would find a way to include all of us or it would be split with Saul getting half and Brian and Adam dividing the other half. I certainly knew how the rules worked, so whether this was really the fair way to award the Prize or not, I had plenty of time to get used to it.

Your book, The Extravagant Universe, *describes the history of the major discoveries that led to the Nobel Prize in 2011, in an interesting and engaging way. I really enjoyed the read, and appreciated the fact that it's not just a dry account of science in the alleged ivory tower; rather, you discuss real people and real emotions. Could you briefly describe a few highlights of your book and your main point(s)?*

I am delighted you've read *The Extravagant Universe*. As I mentioned, many of the members of the High-Z team had been my students or postdocs and I wanted to make sure our story got told. There had been a lot of press accounts of this research and not all of it accurate. Plus I wanted to show how much fun we have doing research.

The key moment came at the beginning of 1998. Adam Riess had been calling me up through November and December, saying it looked like the data were pointing toward cosmic acceleration. This could be the result of a "cosmological constant," or something like it. Einstein had invented the cosmological constant to make a static universe, then abandoned it when Slipher, Humason and Hubble showed there were big redshifts that got bigger with distance, (as Lemaitre had shown you would get in a solution to Einstein's equations in an expanding universe.) So the cosmological constant was a kind of theoretical poison ivy that nobody wanted to touch. Or, as my mother said, "Bobby, do you think you're smarter than Einstein?"

But Adam wasn't intimidated. After Brian had a chance to check the results, we had a lively discussion inside the team on what to do. Some of the e-mails are in the book. We could wait for more data, but we knew Saul's team [at Lawrence Berkeley Lab] had more data in hand. I thought it was worse to be wrong than second. Saul's team had already published a result in July of 1997 that said the supernovae showed the universe was slowing down. Were we confident enough to contradict them? Anyway, we went ahead. You can read about it in the book.

Compare this to the guys with the superluminal neutrinos -- they decided to go ahead and publish, but they ended up with egg on their faces. Maybe they should have wiggled a few more cables. Or, on the other side, we have the decision to go ahead and show the recent data from Large Hadron Collider, which may or may not be the Higgs, but surely is something real.

Anyway, the main idea is that we can now make measurements to test our ideas about the universe. This is mostly due to advances in technology: telescopes like Hubble, CCD detectors like the one built for Cerro Tololo, computers to help sift haystacks of data for the sharp needles of supernovae. We're not smarter than Einstein or Hubble, but we have much better data!

Can you briefly explain the science of "standard candles" and the Hubble shift data that led to the now widely-accepted conclusion that our universe is not only expanding, but is accelerating in that expansion?

The great breakthrough in understanding the Universe came in the 1920s when Edwin Hubble figured out how to measure the distances to galaxies from the apparent brightness of the stars they contain. If you know the energy output of a certain type of star, you can gauge its distance from the energy you receive from it each second. If you look out over a desert highway, you see distant cars with faint lights and nearby ones with brighter-looking lights. If they're all really the same, you can do a good job of judging distances. For our work, we used a particular kind of exploding star, which erupts in an immense nuclear explosion. These are more-or-less the same intrinsic brightness, but a million times brighter than the stars that Hubble used. The apparent brightness goes down like the square of the distance, so this means we can see these Type Ia supernovae a thousand times farther away than the Cepheid variable stars Hubble employed. Instead of measuring distances to the nearby galaxies of a few million light years as Hubble did, we can use supernovae to measure the distances to distant galaxies a few billion light years away-- roughly half way back to the Big Bang.

The other half of the expanding universe [methodology] is to measure the velocities of galaxies. This was done in the 1920s by Vesto Slipher at the Lowell Observatories, and then later, with Hubble's encouragement by Milton Humason at Mount Wilson. The amazing thing is that on average, the velocity of a galaxy is proportional to its distance, as measured from Cepheids or other methods. We interpret this as evidence for an expanding universe. But the details of the relation between velocity and distance depend on the history of cosmic expansion. The light from distant objects has been traveling to us for a long time, so it reflects the conditions when it left. By carefully tracing the relation between velocity and distance over a large span of cosmic time, we can find out whether the universe has been slowing down (consensus favorite in 1990), staying the same, or speeding up. By 1998, our High-Z Team had enough measurements, each of which was precise enough, to show that the expansion of the universe has actually been speeding up over time -- there's cosmic acceleration.

I get the impression from your book, and from other accounts, that you have a very hard nose when it comes to aiming for the most rigorous science. In other words, you're always pushing for more data and making sure everyone is extremely comfortable with conclusions before they're published. Would you describe your role on the High-Z team, and more generally, in this manner?

Well, it certainly is true that I hate to be wrong. It's OK for a theorist to be wrong, as long as they are interesting, but an observer (which I am) should be a reliable source of information. I told Adam Riess that the penalty for being wrong should be as big as the reward for being first. But when you are sitting on top of a big discovery, like cosmic acceleration, you don't want to be too slow, either. As you know, there were two teams at work and the other guys had already published a paper in the Astrophysical Journal, in July 1997, that claimed their measurements of distant supernovae showed the universe was slowing down and there was no need for a cosmological constant. When we started to see the opposite, in the Fall of 1997, we had to overcome our own reluctance to contradict this work, plus my personal revulsion for the cosmological constant (after all-- Einstein had said it was unsatisfactory and banned it from serious discussion in 1931!), to be certain we had a valid result. In my book, there are some verbatim e-mails from the discussion inside our group. In the end, we decided that we should go for it, but not make any public statement until we had the scientific paper describing our work ready to submit to a professional journal. So we made poor old Bruno Leibundgut say "we're working on it" in January at the Moriond meeting where he reported on our work, and waited until the Marina Del Rey meeting in February to announce that we saw acceleration. The results were quite astonishing -- the press really picked up this announcement and pretty soon Adam Riess was on The News Hour. We submitted our paper in March and it appeared in The Astronomical Journal in September 1998. The other guys submitted a paper in September 1998 that came out in the middle of 1999 with similar results.

Along the same lines, you mention the problem of cosmic dust many times in your book and you leave this issue unresolved in your book because the science was still unsettled by the time you went to press. Has this issue been settled now or is it still possible that other explanations may be offered, such as interstellar dust, for what is currently interpreted as evidence for accelerating expansion?

Yes, dust is really important. It can only make objects dimmer, which you might mistakenly interpret as a greater distance from the standard candle idea. So you must have a way to measure dust if you are going to learn about cosmic acceleration (which also makes the more distant objects appear fainter).

When Adam was a graduate student, this is what he worked on with Bill Press and me -- how to measure distances accurately even when there is some dust in the way. It turns out dust absorbs blue light more than red light, so you can tell how much dust there is by measuring how it changes the color of a distant supernova. You have to measure the supernova through different color filters and figure out how much dust. Adam figured out a neat way to do this. So did our colleagues working in Chile.

Our competitors had not absorbed this lesson, and made their earliest measurements through just one filter. With just one measurement you cannot tell the difference between a supernova that is dimmed by dust and one that is dimmed by the effect of an accelerating universe.

More recently, we've been measuring the light from supernovae at wavelengths beyond visible light -- out in the infrared. It turns out that the dust is less important there, and, as an unexpected bonus, the supernovae are also better standard candles at infrared wavelengths. This means the infrared is the place to make the most accurate measurements of cosmic acceleration, and use those to figure out the properties of the dark energy. Is it the cosmological constant or something else? You need very reliable measurements to find out. I am the Principal Investigator of a big program on the Hubble Space Telescope that will use infrared measurements of distant supernovae for this purpose. Maybe I will have something interesting to tell you about this in a year or two.

I look forward to learning more about your work on infrared imaging of distant supernovae as this develops. You mentioned in your book that the issue of pink dust (what you also call playfully "pixie dust") was still being worked on at that time. Has that issue been resolved or is this what your work on infrared imaging hopes to achieve?

I think this issue is pretty well settled by the wide-wavelength span of our observations. But there still is the puzzling matter of different behavior of dust in cases where there's a lot of it. In those cases, it looks as if light is scattered more than once, leading to some significant differences in the right way to correct for dust. Overall, these have very little effect on the cosmological evidence for acceleration, but we will need to do better if we want to get really reliable constraints on the nature of the dark energy.

More philosophically, how do you personally conceive of dark energy? Do you view it as a repulsive property of space itself, akin to some type of "new ether" (the phrase Einstein used later in his career to explain the properties of space)? How convinced are you that dark energy is the right theoretical construct to explain the supernova data?

Well, calling it the dark energy is meant to convey the possibility that it could be something different from Einstein's cosmological constant. But I would say the cosmological constant is the leading contender. The modern view of the cosmological constant would be a pressure (negative pressure) associated with the vacuum, just as Lemaitre discussed in the 1930s. Another possibility is a light scalar field that has similar properties. (The Higgs field is a scalar field-- so this idea has some traction.) But there are so many possibilities, it is hard to know how to weed out the ones that are wrong. So the best we can do for the present is to see if the properties of the dark energy do or do not match the predictions of the cosmological constant. If the observations show something different, that would be really interesting.

There's also the possibility that gravity does not behave exactly as Einstein imagined. While it is hard to come up with a theory that is better than General Relativity and that passes all the known experimental tests, some people are exploring this path.

I must admit I'm always interested in maverick physics theories, as it certainly seems to me that there is plenty of room for debate about what is still a pretty nascent state of the art in cosmology, and what is a maverick view one day often becomes mainstream a few years later. When it comes to the accelerating expansion of the universe, have you followed developments in plasma cosmology at all? In plasma cosmology, developed by Nobelist Hannes Alfven and others like Eric Lerner, the electromagnetic influence of plasmas (which is of course what all stars are comprised of) at the largest spatial scales is considered to be far more important than gravity - an idea which is hard to accept for most physicists who are used to gravity being the only relevant force at the largest scales. Do you think there is any merit to plasma cosmology?

No.

The correct solution to understanding why the cosmological constant is so small eludes us at the moment. When the correct explanation is developed, it will be a new idea, and may seem strange at first. But this does not mean that all strange ideas are correct. The most important thing is to work out their consequences and confront the ideas with the data.

Also, the convergence of many independent lines of evidence -- from galaxy clustering, from the properties of the cosmic microwave background, and from the history of cosmic expansion that the supernovae trace -- all point to a mixed dark matter/dark energy universe with a pinch of ordinary matter that allows us to see what is going on. There's a lot less room for speculation in cosmology than there was thirty years ago. This is a good thing -- it shows we're beginning to understand how the universe works.

I hope you don't mind if I shift toward the philosophy of science in my next few questions. As a non-physicist but someone trained in science (I have a background in biology as well as law) and someone who has read widely in physics for many years, I can't avoid the impression that today's cosmology lacks a strong foundation. The word "epicycles" comes up a lot in Richard Panek's book, The Four Percent Universe: The Race to Discover the Rest of Reality. Many of the physicists quoted used this term in reference to dark matter and dark energy because these are, of course, very substantial modifications to general relativity. In other words, they're late additions to make Einstein's equations of general relativity, our prevailing theory of gravity, match observations of universal expansion and galactic rotation and formation. Do you feel this charge is unfair (most of Panek's discussants end up accepting these additions to general relativity at some point)? Are you optimistic that we are well on our way to firming up the foundations of modern cosmology?

The observations are firm enough -- there's strong evidence that the masses of galaxies are much bigger than the mass of the luminous matter they contain. But it is true that the nature of the dark matter remains obscure.

It certainly would help if we detected the dark matter particles. People take these ideas very seriously and have built subtle experiments to find the mist of dark matter particles through which the Sun and Earth are moving as we orbit in the Milky Way. This could happen in the next few years.

Similarly, while the data are now quite solid for cosmic acceleration, it would be very helpful if there were a strong theoretical notion for the mechanism that makes the cosmological constant small (but not zero.) There are many theoretical ideas, but none of them seems compelling. Still, I think the way forward is to make more reliable measurements that could tell the difference between a truly constant cosmological constant and something that is subtly different. Looking ahead, it could be that ten years from now, when we've pinned down the properties of dark energy with ten times the precision, it still looks just like the cosmological constant. At that point, I suppose people will begin to look elsewhere for exciting observational programs.

Do you have a preferred approach to the philosophy of science? Thomas Kuhn's approach, fleshed out in The Structure of Scientific Revolutions and other works, suggests that scientific paradigm changes occur (abruptly rather than incrementally) not due to rational debate and accumulation of evidence, but more due to an accumulation of evidence contrary to the prevailing view that is ignored for a long time but at some point becomes too strong to ignore and, so to speak, the dam bursts and a new paradigm is born. Do you see any merit to Kuhn's thinking with respect to physics? Do you view the now widely accepted notion of accelerating expansion as a paradigm shift?

I suppose you could talk about the dark energy in those terms. In 1997, I certainly was unhappy that our data were pointing toward a cosmological constant -- this was both contrary to the published work of the other team and leading us into the theoretical poison ivy that Einstein had banished from the discussion. But another way to think about it is that the theorists (Lawrence Krauss & Michael Turner for example, or Jerry Ostriker and Paul Steinhardt in a *Nature* paper in 1995) could see how the pieces of the cosmological puzzle would fit together neatly if only there were a non-zero cosmological constant. Then you could get the Hubble constant to agree with the age of the Universe and have a flat, Euclidean geometry for the universe even though all the evidence was that there was too little matter (including the dark matter in galaxies and galaxy clusters) to do this. The balance would be made up by dark energy. So the problem was not conceptual -- it was that Perlmutter's group kept saying at conferences, and finally in an *Astrophysical Journal* paper in 1997 that they had done the measurement with supernovae and found the universe was decelerating. So I think the important step forward was not an irrational flash of insight, it was a correct measurement of the properties of supernovae.

Everybody was ready for this to be the correct answer.

The cosmological constant and dark energy debate is an interesting case of how physics evolves over time. The history is well-known: Einstein proposed the cosmological constant in his initial work on cosmology in order to preserve a static universe, which was the prevailing view at the time and a view that matched his intuitions about how nature should be. However, he later rejected the cosmological constant as the biggest blunder of his career due to new evidence suggesting that the universe was in fact expanding. Now, many decades later, there is a broad consensus that Einstein was actually right the first time due to the evidence from supernovae that your team and others have collected in recent years. In light of this history, and many other similar evolutions in physics, how confident are you that we generally "have it right" in our views today? Do you see physics changing very dramatically in the next few decades?

It would be pretty silly to say "everything has been turned upside down since 1990, but now we understand everything perfectly." Surely, a more modest view is appropriate. The evidence for an evolving universe where the visible world traces the effects of dark matter and dark energy is very strong. But, as you suggest, there's a lot we don't know. This is a great situation -- for a scientist, ignorance is opportunity. Fortunately, we have terrific ideas for more powerful telescopes and experiments that can tell us which picture is right, and help guide our thinking. Unfortunately, some of these instruments are very expensive, but I think that deep down, people want to know how what the world is made of and how it works. Aside from the economic benefits that investment in science and technology brings, it would be a good thing to continue this quest.

I like your statement that "ignorance is opportunity" and I read recently somewhere that science isn't about knowledge as much as it is about identifying more precisely what we don't know. You've mentioned dark matter and I wanted to ask about this sister concept to dark energy: isn't the argument for dark matter almost entirely circular? In other words, dark matter was originally posited to explain anomalous observations about galactic rotations and other large-scale motions and then this same evidence is often used to support the dark matter concept. Experiments designed to find the stuff that constitutes dark matter have, I believe, turned up empty-handed. Am I being unfair here?

On dark matter I think you are missing some important points. First, there's no question that you either give up on Newton's gravity or you need a lot of dark matter on the scale of galaxies to account for their rotation curves. Next, you find that big clusters of galaxies exhibit the presence of matter three ways-- by the motions of the galaxies, by the temperature of the hot gas that falls into the gravitational pit formed by the dark matter, and third by the warping of background images as gravitational lensing. And the same amount of dark matter that you infer from the clusters is just what's needed, when added to the dark energy density, to account for the flat (Euclidean) geometry of the Universe at large.

Now, the hard part is saying what the dark matter actually is. The experimental searches are only now beginning to probe the most likely regions for some kind of weakly-interacting dark matter particle. So it's not surprising that they haven't seen anything. But as the searches get better, and we learn more about the world of particles by experiments at the LHC, so we know what to look for, this subject should get a lot more interesting very soon.

On a different note, cosmology is important to scientists and laymen alike perhaps most importantly because of what our theories say about the ultimate fate of the universe. The Big Bang cosmology was for some time complemented by the "Big Crunch" vision of the end of the universe resulting from gravitational collapse trillions of years hence. With the new data supporting an accelerating expansion, this vision has given way to a constantly expanding universe that will eventually end in a whimper, not a crunch, what is sometimes described as "heat death" as all motion eventually comes to an end and matter and energy eventually simply dissipate into nothingness. Yet another vision that is still considered possible is the "big bounce" cosmology (one I find appealing), in which universes come and go over unimaginable timescales. How much do you think personal intuitions about the fate of the universe influence cosmologists, if at all? What would your preferred "end of the universe" be, if you could actually choose one regardless of the data?

The present information on the nature of the dark energy does not tell you if the universe will expand forever or end in a big crunch. But, if the dark energy is really the cosmological constant, then the expansion will be literally exponential, so that distant galaxies will have their light stretched to the red and then out of sight. The universe will become a dark, cold, lonely place. If this is right, eventually, after Andromeda smashes into the Milky Way, there will be just one large galaxy in our observable universe: much like the picture Einstein started out with in 1917. This is a reason for funding cosmology now!

The universe doesn't care what you (or I) think, and it is not required to make any sense to beings who have grown up on Earth, which is far from a typical site in the Universe. Our "common sense" is good for predicting the trajectory of baseballs, but very poor at telling us how the universe should behave.

Last, what do you see as the most pressing issues facing physics today? Quantum gravity? Figuring out what results in the observed accelerating expansion? Making string theory an empirical theory? Or something else entirely?

I think the dark energy points precisely at the unsolved problems that lie right at the junction of quantum physics and gravity. Everybody knows we don't have a quantum theory of gravity, and if we did, there might be some way to see why the cosmological constant must be so small. I am hopeful such a theory will emerge. At the moment, we have a very wide range of speculations and very few ways to weed this lush garden of ideas. So the path forward is through measurement -- trying hard to pin down whether the cosmological constant is or is not a sufficient explanation for cosmic acceleration. So far, all the data are consistent with the dark energy being the cosmological constant, but the precision of the measurements is not very good. I am working on better measurements, using infrared observations with the Hubble Space Telescope.

Chapter 34

The Rainbow and the Worm:

A Conversation With Mae-Wan Ho

What is life? Many have asked this question, and no definitive answer is yet widely accepted. Is life something truly distinct from non-living stuff, as many dualists have suggested for millennia? Is there an *élan vital* that distinguishes living from dead stuff? Or is life about certain types of organization, metabolism, reproduction, goal-oriented behavior? None of these answers have yet won the debate.

There is, however, an intriguing new set of ideas that has been developed by Mae-Wan Ho, a biophysicist and science activist (as she calls herself) based in London. Ho's basic assertion is that life exists on a spectrum and is, at its root, organized and quantum coherent energy. Ho's work attempts to bridge the gap between physics and biology by recognizing that there is no real gap at all – just a gap in current methods and habits of thinking.

In researching and developing my own views on the nature of life and on evolution, I've found Ho both a kindred spirit on many issues and also a goad to further research and thought. The increased interest in quantum biology in recent years is perhaps an indication that the ideas that Ho has been developing for some decades are catching on.

One of Ho's key ideas is that quantum physics does indeed have macro-level effects, and life itself is in many ways defined by its ability to bootstrap quantum communication to the macro level.

Ho is strongly inspired by Alfred North Whitehead, the British philosopher, mathematician and physicist who developed an extraordinarily detailed and far-reaching vision of nature that is quite different than the materialist views that hold sway in many quarters today. I've also been inspired by Whitehead and it is intriguing as I make my way through readings in biology, physics and philosophy to see how many thinkers have been influenced by Whitehead.

I highly recommend Ho's books to anyone interested in cutting-edge biology or biophysics, or anyone interested in related philosophical issues. Ho is a brilliant researcher and synthesizer who I feel will be lauded widely as her ideas achieve broader acceptance in coming decades. She can tend toward the mystical and artistic at times in her work, which I find intriguing and effective in helping to create a broader understanding of nature and our place in it, though this tendency is unusual among most working scientists. I urge those readers who are not used to this style to give it a chance. The effort will be rewarded.

I had the pleasure of interviewing Mae-Wan via email about her books, *The Rainbow and the Worm: The Physics of Organisms* (now in its third edition) and *Living Rainbow H$_2$O*, her newest work about the startling properties of water and its relation to life as we know it.

How did you decide to focus on the "physics of organisms" as a career?

I've dreamt of understanding life ever since hearing of Szent-Gyorgyi's remark that "life is interposed between two energy levels of an electron" as a biology undergraduate in Hong Kong University. I did a Ph.D in biochemistry, but biochemistry did not and still does not address the question *What is Life?* that quantum physicist Erwin Schrödinger asked in his 1944 book of that title. Szent-Gyorgyi is the father of biochemistry, and as I got deeper into my research, I realized that the two scientists were way, way ahead of their time, and got a lot of things right.

What is your personal background and primary inspiration for your work?

I grew up in Hong Kong when the 'bamboo curtain' was in place. The then British colony was a cultural desert with Coca Cola adverts and Hollywood movies filling the vacuum. My parents, aunts and uncles were typical of well-to-do middle-class Hong Kong Chinese caught up in the drive to be 'modern' ("more dung" in Cantonese pronunciation), while my grandparents' generation clung on to the old ways for better or for worse but without much conviction. China, after all, lost the war to the West, to modernism, and lost very badly indeed. To this day, the humiliation suffered at the hands of Western foreigners (and the Japanese) is still palpable among the older Chinese, and with that, the fear of being backward, and not keeping up with modernity.

I had six grandmothers on my mother's side and one on my father's side. My biological grandmother was the 5th grandmother, a concubine gifted to my grandfather by his friend who had bought her as a maid. She was my lifeline. A devout Buddhist, she was beneficence incarnated. She gave and taught me unconditional love, and simultaneously freedom and spontaneity. Fifth Grandmother was the yardstick, the golden standard against which all else was to be measured. I am not a Buddhist, but discovered instead that I am thoroughly a Taoist by nature, which is strange, as I was never, ever trained in Taoism. I think it must be part of a collective unconscious, or I would now say, the quantum memory of millennia written into the vacuum field that I have access to. My physics of organisms presented in The Rainbow and the Worm was strongly influenced by this quantum memory. (The 'physics of organisms' is to be distinguished from 'biophysics', which is about more mundane things like X-ray diffraction and other physical instrumentation applied to biology, so I am not a traditional biophysicist.) I found my way back to the holistic knowledge of my own culture via contemporary Western physics, which convinces me that I was rediscovering something universal.

What are the key points of your books The Rainbow and the Worm: The Physics of Organisms *and* Living Rainbow H_2O?

The Rainbow and the Worm set out to answer the question, what is life?, that Schrödinger asked. Most people thought he provided the answer by postulating DNA as the genetic material. That was only part of the answer. The other part he suggested was quantum coherence, a state of being whole that involves molecules acting in perfectly correlated ways, and a special thermodynamics of life, which he referred to a 'negentropy', or 'negative entropy'. Following these leads, I extended conventional quantum physics and non-equilibrium thermodynamics to provide the tentative answer, drawing on the work especially of Herbert Fröhlich, Fritz Albert Popp and Kenneth Denbigh, and empirical evidence from the scientific literature and my own research.

Life, in the ideal, is a domain that captures and stores energy and mobilizes it quantum coherently in perfectly coupled cycles that generate no entropy. This is a very compact statement, but it took years and several editions of the book to get to this conclusion, and the implications are rich, which is why it took the entire book to develop. They range from the physics of sustainable systems to the naturalistic ethics universally adopted by all cultures, that of doing no harm to others. In a quantum coherent universe, all beings are both localized as particle/solid objects and delocalized as quantum wave functions spread ultimately throughout the universe. Hence all beings are mutually entangled and mutually constitutive. Thus, harming others effectively harms ourselves, and the best way to benefit oneself may be to benefit others.

Living Rainbow H2O is a sequel to *The Rainbow and the Worm*, concentrating on the latest findings in the quantum physics and chemistry of the liquid crystalline water in the living matrix that enables noiseless, rapid intercommunication to take place, as required of quantum coherent system. Water also provides the electricity that energizes and animates life. That is why water is "the means, medium and message of life." It is the "rainbow within" because its liquid crystalline state enables molecules to line up and move coherently together, creating interference colours when viewed under the polarizing microscope, which are the stuff of rainbows. A whole new cell biology and biology of life is emerging, based on water, that has been completely left out in the reductionist and overly mechanistic biology of the mainstream

Why have so few people taken up where Erwin Schrödinger, the Nobel Prize-winning physicist and author of the 1944 classic book What Is Life?, *left off in terms of trying to mesh physics with biology?*

Lack of courage in addressing big questions or to disagree with the mainstream, lack of imagination, lack of funding, too much concentration on molecular nuts and bolts, domination of reductionist biology, too much specialization and lack of interdisciplinary training, lack of appreciation of the beauty of nature. In my opinion, to really understand nature, one needs to be both a romantic poet and artist at heart.

One feature of The Rainbow and the Worm *(RAW from now on) that struck me is the common practice in biology of destroying organisms in order to study them and how many of your insights about life arose from examining live organisms with tools that include creating images of the "rainbow worm" of your title, which don't kill the creature being studied. How do your non-invasive techniques compare to the invasive and generally lethal techniques historically used in biology?*

Non-destructive, minimally invasive observation is the key to really knowing and understanding organisms, i.e., with the utmost sensitivity in all of one's senses including one's appreciation of beauty and love, so that the known is most itself as the knower is most herself. That is also the highest order quantum coherent state of being one with the known. Discovering that truth made me realize the violence we do, not only to nature but most of all to ourselves. Through traditional invasive techniques, we lose the sensitivity that makes us most alive, and most ready to be inspired.

Perhaps your most important definition of life offered in RAW *(of a few complementary definitions that you offer) is this: "The organism is, in the ideal, a quantum superposition of coherent activities over all space-times..." Can you explain briefly how you came to this conclusion and what it adds to the thoughts offered by Schrödinger in his 1944 book?*

Many people following Schrödinger have proposed that the organism is quantum coherent, prominent among them, Fritz Albert Popp, Emilio Del Giudice and Fröhlich, all of whom I learned a great deal from, though not always what they intended to teach me. However, *RAW* was the only book that connected and reinterpreted conventional biochemistry and physiology, physics, chemistry, and mathematics, as well as everyday experience, with quantum coherence. Living activities span a wide range of space and time scales. The nearest analogy to the quantum coherence of a living system is a laser that becomes coherent simultaneously in more than one frequency, and all the frequencies are coupled together.

You offer a number of arguments for viewing life as essentially quantum coherent systems, based primarily on the degree to which the various parts of organisms are able to work autonomously but still remain highly coordinated - and you analogize the functioning of organisms to highly intricate jazz ensembles playing over a range of 74 octaves. I certainly like the poetry of this description, but I must admit that I'm not yet convinced by your arguments that quantum coherence must be at play at the macro level or intermediate level in organisms. Aren't there other possible forces/mechanisms/information pathways at play that don't have to involve quantum coherence?

There aren't really other possible forces/mechanisms/information pathways that don't have to involve quantum coherence when you take note of the liquid crystalline (condensed state) of the living matrix (both intracellular and extracellular). I am not saying organisms are perfectly quantum coherent, i.e., coherent to nth order where n is a very large number approaching infinity. If that were the case, they would never age and never die. In other words, there are degrees of quantum coherence, and the higher the order, the less quickly the organism ages. *RAW* is a very radical book; it contains other proposals – apart from the main ones regarding quantum coherent organisms and circular thermodynamics – especially about space and time. Notably, I suggested that both space and time are created by organic processes; time's arrow arising from entropy generated by the incoherence of process. Hence an individual's biological time can be very different from external mechanical time. People who live more coherently may age more slowly.

On a similar note, you argue that quantum coherence allows instantaneous transfer of information, and thus the development of highly coordinated organisms across many scales of space and time. Yet quantum coherence doesn't have to be instantaneous in nature. Salart, et al., a Swiss team studying quantum entanglement, found in 2008 that entanglement operates at speeds at least 10,000 times the speed of light (which doesn't rule out instantaneity, of course). Does it matter to your theories about biophysics whether entanglement operates instantaneously or "merely" at many orders of magnitude faster than the speed of light?

Again quantum coherence can exist to different degrees (order), my zero-entropy (perfectly quantum coherent) theory of the organism is an ideal that can be achieved perhaps once or maybe several times in a lifetime, in an especially inspired state, or in an emergency. So instantaneous transfer of information is similarly an ideal towards which the living system approaches (asymptotically). However, *RAW* also proposed, following quantum physicist Wolfgang Schommers, that there is a time-energy uncertainty relationship in parallel with the usual Heisenberg position-momentum uncertainty, that involves real uncertainty in time, so much so that time can go backwards.

Staying with the issue of instantaneity versus merely faster than light transfer of information, isn't this a pretty crucial distinction for both physics and biophysics? Can instantaneity make sense logically? It seems that if we have distinctions in the physical world, as we do, with matter/energy existing in an "extensive continuum" (to use Whitehead's phrase), that instantaneous transfer of information or causation may be logically impossible.

From the observer point of view, there is no distinction between traveling faster than light and instantaneity. The whole of quantum encryption and quantum information transfer, and even teleportation, depends on instantaneity. These experiments have already been done in the real world. I am among those scientists that do not believe there is a distinction between the classical world and the quantum world, as quantum effects have now been demonstrated at the macroscopic level, say, in superconductivity, and also quantum interference and wave particle duality for particles as big as viruses. We live in a quantum world, and we only observe classical effects because we insist on applying mechanical and mechanistic methods to relate to it. As someone said, if your only tool is a hammer, then everything looks like a nail.

Whitehead is indeed right, that we cannot understand the physical world except from the point of view of an organism. The important point to stress is that organisms are macroscopic quantum objects with a macroscopic wave function that evolves as we entangle other quantum beings in our environment. That is why he said something like: each volume of space has reference to every other volume of space, and each interval of time has reference to every other interval of time. There is ultimately a universal simultaneity in which no space-time separation exists, in a state of complete quantum coherence. Some of us may reach this state via a religious or mystical experience. Others like me touch this sublime state during an intense aesthetic experience (see my article "In Search of the Sublime").

I was fascinated to read in your book about the "liquid crystalline" structure of organisms, with water as the basis for this structure, allowing much faster communication between parts of the organism than electrochemical signaling or other signaling paths allow. Can you briefly describe this feature of your work, including the idea of proton conduction and its role in achieving coherence in organisms?

The liquid crystalline structure of organisms depends essentially on the liquid crystalline water that aligns itself along the enormous amount of interfaces. It is excited water that is easily split by infrared photons absorbed in photosynthesis, into protons, electrons and oxygen. The protons and electrons are positive and negative electricity that basically power molecular machines that, because of the water associated with them, can transfer and transform energy at close to 100% efficiency. The pervasive liquid crystalline water also enables the molecules to act in a highly coordinated way, approaching quantum coherence.

Walter Freeman at UC Berkeley has long argued that his work on rabbit brains demonstrated that certain brain signaling must be faster than is allowed for with neuronal electrochemical signaling. Is the proton conduction structure that pervades animal bodies a likely candidate for this phenomenon or are there likely other pathways at work?

Precisely, only quantum coherent proton and electron transport can account for the instantaneous or faster than light intercommunication that enables distant neurons to fire together, which is not different from distant muscle fibres acting together in a perfectly coordinated way. At bottom, the entire organism - brain and body - is a coherent quantum electrodynamic field that organizes all the genes and molecules. This enables ultimately each individual molecule to intercommunicate with every other, and water holds the key to the intercommunication, as well as memory of the macroscopic wave function that characterizes the individual organism.

Your recent book, Living Rainbow H₂O, *focuses in on the details of water as crucial to the fine-tuned coherence of organisms. You describe a number of features of water that are in some ways anomalous, including its melting point and many other anomalies. Do you believe the amazing properties of water support some version of the Anthropic Principle or would you suggest some other conclusion?*

There is no need to invoke the anthropic principle. That's the refuge of the ignorant and ultimately, the intellectually lazy. When we really understand the physics and chemistry, the most amazing patterns and stable forms arise, spontaneously and naturally. That's what my entire work is about. It is to remove the superficially mysterious to get at the really deep mystery of life, the universe, and everything. Maybe we shall never arrive at the ultimate mystery, but it is a life-long love affair I have with nature, so I shall never give up trying.

You venture into discussions of more philosophical concepts in your books, including the nature and evolution of consciousness. You include a chapter on time and free will in RAW, adopting a Bergsonian and Whiteheadian view of time as pure duration, and suggesting that time is actually quantized rather than continuous, as is matter and energy. Could you describe a little further how you conceive of quantized time and its place in your ideas on consciousness?

The quantization of time that I envisage goes way beyond the usual quantization of action in Planck's constant, and is a speculative idea in thinking of space-time as fractal, as consistent with the fact that different actions have discretely different characteristic time (and space); and the idea that organic processes create space-time. It is also consistent with the finding that living processes and structures as well as non-living processes are indeed fractal, as mathematician Ian Stewart and others have shown.

Fractal dynamics characterizes intracellular structure, and is the organizing principle in physiology and ecology, as shown by Geoffrey West and colleagues. French astrophysicist Lauren Nottale presented a convincing case that the universe itself is fractal. Thus, we have fractal space-time structures on all scales from the universe to the smallest cell and perhaps even fundamental particles.

From the perspective of the entire universe, its duration (present) is still on-going; whereas galaxies have been formed; stars have come and gone; numerous species have originated and become extinct; and astronomical numbers of individual organisms have lived and perished.

Regarding Walter Freeman's work, isn't it a big step to go from transfer of information that is too fast for traditional electrochemical pathways to an assumption that such transfers must be either instantaneous or faster than light? Isn't there a vast middle ground that should be explored first?

The big difference is between conventional explanations based on 'electrochemical pathways' – presumably neurons and nerve fibres – and electrodynamical fields. Field effects do not require 'instantaneous' intercommunication, but they certainly act much faster than conduction via nerves and synapses. The point is that quantum coherence automatically includes field effects and beyond.

You suggest that time has a fractal nature. With respect to human consciousness, how does this fractal nature of time manifest itself? Is it amenable to scientific investigation?

Natural processes are fractal. Since the publication of the first edition of *RAW* in 1992, this is now widely accepted. Processes are fractal because they have characteristic time scales, i.e., natural process time is fractal. The fractal nature of organic time is what Bergson meant by 'duration', which one can experience by introspection. In neuroscience, for example, the duration of conscious perception is about 0.5 seconds. Within that duration is a cascade of nested processes each with its own characteristic timescale, and they bear a fractal relationship to one another. In my book, I gave the example of the healthy heartbeat, which has fractal and multi-fractal structure, i.e., self-similarity on many scales. That is the basis for diagnosis of dynamic diseases, which involves a loss of this coherent fractal structure.

Last, what is, in your view, the role of consciousness in the evolution oaf life, and where are we likely to go as a species in terms of the ongoing evolution of our consciousness?

Consciousness involves a perception of "I", despite the multiplicity of cells and molecules making up our body. In other words, it requires quantum coherence. That was clear to Erwin Schrödinger, and I am happy to follow in his footsteps. In my article "Quantum Coherence and Conscious Experience," published more than 15 years ago, I showed why quantum coherence is a prerequisite for conscious experience. It is interesting to note that Whitehead, who argued that the universe is an organism, containing subordinate organisms all the way down to fundamental particles, endowed even electrons with a kind of primal perception which he referred to as 'prehensive unification'. More importantly, because we are conscious we can shape and create reality, being entangled with all there is. That is what I regard as the biology of free will. Neither determinism nor randomness rules, only the most sensitive and informed action. Informed actions are those that are maximally coherent with the universe, when we, the knower, are most ourselves and the known universe is most itself. In a Whiteheadian universe, all organisms, including the fundamental particles, are involved in co-creating the universal future, and I am quite comfortable with that view.

Chapter 35

Time Reborn:

A Conversation With Lee Smolin

What then is time? If no one asks me, I know what it is. If I wish to explain it to him who asks, I do not know.

St. Augustine

Time is like water to a fish. We're so immersed in it that it's extremely difficult to even think about it except as the entirety of our lived experience. And yet there has been a concerted effort over the last few hundred years to demonstrate that the lived experience of time is ultimately an illusion!

When we get down to brass tacks there seem to be only two things we know with certainty: that there is consciousness, here, now; and that the contents of consciousness change. We call this process of change "time." Everything other than these two basic features of reality is, literally, inferred, by each of us as we go through our lives moment to moment.

So how can it be that the majority of physicists today believe that time is an illusion? Well, that's a good story and Lee Smolin's new book, *Time Reborn*, delves into this story in detail. Smolin is an American theoretical physicist, a researcher and founder at the Perimeter Institute for Theoretical Physics, in Waterloo, Canada, and an adjunct professor of physics at the University of Waterloo. He's written a number of previous books, including the 2006 book, *The Trouble With Physics*, an extended critique of string theory and a tendency toward groupthink in physics today.

Smolin's new book is a cornucopia of big ideas, expressed clearly and compassionately. Smolin truly wants to understand – and to help you, the interested reader, to also understand – the big questions in physics today. And, ultimately, physics is not just for physicists. Physics is, when we get down to it, about the nature of reality and our place in it. Time Reborn is, for these reasons, fundamentally a book of philosophy and even of spirituality – but without any woo woo. Well, maybe a tiny bit of woo right at the end, if we consider discussions of the nature of consciousness woo.

Smolin's is a really rare book: one that is accessible and designed as much for lay readers as it is for physicists, but also a book that proposes new, ground-breaking, theories. More than that, Smolin is suggesting, explicitly and clearly, with fairly convincing arguments, that much of modern physics is either incomplete or wrong. That's a heavy lift, but he pulls it off well.

I've written previously, as a philosopher of science, about my concerns with the common view that time is an illusion, and my own objections to relativity theory. Smolin is politic about these issues in his book, but he's also suggesting that the prevailing views about the nature of time and relativity theory need some substantial corrections.

Smolin writes like a dream and his tone is spot on for someone who is trying to change a lot of minds about some really big issues. I had the pleasure of interviewing Smolin via email from his home in Toronto.

Why should we care about time anyway? Do different theories of time really impact our lives that much?

How we think about the future and the past determines everything about how we think about our situation as human beings. Are freedom, agency, will, discovery, invention, surprise, genuine? If time is an illusion so are they, and hence so are many of the human qualities we cherish.

Einstein famously stated that the distinction between past, present and future is a "stubbornly persistent illusion." Why is it, do you think, that the idea of time being an illusion has such appeal among physicists and regular people alike? Time is, as you write, one of the most real things we know. We can't, as conscious beings, exist except to exist in time, and everything about our existence suggests that time is real. And yet the idea that time is ultimately an illusion is pervasive.

The first part of the book is aimed at answering that question. It is a good question. One part of the answer is the very common tendency to look down on what is changeable and temporary and admire those things we imagine are timeless. Some of us have a great desire to transcend the time-bound realm we experience directly for fantasies of eternal beauty and truth.

How much should the human experience of time factor into our physics?

The book argues that the experience we have of time flowing from moment into moment is not an illusion but one of the deepest clues we have as to the nature of reality.

Many of our physical laws are said to be "time-reversible" because the equations work equally well when run forwards or backwards. Many people consider these equations and say something like: "Look, time is reversible! Time is an illusion and there is no free will." But this ignores of course that the universe we live in is entirely uni-directional. We proceed from the present into the future. We remember the past. There is nothing in our universe that proceeds from the present into the past, as far as we know. So these equations, it seems, are wrong in their time-reversibility because they don't fully describe the world we live in. Why do we so commonly mistake incomplete models of reality for reality itself?

In the book I propose that the time-reversible laws whose action we observe are approximations and that there are more fundamental laws that are time-irreversible. This seems a better explanation for the arrows of time than the standard one, which has to posit that the universe began in a highly improbable initial state. I won't try to answer your more general query. We all do our best with the theories and models we have.

A key factor in the commonly held view of time today, that time is an illusion, is the notion that the speed of light is absolute, a postulate of Einstein's special theory of relativity. The previously held view was that space and time are absolute but Einstein flipped these assumptions around, making the speed of light universal for all observers - no matter what their motion is in relation to the speed of light. This flipping of assumptions requires that time and space become malleable because the speed of light is of course, by definition, distance (space) divided by time. Setting aside any other debates about relativity theory for the moment, why would the speed of light be absolute? No other speeds are absolute, that is, all other speeds do indeed change in relation to the speed of the observer, so it's always seemed a rather strange notion to me.

Special relativity works extremely well and the postulate of the invariance or universality of the speed of light is extremely well-tested. It might be wrong in the end but it is an extremely good approximation to reality. This issue is discussed in some detail in the book. We are also working on the website which willl have "on-line appendixes" to give more details of some topics including special relativity. Even if special relativity ultimately is transcended, it is a beautiful experience to comprehend it.

You discuss in your book some of the tension between quantum theory and special relativity, including the fact that quantum theory seems to require some kind of superluminal (faster than light) causation. Doesn't this evidence, generally described as "nonlocality," constitute experimental falsification of special relativity? Or at least falsification enough to prompt serious re-thinking of the validity of special relativity?

This is a pretty subtle issue, as discussed in the book. There certainly is a tension between the relativity of simultaneity and non-locality in quantum theory, but it's not strong enough to add up to a falsification of either side by itself. What is true is that _if_ one demands that there be a deterministic explanation of what causes outcomes of quantum processes, then some physicists, such as Antony Valentini, suggest there is a violation of the relativity of simultaneity. But if you are happy with quantum indeterminacy then there is no problem reconciling them.

Your book is full of delicious iconoclasm, argued sincerely, clearly and compassionately. You argue, essentially, that much of modern physics has been waylaid by bad ideas and theories! I know that it's always hard to criticize relativity theory and to be simultaneously taken seriously as a physicist or a philosopher. And yet you do tackle this sacred cow - along with many other sacred cows - of modern physics. And you are taken very seriously as a physicist. So do you see a new opening for new ideas that view time as real? Do you sense that your colleagues are perhaps more ready now than in years past for new ideas that go beyond or even contradict special and general relativity?

First, the critique I offer of relativity theory is subtle and embraces the experimental success of Einstein's special and general theories of relativity. For example I describe shape dynamics, which is a new way of reconciling the existence of a preferred time that is perceptible at the scale of the universe as a whole, with the validity of the principle of relativity on smaller scales.

You've argued for some time that the particular physical laws we know are likely to be a consequence of "cosmological natural selection," which results from black holes creating new universes, with slightly different laws than the laws in the universe that contains the progenitor black hole. This theory has a number of advantages, which you describe in your new book, particularly compared to alternative theories. However, at a basic level, why would new universes be formed through black holes?

General relativity predicts that time ends inside black holes because the gravitational collapse squeezes matter to infinite density. However, it has long been hypothesized that quantum effects prevent this from happening, causing a "bounce" where the matter stops contracting and starts expanding. This creates a new expanding region of the universe that cannot be seen from outside the black hole. This can be called a new universe. This scenario has a lot of support from the study of mathematical models of quantum effects in the interiors of black holes.

And why would each new universe's laws change a little, after being born from a black hole?

Because I can make that hypothesis without contradicting anything that is known and its implications are interesting.

You argue that Leibniz's "principle of sufficient reason" should be a key criterion for good theories. This principles states that everything that is real must have some reason behind it, and thus some equivalent in our theories. But isn't it rather hard to pin down what qualifies as a "reason"? To be a bit flip, we could argue that the moon is whitish gray because it's made of cottage cheese, and this is a reason - but it's just a really bad reason. How do we use this principle in a way that has teeth?

Leibniz means reason in the sense of an explanation for why the universe has one feature when it might have had a different feature. The classic case, which is discussed in the book, is why the universe was not created ten meters to the right or ten minutes earlier. Since nothing in the actual universe would be changed in these scenarios Leibniz concludes there can be no meaning to absolute position or time.

Hendrik Lorentz, a mentor to Einstein, developed the "Lorentz transformations," the mathematics behind both Einstein's special relativity and Lorentz's own theory of relativity. Lorentz's theory, while considered to be empirically indistinguishable from special relativity, is not widely accepted because it relies on a version of absolute time and space. However, shape dynamics, a theory that you discuss favorably, seems to reinterpret general relativity in a way that mirrors Lorentz's theory of relativity in that it takes time as fundamental. Can shape dynamics be viewed as a generalization of Lorentzian relativity?

No, because the preferred time in shape dynamics is not absolute, it is determined dynamically as a result of the distribution of matter and fields in the universe.

The general view in the philosophy of science is that new theories that gain acceptance do so not by replacing but by going beyond the old paradigm - Einstein's general relativity (GR), for example, doesn't falsify Newtonian gravity, it goes beyond Newton by showing that Newton's gravitational theory is a limiting case of Einstein's GR. However, sometimes theories are simply replaced by new ones because there are, of course, an infinite number of possible theories for explaining any given set of data and sometimes new theories are simply better than old theories at explaining the data. For example, Copernicus' heliocentric view of the solar system has entirely replaced Ptolemy's geocentric epicycle view because, even though Ptolemy's model was highly accurate in terms of explaining the data, it makes far more sense to suggest, as Copernicus did, that the Sun is in fact the center of the solar system, for a variety of reasons. You criticize GR in some ways in your book, but you also suggest that much of the theory has merit. Could it be, however, that it's in need of replacement whole cloth, even though it makes many correct predictions, like Ptolemy's view of the solar system?

This is the kind of question best answered in retrospect. Let's see what happens.

I hate to pick on Einstein because he was in so many ways a great man: a great physicist, a great humanitarian and all around a great human being. But I agree with one of your key points in your book: that Einstein's view that time is ultimately an illusion is not only wrong but very damagingly wrong because of the consequences that flow necessarily from the view that time is an illusion: free will is an illusion and, arguably, human consciousness becomes an illusion because we seem to have no way to reconcile the view that time is an illusion with the obvious flow of time that is the foundation of human consciousness. So let me pick a bit more on Einstein and ask you this: you write (p. 56) that Einstein showed that simultaneity is relative. But the conclusion of the relativity of simultaneity flows necessarily from Einstein's postulates (that the speed of light is absolute and that the laws of nature are relative), so he didn't really show that simultaneity was relative - he assumed it. What do I have wrong here?

The relativity of simultaneity is a consequence of the two postulates that Einstein proposed and so it is deduced from the postulates. The postulates and their consequences are then checked experimentally and, so far, they hold remarkably well.

You argue against Platonism, the notion that our reality is a corrupted reflection of a timeless perfect reality, and I tend to agree. Yet you also state or imply frequently that laws "guide" physical outcomes. This seems to me to be reverting back to Platonism. Aren't laws better viewed as human creations based on observed behaviors in the universe around us? And behaviors are simply built in to the constituents of our universe?

Please let's be careful here. When we human beings hypothesize that a law of nature holds – even temporarily or situationally – we are creating an idea, but we are also making an hypothesis about how nature behaves, whose truth or usefulness has nothing to do with what we know or believe.

Turning to the philosophy of science, I'm curious if you or anyone else has thought about putting the evolution of scientific theories under the spotlight in terms of memetic natural selection. There are various theories of how scientific change occurs, but to my knowledge no one has done any detailed study (testing and falsification) of these theories of memetic change in the real world. Could this be done? Would it be useful in order to better understand how scientific progress really occurs?

I recall in graduate school hearing Quine and others discuss evolutionary approaches to epistemology, but I haven't thought seriously about it since then.

You view the universe as ultimately indeterministic – contrary to the prevailing view that all things are ultimately determined – based essentially on your view that the laws of physics are always changing. How important to your general worldview is it to understand that we, and the universe we live in, are ultimately free to choose our own course?

Personally, I have become fond of this view. I find in it a kind of consolation that goes some distance to replacing what is lost by rejecting both the consolations of religion and the consolations of aspiring to transcendence to a timeless reality.

You venture far beyond physics in your Epilogue, including some musings on the nature of consciousness. You discuss David Chalmers favorably, a well-known panpsychist (this is the view that all matter has some associated mind/subjectivity and vice versa). You also discuss Leibniz, Spinoza, and Peirce, all of whom were also panpsychists of various stripes (see David Skrbina's Panpsychism in the West). *Would you like to take this opportunity to "out" yourself as a panpsychist?*

In college I wrote a long essay on the body-mind problem where I invented for myself an idea that I've later come to understand is a form of panpsychism. It is expressed on page 270 of *Time Reborn* as:

The problem of consciousness is an aspect of the question of what the world really is. We don't know what a rock really is, or an atom, or an electron. We can only observe how they interact with other things and thereby describe their relational properties. Perhaps everything has external and internal aspects. The external properties are those that science can capture and describe — through interactions, in terms of relationships. The internal aspect is the intrinsic essence; it is the reality that is not expressible in the language of interactions and relations. Consciousness, whatever it is, is an aspect of the intrinsic essence of brains.

This is as far as I am willing to go now, on an issue where I don't know the literature well, and I haven't thought enough about.

Last, you write that an entirely new approach to physics is needed, and that mathematics needs to be demoted a little in favor of more conceptual approaches to physics, and yet you don't seem to offer an alternative! Is this your next book?

I disagree. I do discuss alternative approaches to physics along the lines of the principles I propose. Because I am a scientist they are developed as explorations of models and hypotheses. Those discussed in the book include cosmological natural selection, the principle of precedence, the real ensemble interpretation of quantum theories as well as the responses to the metalaws dilemma I describe including the idea of the universality of metalaws and the merging of the concept of state and law. All of these have been the subject of scientific papers which are referenced in the notes.

Chapter 36

Expanding Our Notion of Existence:

A Conversation With Novelist David Brin

Finding a good novel gets harder and harder the older I get. Part of the problem is that I read mostly non-fiction and I find that most fiction doesn't have the "meat" that I'm looking for in non-fiction. That is, much of what comprises fiction is stuff I tend to skip over because I'm generally reading for what I consider to be the most important points!

I realize that this is no way to enjoy a good story, but I think a lot of us fall into this same category nowadays. The science fiction genre still holds some hope, however, for keeping our attention.

I recently listened to David Brin's latest novel, *Existence*, a very large novel – in ideas, content and pages – about the not-too-distant future of humanity. It hooked me right away and I've been running a lot more lately because of my looking forward to listening to the novel on my iPod as I run. Now I've finished it I'm not sure I can find a similarly enthralling listen.

David Brin first hooked me as a teenager almost thirty years ago when I read his Uplift series of novels – *Sundiver*, *Startide Rising* and *The Uplift War*. Brin's *Uplift* series is a classic now, and he won the Hugo Award, one of science fictions highest honors, twice for this series, along with many other awards. Brin is also a working scientist, with a Ph.D in space science from UC San Diego (also my alma mater). His website contains a lot of content on topics from science to science fiction to politics.

Brin is considered one of the more prominent hard sci-fi writers today and he firmly believes that good sci-fi should explore themes that are relevant to all of us. Existence explores a number of scenarios regarding alien contact – a perennial sci-fi theme. His ideas, story and conclusions are, however, quite new. I highly recommend the book.

I had the pleasure of interviewing Brin via email, the first in my interview series with a novelist.

Your novel, Existence, *is a big story in the "hard sci-fi" genre, and it's really well done. It's highly entertaining and suspenseful, and also quite believable. It's a novel of ideas set in the not-too-distant future, and I'm curious what inspired the novel and your decision to make it as much, or perhaps more, about ideas than about traditional plot arcs?*

Of course *Existence* was a difficult project to write and especially to make smooth and easy for the reader. In order to portray richly the world of 2048, I go back to the juggling act that worked so well in Earth [a previous Brin novel]. This method -- citing fictitious news accounts, books and arguments between the chapters -- got its start with the novel USA by Dos Passos and was brought to stunning fruition by the titan of 1960s science Fiction, John Brunner, in his fantastic *Stand on Zanzibar*, a work that deeply inspired me, using many characters and media extracts to give a sweeping panorama of a world we may yet live to see.

Existence *is centered on the discovery in earth orbit of a football-sized alien probe, and the dialogue with other races that ensues. Do you think this is in fact the most likely scenario for alien contact, if and when it happens?*

I have explored concepts of human contact with the alien in my work as an astronomer, surveying such possibilities in our galactic neighborhood and through involvement in the SETI program. (See articles and speculations by David Brin about the Search for Extraterrestrial Intelligence (SETI)) As it happens, such contact might not happen first via radio waves. There are serious calculations suggesting that physical probes, small, compact and long-lasting, might be a principal means by which species make others aware of them. I explore this possibility, in a wide range of possible ways.

What is the likelihood, in your view, that there are artifacts like the ones you write about in your novel, in Earth orbit right now? Or elsewhere on our planet?

Landing on Earth might be a challenge for such probes, but it has long been pondered whether some - perhaps millions of years old - might be "lurking" in, say, the Asteroid Belt or under the surface of the moon. It is a remarkably efficient approach and one that Arthur C. Clarke explored a little in *2001: A Space Odyssey.* I merely explore it in further detail, using the best science we've come up with, so far.

Do you think it's at all likely that we are in fact alone in our galaxy, as an advanced civilization? Are we cosmically alone?

It's a daunting possibility, isn't it? Either way... if we seem to be alone, or if we make contact with neighbors out there... Either way, the universe is sure to be unnerving as we forge outward. No wonder some of our fellow citizens quail from thinking about the cosmos, or the future, and some even deny there will be a future at all. It arises from a desperate unwillingness to think about the grand context for all our little struggles.

What is your process for writing a big novel like this one? Do you have research staff?

I do all my own research. And most of it consists of just one thing. Being interested in absolutely everything. I highly recommend it!

Let's dive into some of the big themes covered in your book (no spoilers yet). I was really intrigued by your discussion of "smart mobs," which are virtual mobs that provide information or advice as requested, based on the statistically most popular answers provided by the mob. How is this different than searching Google today? Is it the active choice of which mob to consult that makes it different? Or the possibility to have a mob along with you as you engage in activities that require advice?

The smart mob concept assumes that a certain fraction of the population will grow tired of just relying upon Google, YouTube, and snarky jpeg slides that they share on Facebook. That is not what skilled professionals do, say the police when comparing notes with each other to solve a crime, or CIA officers pooling their expertise to hunt down a terrorist. Or top Wall Street firms analyzing which companies will rise or fall. These professionals use advanced analytical tools and share data with each other across the world, at lightning speed. They build models of real-time events in which dozens or even hundreds of consultants and team members each contribute some special knowledge or skill. I never cease to be amazed, in times of rapid change, how people cling to the notion that further change won't happen. But all of those analytic and collaboration skills will eventually reach amateur and private hands. The way video photography reached us in recent decades. Most of us will ignore the power of these tools. But millions will grab and use them.

You've described yourself as a "heretical libertarian" so how do you see the libertarian ideals of smaller government and greater freedom unfolding in the next few decades? You discuss in your book how the new oligarchy, made possible by the extreme disparities in this country and others, may lead away from more democratic forms of government.

Today's main branch of libertarianism has turned an intellectual movement into a brainless thing. "I'm for liberty!" is the shouted credo, followed by the relentless implication that "government" is the only possible threat to that liberty. What they thus do is: (1) imply that other people aren't for liberty, a grotesquely self-serving insult. And (2) they ignore 6,000 years of human history, in which 99% of cultures saw freedom and markets destroyed not by government bureaucrats, but by inherited owner oligarchies. But today's movement is led by folks who desperately ignore that fact. Instead of waving the vague apple pie image of "liberty" (yes, we are all for it ... well, most of us are) we should take the love of freedom as something shared by many. So what separates (true) libertarians [from the inauthentic type that is common today]? I suggest the following: an appreciation of competition, the most creative force in the universe, the force that made us, that propels evolution, markets, democracy and science. It is the only thing that ever cuts through the human penchant for self-delusion. There we see a split, all right. The left emphasizes cooperation - another admirable human trait, but steeped in problems. The right keeps trying to deliver us back into the hands of owner oligarchs. A true libertarian movement would actually read Adam Smith and realize that our Enlightenment must defend the competitive arenas of markets and democracy and science that gave us everything. And if you think about it, you realize that government often helps competition. And idolatry of unlimited personal wealth often hurts it.

You discuss in your novel the "diamond class" model that seems to be your ideal social model, in which a large middle class (the bulge in the diamond) narrows in numbers as we go up in income (the top of the diamond) and narrows similarly to the bottom as we go down in income (the bottom of the diamond). What policies today, political, technological, economic, etc., do you think will ensure that the diamond class ideal continues, and improves, into the future?

Government policies helped make the American middle class. In the 1930s it seemed the US would tumble into class war and either communism or fascism. We were rescued by our native practicality, plus a man who helped us create the flattest social order in human history – Franklin Roosevelt. After FDR, in the 1950s and under high tax rates, the middle class boomed and market investments created a spectacular creative capitalism. Yet we are now told, relentlessly, that he was Satan. Funny thing, the Greatest Generation adored him. I am not approving of all things FDR did. But careening back into feudalism is not the way to fix things.

Your book is, in some ways, a re-telling of the Pandora's Box cautionary tale about the perils of knowledge and technology. You also suggest (though not without much hedging) that advanced civilizations can't last very long. Certainly the history of civilizations on our planet supports this view, but isn't there a good possibility, if we survive the next few decades, that our probes and some (possibly a great many) individuals will escape this beautiful planet we call home, on a permanent basis and before too long spread far and wide in our solar system and eventually to nearby stars?

I see nothing in your question to disagree with. Except that I think we will manage (barely) to grow up in time to not only take the stars, but save ourselves and our planet. And save freedom at the same time.

You also suggest (spoiler alert, watch out) that the future for advanced civilizations may be entirely virtual. Is this in your view a likely future for humanity? Or are you more optimistic that we can live a more corporeal existence far into the future, as well as living in parallel virtual realities if we choose to do so?

Sounds good to me! Every decade that I live, there is some great new idea that expands our concept of the possible. Blending science and fiction and history and curiosity... it's fun!

Stephen Hawking made news last year by suggesting that space-faring alien species are more likely than not to be hostile to us, much as the history of human civilization has revealed scant regard for weaker human populations. I'm inclined to agree and, if this is the case, it would weigh heavily in favor of us doing everything we can to not advertise our presence, at least until we are far more technologically advanced. Do you agree?

I found Professor Hawking's particular scenario to be very unconvincing. But that does not matter. There are more than a hundred theories to explain the "Fermi Paradox" regarding why the skies seem so empty of civilizations that ought to be out there. And three-fourths of those theories are at least disturbing, some of them downright scary. That is not to say that we shouldn't stay optimistic! I support the SETI search ... but not recent foolish efforts to shout into space. Listening is not shouting.

For (much) more, see my articles and speculations about the Search for Extraterrestrial Intelligence (SETI) http://www.scoop.it/t/seti-the-search-for-extraterrestrial-intelligence

How do you think rejuvenation/immortality technologies will unfold? You don't seem to believe that thinkers like Ray Kurzweil, who suggest that biological immortality may just be a couple of decades away, are right.

The folks who think we are about to become immortal may turn out to be right. Many of them are very clever and some interesting science is spilling forth. Still, their passion is familiar from 6,000 years of transcendentalists shouting promises that were never kept. Elsewhere, I go into a dozen reasons why extending human lifespan by more than a decade or two may be harder than we thought. http://www.davidbrin.com/immortality.html

You discuss some scenarios in which certain types of alien probes may mutate into all-consuming artificial viruses, eating up everything in their path - kind of like Galactus, the world-devouring bad guy in the Fantastic Four comic books. It seems that since this hasn't happened yet, in 14 billion years or so, that it's unlikely to happen now. Or is this view too Pollyanna-ish?

The simplistic eat-everything alien probe was never mine. It is an old cliché and yes, the existence of the Earth we are standing on disproves it. But there are much more subtle forms of predation and some might arise out of basic misunderstandings. If we are to avoid such errors, it would be wise to first think them through. That is one purpose of high-level science fiction.

You made me laugh out loud in your discussion of relic fragment lawyers, artificial attorney bots, essentially, since I'm one of the old school carbon-based lawyer types. How far are we from having expert systems sophisticated enough to replace many duties commonly performed by lawyers, doctors or sci-fi authors?

I haven't a clue. It may already have happened and we are living in a simulation. Or else it may be that modeling the human mind is much more complicated than anyone expected. It is that vast realm in between that seems worth exploring: the realm of idea space.

You discuss the possibility of simulated worlds, and this idea has taken off since the Matrix movies. It's an intriguing notion and it seems that we could never rule out the possibility that we are living in simulation. That said, could we ever devise tests (something a bit more realistic than red pill/blue pill) to probe our reality and find out if we are in fact living in a simulation?

There are a few tests. Alas, so far all of them are favoring the simulation theory. Like the weird fact that the universe has an upper speed limit. (The speed of light.) It effectively limits the size of the needed simulation space, which is what super beings would have to do, to save resources. There are half a dozen other traits of our cosmos that make us physicists go... "huh! Well, maybe..."

Last, what is your advice for aspiring sci-fi authors?

What I can do is point you to an "advice article" that I've posted online, containing a distillation of wisdom and answers to questions I've been sent across 20 years. (Note, most authors never answer at all.) This article is at: http://www.davidbrin.com/advice.htm.

Many people have found it extremely helpful.

Sci-fi is the literary genre that explores possibilities and the affects of change upon human beings. Any genre that doesn't contemplate how things might be different and how people might react... of what value is such navel contemplation in such times as these? Well, I suppose cowardly agoraphobia has its place. But I have the universe and time and the human mind and soul and heart as a playground. Why limit myself?

Chapter 37

Alternative Cosmologies Part 1:

A Conversation With Reg Cahill

The term "ether" is unique in the history of physics not only because of the so many different meanings in which it has been used but also because it is the only term that has been eliminated and subsequently reinstated, though with a different connotation, by one and the same physicist [Einstein].

Max Jammer, in the Foreword to *Einstein and the Ether* (2000)

Physics is considered the hardest of the sciences, in terms of the degree of precision and certainty regarding its data and theories. Physics is not, however, as "hard" a science as most people like to think. In fact, physical theories, like all theories, are human creations that approximate reality and, as such, are never the whole story. There is always more than one theory that can explain the available evidence – far more than one, in fact. The difficulty is finding a theory that is self-consistent, explains the evidence at issue and fits within a broader explanatory framework.

In reading books like Brian Greene's *The Fabric of the Cosmos* and *The Elegant Universe*, or Lee Smolin's *The Trouble With Physics*, we realize that the one certainty in physics is this: our physical theories will continue to change over time. We will never – literally – have a complete description of the universe and its workings because we simply don't know the full extent of what we don't know. And we will never know the full extent of what we don't know.

It's important to keep in mind also that all theories, including physical theories, rest on assumptions about the nature of reality, generally called "postulates" or "principles." If the assumptions turn out to be wrong, the theory will very likely be wrong. Last, theories can never be proven – they can only be supported by experimental evidence or disproved by experimental evidence that contradicts the theory at issue. The degree to which theories are rejected as invalid depends on the degree to which experimental evidence disproves key features of the theory.

For example, even though there is a fairly strong consensus among cosmologists that the universe is expanding at a faster rate than previously predicted by General Relativity (the prevailing theory of gravity), very few physicists were willing, based on this difficulty alone, to reject General Relativity as a theory. Rather, various fixes, including the now widespread concepts of "dark energy," have been developed to reconcile General Relativity with the unexpected data about accelerating expansion (which led to the 2011 Nobel Prize in physics) and other gravitational anomalies. Dark matter is a similar patch to General Relativity, for which there is even less evidence.

There are many other possible views, however, that can explain the data as well or better. Reg Cahill, my interviewee for this first installment of a new series on alternative cosmologies, for example, has pointed out that the supernovae data relied upon for the accelerating expansion model of the universe, can equally support the view of a universe expanding at a constant rate. A later interviewee, Jayant Narlikar, a supporter of the Quasi Steady State Cosmology, believes that we may be fundamentally misinterpreting Hubble's Law on redshift, which is the basis for the prevailing view that the universe is expanding.

While even scientists and science journalists often speak sloppily about theories being proven, it simply is not the case that any theory – even theories that rise to the level of "laws," due to very strong experimental support – are ever proven. Richard Feynman, a Nobel Prize-winning physicist, stated: "[E]ven those ideas which have been held for a very long time and which have been very accurately verified might be wrong .... [W]e now have a much more humble point of view of our physical laws – everything can be wrong!"

There remains a chorus of discontent over the state of physics today. David Gross, another Nobelist and a physics professor at UC Santa Barbara, ended a 2005 conference on string theory, the dominant research interest for most theoretical physicists over the last two decades, by saying: "We don't know what we are talking about.... The state of physics today is like it was when we were mystified by radioactivity.... They were missing something absolutely fundamental. We are perhaps missing something as profound as they were back then."

Reg Cahill is a professor of physics at Flinders University in Adelaide, Australia, Reg has for many years now challenged the mainstream physical consensus in many ways. He's published widely, but generally in "dissident" physics journals (yes, there are dissident journals in physics) because he challenges ideas that are generally considered to be settled. While Cahill is a proud maverick in his field he has nevertheless received recognition for his achievements and was awarded a Gold Medal in 2010 by the Telesio - Galilei Academy of Science for his development of the "Process Physics" model that is his signature achievement.

I had the pleasure of interviewing Reg, by email, on his Process Physics, why he believes Einstein got it wrong on gravity, and why a new understanding of the nature of mind is key for a more accurate physics. I am also working on a book about Reg, his physical theories, and process philosophy as an alternative to the prevailing materialism of our era. I am highly intrigued by Reg's ideas, but I am not equipped at this time to make my own determination about their validity, let alone their superiority to the mainstream views. Reg seems to me to be overly categorical in his pronouncements at times, and can tend toward the grandiose at other times. It is, however, clear to me that Reg's voice should be part of today's discussions about cosmology and physics more generally.

What led you into physics?

At a very young age, maybe five or six, I was fascinated by questions of how things worked – my first case was the radio. I thought it was an astounding process. Others, it seemed to me, didn't ask such questions. From there my interest in physics simply developed. On leaving school I was initially planning on being an electrical engineer, but dropped that very quickly when the University of New South Wales (in Australia) offered me a scholarship to do a physics degree, and then stay to do a PhD. During the latter years of school and early years of university I was involved with radios, etc., as a hobby – and built my own oscilloscope, and later modified a military aircraft scope to work on mains voltage.

Who is the most influential thinker with respect to your own worldview, or your own brand of physics?

I don't think there was any one person. My research over the years has simply gone deeper into fundamental issues – first doing low energy nuclear physics, then high energy particle physics: quarks and gluon theory, and finally now into developing new understandings of space and matter – at the "Process Physics" level. So this was an ongoing process of following the clues deeper and deeper. I came at the Process Physics point of view independently, and then was amazed to learn that Alfred North Whitehead, and other similar process thinkers, including Heraclitus of ancient Greece, had arrived at the same sort of thinking, but by very different routes.

Could you describe briefly your "Process Physics" and how it differs from mainstream views in physics?

My Process Physics perspective is fleshed out in a number of papers and my 2005 book, *Process Physics*. Basically, conventional physics uses a syntax-based model – where symbols stand for things: matter, space, time... The physical laws are encoded in rules of manipulations of these symbols [as described by the equations of various physical theories]. In Process Physics, to the contrary, one is modeling, at the deepest levels, that nature is all about process – processes involving the generation of patterns, their interaction by means of pattern recognition, and change – so this is an information-based model. It is not, however, about our knowledge or information about reality; rather, it is about interacting patterns, where the structure of the patterns determines their interaction and evolution over time. This is a semantic information theory, whereas conventional physics uses syntactical information. Also, Process Physics does not begin by assuming the existence of space, matter, etc. It assumes only a cosmic-indexing type of time, which is emergent. These phenomena, in my theory, emerge from the more fundamental level of reality.

Physics has been in the news a lot lately with the discovery of evidence supporting the existence of the Higgs boson. Could you explain this finding and how it impacts, if at all, your Process Physics.

The standard model [of particle physics] starts by assuming that the equations have a certain symmetry. That symmetry requires all particles to be massless – which they are not. To avoid that outcome, a new field is introduced which, in an *ad hoc* way, forces most particles to have mass. So the whole procedure lacks elegance. This field in turn results in the supposed existence of a new particle – the Higgs boson. Given the manifest inelegance of this model I would be very surprised if the claimed discovery of the Higgs boson survives scrutiny. As for Process Physics I doubt the new Higgs field data has any significance.

Is the Higgs field a modern name for what was previously called the "ether" and perhaps wrongly dismissed? How does your work relate to ether-based theories of physics?

No. The "ether" in Process Physics has been replaced by the term "dynamical space." In conventional physics, space is a geometrical "container," to the extent that its existence is even acknowledged. The 19th Century notion of the "ether" was considered to exist in the "container" of space. The "dynamical space" is, however, a complex fractal system, which only manifests geometrical properties at the higher level. Dynamical space is not just a concept. It has been detected repeatedly for more than 120 years without being widely acknowledged. Contrary to the widespread views on this issue, the speed of light is in fact anisotropic [not constant for all observers], when measured by an observer moving through the dynamical space. For example, the famous Michelson-Morley experiment did in fact, when analyzed correctly, find evidence for light anisotropy. And the dynamics of dynamical space have also been discovered. I would expect that it is the dynamics of this new type of space – in particular its detected fractal texture – which causes particles to have mass. I am working on this conjecture.

There are many notions of the "ether," and ultimately terminology is far less important than the concepts they convey. However, you write in your recent paper, suggesting that Einstein's Special Relativity theory has been falsified, and Lorentz's competing theory of relativity supported, the following as your introduction: "Physics has failed, from the early days of Galileo and Newton, to consider the existence of space as a structured, detectable and dynamical system, and one that underpins all phenomena..." This sounds to me like the ether that Lorentz himself advocated, so is it not fair to call your neo-Lorentzian theory a type of ether theory?

Aether theories are [generally] dualistic – they have both a space and an aether embedded in that space. Indeed, physicists find it almost impossible to abandon this dualism, except in Special Relativity and General Relativity where both space and aether were abandoned in favor of space-time [a four-dimensional reality that views time as akin to an additional spatial dimension]. Lorentzian relativity is also a dualistic theory with an aether embedded in a space, but with time a separate phenomenon. In neo-Lorentzian relativity [which is a fair characterization of my Process Physics] we abandon this dualism by positing a structured dynamical space [as the fundamental level of reality]. This dynamical space appears to be fractally textured – according to experiment and theory. This dynamical space is different from both the older notion of space (as a perfect geometrical system) and to an aether, as some form of particulate system embedded in and possibly moving through the geometrical space. In neo-Lorentzian relativity, the "geometry" of the dynamical space is emergent – including its three-dimensionality [and other properties].

More generally, hasn't physics come around in recent decades to the idea of space as a real entity and not simply a vessel for matter and energy? Mainstream publications like Brian Greene's book, The Fabric of the Cosmos, *focus on the fact that empty space has certain properties. Einstein also later repudiated his own suggestion, in his seminal 1905 paper on Special Relativity, that space has no properties.*

To the contrary, conventional physics focuses on spacetime, not space as a separate entity. The very concept of "space" is actually rejected by Special Relativity and General Relativity, although sloppy language often confuses the issue. So referring, in Special Relativity and General Relativity, to empty space as having properties is actually misleading. In other words, what one observer identifies as a spatial part of spacetime, is different from another observer's space part of that same spacetime.

Why is relativity theory so hard to challenge in mainstream physics journals? Are physicists generally group-thinkers who are highly resistant to challenges from the fringes, as respected thinkers like Lee Smolin and Thomas Kuhn have suggested?

In my view, few physicists actually understand Special or General Relativity. Most physicists' complete belief in these theories is just that: belief without deep understanding – and they defend that belief with ferocity. Indeed, most physicists appear not to accept the scientific method – namely that ongoing experiments should decide whether a theory survives or not. Of course, Special Relativity, in particular, has been the foundation of physics for more than 100 years – and most physicists would say that its falsification would be incredibly unlikely. However, my recent paper on neo-Lorentzian relativity ("Dynamical 3-Space: neo-Lorentz Relativity") shows just that – that Special Relativity is exactly derivable from Galilean Relativity, and Special Relativity does not do the job claimed for it – meaning that its predictions are inconsistent with experiment.

Can you describe briefly your recent work suggesting that Einstein's Special Relativity has been falsified?

Special Relativity, rather than being a fundamentally new theory, is exactly derivable from Galilean Relativity by an exact linear change of space and time coordinates, which mixes the Galilean space and time coordinates. So it turns out that there is no new physics in Special Relativity that is not already in Galilean Relativity. In particular, the various so-called relativistic effects (length contraction, time dilation…) are merely coordinate artifacts. Such actual phenomena cannot emerge from merely a change of coordinates.

One can also show experimentally that these supposed "relativistic effects" are not those actually detected in experiments. One example is that the length contraction effect in neo-Lorentzian Relativity is determined by the speed of an object relative to the dynamical space (which is some 500km/s for an object at rest on earth), whereas the Special Relativity length contraction is determined by the object's speed with respect to the observer, which in most experiments is 0 km/s. This extreme contrast in predictions is manifestly checked by comparing results from Michelson interferometer experiments with spacecraft earth-flyby Doppler shift data: the outcome is that the Special Relativity prediction is falsified, and the neo-Lorentzian Relativity prediction is confirmed.

Your Process Physics aligns well with Alfred North Whitehead's work in philosophy, mathematics and physics. Whitehead was a well-known panpsychist in that he believed that all matter has some mind associated with it such that as matter complexifies so mind complexifies. How important is panpsychism in your Process Physics? Is this idea captured in your notion of "semantic information"?

I developed Process Physics before I became aware of Whitehead's philosophy – I was more aware of the work of Heraclitus at that time. Nevertheless, I was happy to acknowledge the philosophical ideas of these and other process philosophers, when I became aware of them, and I now have an ongoing working relationship with various process philosophers. One should note that of course these philosophers had no detailed/mathematical/ implementation/theory/model for their philosophies and this is what my Process Physics attempts to provide. I also suspect that panpsychism is a valid property of reality, and yes it is an aspect of "semantic information."

John Archibald Wheeler made famous the notion that information may be fundamental to reality with his phrase "it from bit." Do you agree with this idea and if not how would you modify it?

I agree, although Wheeler did not have an implementation mechanism or [detailed] model. In any case one must carefully distinguish between syntactical information, which I suspect is what Wheeler was referring to, from semantic information.

What do you mean by "semantic information" and how does this idea relate to the philosophical view known as panpsychism?

Process Physics is about self-generated patterns – and how these patterns interact. So the theory and the reality it models are about active information - information has meaning for the system, and so is called semantic information. Syntactical information is that stored by way of symbols, and then "interactions" are by way of rules, i.e., equations. Equations always presuppose some a priori syntactical rules, and so cannot be fundamental. Semantic information, being active, suggests that the universe is self-aware in some manner, and at all levels. This is my preferred concept of panpsychism.

At the risk of beating this horse to death, another question on the nature of the ether and ether theories. I see the ether concept, or what you call dynamical space, as pretty key for the development of a more ideal future physics, and this is one of the key reasons I was intrigued by your Process Physics when I first came across it. Einstein stated in a 1919 letter to Lorentz that "with the word ether we say nothing else than that space has to be viewed as a carrier of physical qualities." Do you agree with Einstein here? Would you agree that your "dynamical space" could be described in the same way, as a carrier of physical qualities, which are necessary for an accurate view of nature?

The (new) ether is, in my theory, a dynamical system, the "dynamical space" I've described above – which has a very complicated structure at the deepest level. I describe it as a "quantum foam", meaning that at a deep level the dynamical space is describable by a wave-function whose time evolution is described by a Schrodinger-type theory. On larger scales the dynamical space can be described as being somewhat geometrical, i.e., having three dimensions, etc. It is this aspect that we use as spatial coordinates x, y, z. I would agree with Einstein's above statement except that dynamical space is not the "carrier" of these properties; rather, disturbances of the dynamical space are in fact what we generally call "physical stuff".

You stated above that you are working on the concept that the fractal nature of dynamical space may be the underlying reason that particles have mass. Can you flesh out this idea and contrast it with the Higgs field concept that has gained some recent support?

Wave functions propagating through a fractal space will have their energy changed. My conjecture is that this is equivalent to giving "mass" to the wave function. In the Higgs model there is no such structured space, only a smooth space-time, and so the Higgs field is, incorrectly, in my view, constructed to provide mass to massive particles.

You have been a consistent critic of Einstein's relativity theories. Can your Process Physics be viewed as a full substitution for Einstein's theory of gravity, General Relativity? If so, what kind of real world/technological changes would this substitution lead to?

This is a complete change: Einstein's Special Relativity and General Relativity have failed in almost every case to explain the observed data – and this contrary evidence grows stronger every day. The Process Physics perspective could lead to a fundamental revolution in physics – and there isn't much that will not be changed if these ideas are adopted. Process Physics will also have impacts outside of physics – such as in providing a more firm theoretical basis for non-local interactions ["entanglement"] that are often denied by physics at present, and a broader interconnectedness of the universe that is not acknowledged at present.

Chapter 38

Alternative Cosmologies Part II:

A Conversation With Jayant Narlikar About Quasi-Steady State Cosmology

[The] Big Bang hypothesis ... is an irrational process that cannot be described in scientific terms ... [nor] challenged by an appeal to observation.

Fred Hoyle (1949)

We are at the cusp of becoming a truly space-faring species. SpaceX, a private space firm headed by Internet entrepreneur Elon Musk, made history in 2012 by winning a major NASA contract, which effectively replaces the retired shuttle program, by demonstrating that his private rocket technology could cost-effectively ship people and goods into earth orbit. Another private effort is planning to mine nearby asteroids for critical resources. Yet another private effort is planning a human Mars colony by the early 2020s.

Even though the US space program has moved away from manned missions, it is still pursuing aggressive robotic exploration programs of Mars and other stellar bodies. At the same time, nations like China are quickly trying to catch up with Western space programs.

It's extremely exciting to contemplate the next obvious steps in our race to the stars: establishing a permanent colony on the moon, colonies on Mars and other objects in our solar system. Eventually we'll make it to Alpha Centauri, the nearest star system to us and – at some point in the not-too-distant future – we will probably spread out to the rest of our galaxy.

It is not, then, premature to consider deeply what our universe looks like, where it came from and where it's going. This is what constitutes cosmology – the science of the largest scales of space and time.

Even as someone with no formal training in cosmology, I feel comfortable stating that the mainstream Big Bang Cosmology (BBC) has some serious problems. Dark matter appears to be an *ad hoc* addition to general relativity, our prevailing theory of gravity. Today, many decades after it was originally proposed there is still almost zero hard evidence for dark matter, despite ongoing vigorous efforts to discover exactly what constitutes dark matter.

Dark energy, the posited force behind the accelerating expansion of the universe, is also somewhat fishy, but seems to me to have a better theoretical basis than dark matter.

It is these reasons and more that have led me to explore alternative cosmologies and reach out to the physicists I'm interviewing for this series. Part I of this series explored the ideas of Reg Cahill and his Process Physics. Cahill's ideas contravene many key concepts of the Big Bang Cosmology, most importantly the idea that the speed of light is absolute, a key postulate of Einstein's theories of relativity. From this difference alone, a very different cosmology results.

Part II explores the Quasi Steady State Cosmology developed primarily by Fred Hoyle, Geoffrey Burbidge and Jayant Narlikar, as a successor theory to the Steady State Cosmology. The original Steady State cosmology, which was the primary challenger to the Big Bang theory during the middle part of the 20th Century, faced many difficulties with various observations in the second half of that century – prompting development of the Quasi Steady State Cosmology as a replacement during the 1990s. Narlikar has been integrally involved with developing both theories since the 1960s.

I enjoyed Narlikar and Burbidge's book, *Facts and Speculation in Cosmology*. It is accessible to lay readers but also presents more in-depth information that challenges some of today's widely-accepted ideas about cosmology. They even suggest that one of the fundamental concepts in modern cosmology, Hubble's Law, which relates redshift to acceleration (the more redshift observed in the spectrum of distant stars, the faster they are moving away from us), may actually be wrong.

Narlikar earned his Ph.D from Cambridge University under Fred Hoyle, is past president of the Cosmology Commission of the International Astronomical Union, is a former professor at Cambridge and other institutions, and author of a number of textbooks in cosmology. He now lives in India. I interviewed Narlikar via email.

Is cosmology a mature science yet? It seems to me, in reading fairly widely in cosmology over the years, that a lot of theories rest on quite a bit of speculation. This is of course a key theme of your book, which references "speculation" in its title.

Cosmology, as widely studied today via the standard model [Big Bang Cosmology], is not a mature scientific subject. It rests on very few direct facts and a lot of speculation. That is why I have compared it with the Pythagorean "central fire hypothesis," which suggested (we now know wrongly) that there was a large source of heat and light – that was not the Sun – around which the Earth, Sun and other planets orbited.

Despite the widely held view that the Big Bang Cosmology (BBC) rests on firm observation and theory, you strongly criticize this theory in your book, Facts and Speculation in Cosmology. Could you outline your key objections the BBC?

Let us see what the observations actually are and how they are interpreted. QSSC here stands for the Quasi Steady State Model of cosmology, which is our (Hoyle, Narlikar, Burbidge) alternative cosmology. Here are the key observations:

The cosmic microwave background radiation spectrum is well-established through observation, but where does the radiation come from? To say that it is a relic from an epoch of redshift 1000 is a speculation based on the BBC. It cannot, therefore, be seen as testing the BBC. At best, it provides a consistency check of the BBC. An alternative cosmology like the QSSC provides another viable interpretation of the radiation as relic starlight thermalized from previous expansion/contraction cycles of the universe, discussed further below.

In the period 1960-80, the redshift to magnitude (m-z) relation for galaxies indicated a decelerating universe. The only other serious cosmology in the field then, the Steady State Cosmology, was rejected because it implied an accelerating universe. Post 1998-99, as soon as the supernova data showed that an accelerating universe was consistent with this new data, the BBC supporters changed gears and began to champion the accelerating universe model.

The non-baryonic [baryonic matter is what everything in our normal experience is made of] dark matter postulated in BBC is primarily intended to prop up the BBC against possible disproof involving deuterium abundance and large inhomogeneities of the cosmic microwave background radiation. It has not been detected astronomically nor have accelerators found evidence of dark matter, let alone any observation demonstrating that it constitutes 23% of total matter-energy content in the universe, which is the mainstream view. Yet the idea of dark matter is uncritically accepted to this day.

Last, the inflationary epoch [based on the idea that the very early universe expanded extremely rapidly to almost its present size in the blink of an eye] has been accepted without there being a mathematical model to explain its driving Φ (phi) function, or coming naturally from a fundamental particle physics theory. Inflation theory 'works' when the numbers in this function are put in by hand [that is, ad hoc]. This does not add credibility to the BBC.

You, your co-author, Geoffrey Burbidge, the British physicist Fred Hoyle and others, have since the 1990s advocated the Quasi Steady State Cosmology (QSSC) alternative to the Big Bang – a modification of the Steady State Cosmology that has since been abandoned due to disagreements with observation. Do you still advocate QSSC? What are the key advantages of this theory over the BBC? What observational evidence would provide compelling arguments in favor of QSSC rather than BBC?

I still advocate the QSSC based on the following key observations: QSSC gives an alternative origin of the cosmic microwave background radiation as relic starlight thermalized from previous cycles. It predicts the observed temperature as 2.7K, which BBC cannot. In the BBC, this figure is put in "by hand," that is, it is *ad hoc* rather than emerging naturally from the theory. The supernova magnitude to redshift (m-z) relation is explained by QSSC without invoking an accelerating universe. Moreover, the intergalactic dust postulated for explaining this result turns out to be the same as needed for the cosmic microwave background radiation. The origin of this dust is also explained astrophysically, unlike the mysterious nonbaryonic dark matter postulated by BBC supporters!

Specifically, the QSSC suggests the presence of intergalactic dust in the form of iron needles, which thermalize starlight to produce the CMBR. Laboratory experiments have shown that when metallic vapours cool they condense as solid needles rather than as balls. These needles are highly effective absorbers and radiators at wavelengths around a millimeter, so their expected abundance in the universe around $10^\wedge$-34 gram per cubic centimetres produces a thermalized CMBR. The same dust absorbs radiation from distant supernovae, making the supernovae appear dimmer than nearby ones. Notice that the needles get formed when supernovae eject iron vapour and thus we have a perfect source of absorbers. By contrast, the BBC has no theoretical basis for the origin of nonbaryonic dark matter. In terms of observational evidence to falsify the BBC, I am looking for strong evidence of stars at least 20 billion years old. If these very old stars are found, there will be an obvious problem for BBC. Likewise, modest blueshift (less than 0.1) is expected for very faint (distant) galaxies under the QSSC. These are some of the key observational possibilities to distinguish between the QSSC and the BBC.

How would we identify stars 20 billion years or older? If we did, do you think many BBC advocates would be persuaded that BBC has been falsified?

On the Hertzsprung-Russell diagram, which plots stars with surface temperature on the x-axis and luminosity on the y-axis, such stars will show up on a 'giant branch' turning off from the main sequence (which has the Sun on it) at a height well below the normal giant branch. These stars are interpreted as less massive and are, accordingly, slow burners of hydrogen in their core. So their position on a giant branch means they have finished burning their hydrogen fuel. This allows us to estimate their age and that could be as high as 20 billion years.

BBC advocates will likely try to interpret such evidence differently, such as assuming that the sample is redder because of contamination by dust. We previously had one such very old star sample from the Hubble telescope archives but we could not rule out the interstellar reddening. So we are back to the drawing board looking for other candidates for very old stars.

On a similar note, is the BBC falsifiable even in principle? Aren't large meta-theories like BBC fundamentally unfalsifiable and therefore not truly scientific? Isn't this a classic case of Kuhnian paradigm formation and (possible) destruction - if enough data does eventually accrue that the BBC has been falsified?

BBC has previously been shown to be inconsistent with observations but it has survived by changing its parameters. I assume this cannot go on forever!

You discuss at the end of your book a number of red-shift anomalies, such as nearby galaxies with very contrasting redshifts - which shouldn't happen under the BBC's accelerating universe concept. You also discuss the possibility that we may be misunderstanding at a fundamental level what causes redshift. In other words, you assert that Hubble's Law, which is considered fundamental to cosmology, may be wrong. This would be a huge paradigm shift for physics if it were true. Do you think explanations such as inter-stellar dust or the "tired light" hypothesis may in fact be right when it comes to explaining redshift?

I would urge the conventional observers to closely observe the important cases of anomalous redshifts. If they cannot get rid of the anomalies, then paradigm shift will have to come eventually.

How much do you think the fact that the Western world is still largely Christian, particularly in terms of cultural heritage, affects willingness to accept the BBC?

BBC is of course very different than the Biblical story of creation, but the commonality is creation itself, a start to all things. Your preferred alternative, to the contrary, suggests an eternal universe with no beginning and perhaps no end. I think the three religions that originated in the Middle East somehow make it easier to believe in a universe that was created at some moment of time, as in the BBC. So there may be something in what you suggest. Hinduism and Buddhism, on the other hand, seem comfortable with a universe without a beginning or end. But this division of opinion is not a hard and fast one!

Another "eternal universe" model that I've studied a little is known as Plasma Cosmology and it was developed by Nobelist Hannes Alfven, Erik Lerner and others. The basic idea is that since the large majority of the visible universe is plasma (all stars are plasma), then plasma physics should hold sway at the macro level in the same way as we can observe in labs or in stars. Accordingly, electromagnetism becomes more important at the cosmic scale than gravity. What are your views on Plasma Cosmology?

I have not studied it in sufficient depth to be able to answer this question. But I do not know how the cosmic microwave background radiation is formed in the Plasma Cosmology universe.

The "cosmological principle" (which asserts that we shouldn't think of ourselves as special and, accordingly, the universe should look pretty much the same from where we are in the universe as anywhere else in the universe) is an assumption built into the BBC. It's kind of a reverse Ptolemaic Principle. You criticize this principle as not going far enough in terms of not including the temporal dimension. You suggest that the "perfect cosmological principle" should be adopted, which holds that the universe looks essentially the same in different epochs. But isn't this new principle contradicted by QSSC because the universe is still considered to be expanding in QSSC? Moreover, why should the universe look the same from different locations in space and time? Our common sense suggests that things are indeed asymmetrical in time and space, so why not at the cosmic scale too?

As a supporter of the original steady state cosmology (SSC) [Narlikar was one of the developers of this earlier theory, which was for some time a serious competitor to the Big Bang model] one is tempted to believe in the perfect cosmological principle (PCP). When we (myself, Fred Hoyle and Geoffrey Burbidge) gave up on the SSC and generalized our model to the QSSC, we realized that the PCP has to apply on a longer time scale. The QSSC has a long-term expansion as per the PCP and superposed on it are short-term oscillations of cosmological expansion and contraction. Thus the applicability of the PCP is on a very large scale, just as the spatial cosmological principle applies on a large spatial scale.

In January of this year a research group led by Roger Clowes announced a discovery of the largest structure ever discovered in the universe: a cluster of about seventy quasars ("quasi stellar objects"). This cluster is about forty thousand times larger than our own galaxy and the research team that discovered it suggests that it contradicts the cosmological principle because it shows that at the largest scale the universe is not in fact homogeneous. Do you agree or is it premature to call the cosmological principle falsified?

One could argue that there exist larger inhomogeneities than superclusters. Since the Hubble radius of the universe is around 10 billion light years, in the Clowes example their quoted size is coming close to the above limit, thus making the cosmological principle suspect.

Thinking on longer timescales about the future of humanity, when do you see us venturing out beyond our solar system to explore our galaxy and, eventually, other galaxies? What are the most promising technologies for this leap from little old Earth to the wider universe?

So long as the special theory of relativity is valid, even if we travelled with light speed to the centre of our Galaxy, we will take around 30,000 years to go there and an equal interval to come back. Apart from the logistics of keeping the astronaut living over such long periods, we will not get any benefit from their excursion for we would be long dead before they come back! Our best chance is SETI using radio signals.

Last, what do you see as the most pressing problem(s) in cosmology and physics today?

We need to understand the basic physics at very small scales; then we need to understand where all the matter we see in the universe came from. These are difficult questions and I do not share the enthusiasm of cosmologists and particle physicists that we are very close to the answer.

Chapter 39

Alternative Cosmologies Part III:

A Conversation With Tim Eastman About

Plasma Astrophysics

I began a very ambitious project about five years ago: to write a book that integrated scientific and spiritual views of the universe into a fact-based, rational whole. I'm still plugging away, slowly, and this series of interviews on alternative cosmologies is part of my research on the cosmological section of my book-in-progress, *Cosmic Ecology*.

I met Tim Eastman virtually, through a mutual friend, at the time I began my book project. Eastman is a PhD plasma physicist, consultant and a Wyle Deputy Group Manager for science support at NASA's Goddard Space Flight Center. He has more than 30 years of experience in research and consulting in space physics, space science data systems, space weather, plasma applications, public outreach and education, and philosophy. He has provided key leadership for the nation's research programs in space plasma physics, while program manager at NASA Headquarters and the National Science Foundation. He has published over 100 research papers in space physics and related fields.

I met Tim when our mutual friend recommended me to review some chapters of a book that Tim was working on. Since then I've had numerous exchanges with Tim about my own book project and related questions. Tim advised me, after reviewing some early chapters of my book, on relativity theory and cosmology, to look into the role of plasmas from the stellar to the cosmic scale. With repetition of this point from Tim, I eventually did so.

During the course of my research, Erik Lerner's book, *The Big Bang Never Happened*, made a big impression on me because it presented a strong case that much of today's work in cosmology is highly biased toward Big Bang cosmology (BBC) because this has become the prevailing view and any contrary views are received with great skepticism. Evidence or speculation contrary to the BBC is routinely ignored or misrepresented. I highly recommend Lerner's book. A summary of his arguments is online here.

Lerner's preferred alternative to the BBC is known generally as "plasma cosmology", and is a subset of the less controversial field of "plasma astrophysics." Plasmas are by far the most common naturally-occurring state of normal (non-dark) matter in the universe – stars are made of it, galaxies are made of it, and likely most everything in between. Plasmas are electromagnetically active and these forces are, according to Lerner and others, highly important at both the astrophysical and cosmological scale. Plasma cosmology was developed originally by Hannes Alfven, a Swedish Nobel Prize-winning physicist known for his work on plasmas and magnetohydrodynamics (MHD). Lerner and many others have also contributed to this approach.

This is the third installment in a series on alternative cosmologies and, at this time, I find plasma cosmology's key concept pretty compelling – that electromagnetic forces produced by large-scale plasmas throughout the universe can play an important role in cosmology. I also find very valuable its emphasis on facts and experiment, extrapolated from laboratory experiments, to astrophysical systems, and upward to cosmological-scale observations. A key conclusion of most formulations of plasma cosmology – and the key reason it is considered controversial – is that, as Lerner's book title makes plain, plasma cosmology asserts that the Big Bang never happened. Rather, the universe probably had no beginning. It just is — but it is also in constant flux.

Unfortunately, plasma cosmology can't get no respect among many cosmologists today. In a previous interview, Bob Kirshner of Harvard, part of the team whose work led to the 2011 Nobel Prize in physics, responded to my question "do you think there's any merit to plasma cosmology?" with one word: "No." There is, however, growing recognition, as Tim describes below, of the role of plasmas in at least some aspects of cosmology. And the field of plasma astrophysics is well-established.

There has been some debate (the link is Lerner's reply to a detailed critique of Lerner's views by professor Ned Wright) between BBCers and plasma cosmology proponents, but all too often claims and theories contrary to BBC simply go unanswered. In the spirit of debate and good science more generally, I was honored to interview Eastman via email about plasma astrophysics and the subset of this field often described as plasma cosmology.

How did you come to work in plasma cosmology?

My field of study is plasma physics and space plasmas, in particular. Plasmas are an interactive mix of charged particles, neutrals and fields that exhibits collective effects. Further, plasmas carry electrical currents and generate magnetic fields. Plasmas constitute more than 99% of visible matter in the universe because most stars are plasma entities (see plasmas.org, Eastman's Web site covering all aspects of plasma science and applications, including space plasmas and plasma astrophysics).

Researchers working in cosmology generally do not reference their particular research program (whether Big Bang, quasi-steady state, or other) as part of defining their research discipline, nor should they. In this sense, there are very few researchers who self-designate as "plasma" cosmologists. Ideally, scientifically-grounded astrophysicists who focus on the sub-field of cosmology should seek evidence-based explanations, especially through ever-improved models and analysis to better interpret available observations, augmented with testing of alternative hypotheses.

In the past decade, there have been substantial advances in applying electromagnetism (EM) and plasma concepts, including advances in MHD, to many astrophysical systems. For example, the Topical Group in Plasma Astrophysics of the American Physical Society (APS), formed in 1998, provides one forum among others for scientists focused on applying EM and plasma science to astrophysical systems.

The growing importance of this sub-field has been increasingly recognized in recent years, for example in a 2004 report from the National Academy of Sciences (NAS). [See the two major monographs on MHD, with "applications to laboratory and astrophysical plasmas," by Hans Goedbloed (http://www.differ.nl/users/goedbloed/); also the very high energy portion of the plasma energy spectrum is addressed by contemporary cosmic ray physics, generally using non-MHD particle propagation models.] Within the past couple of decades, there has been a substantial rise in the number of peer-reviewed research papers and major monographs focused on plasma astrophysics. Nearly 5 million hits result from a current Google search on "plasma astrophysics."

What are the key concepts in plasma astrophysics/cosmology?

Plasma astrophysics attempts to build on established results in space plasma physics (primarily in the solar system context) realized over the past half century. This experience has demonstrated multiple processes and scales for which both gravity and EM/plasmas are dynamically important. In contrast, standard cosmology considers only gravity to have a role at the cosmological scale.

Researchers in plasma astrophysics build systematically on the combination of laboratory experiments, observations, modeling, and theory to evaluate applications of EM/plasma science to astrophysical systems.[2] Further, plasma astrophysicists generally apply a bottom-up methodology which, as in Dr. Goedbloed's works, goes from the laboratory, to nearby space plasma tests, to local astrophysical systems, and then progressively to more distant astrophysical systems. This approach contrasts with the top-down methodology most often applied in "standard" cosmology, which begins with a speculative deductive framework from which various consequences are checked against observations (usually with a focus on "confirmation"). In other words, inductive approaches to plasma cosmology systematically adapt well-established lab-tested facts, and nearby space-based tests, to larger and larger astrophysical systems.

What are the key empirical facts in favor of plasma cosmology?

Key empirical results that support plasma astrophysics, including applications to cosmology, include the following, among many others:

Both gravity and EM/plasmas have become well established as dynamically important for several key plasma processes and at multiple scales throughout the solar system. Studies of these systems are part of contemporary space physics (aka "Heliophysics"), which comprises a major division of NASA science programs.

Both gravity and EM/plasmas are increasingly recognized as dynamically important in a broad range of astrophysical systems; e.g., neutron star accretion disks; galactic radio jets, active galactic nuclei, shock fronts, magnetic reconnection, and stellar magnetospheres (see peer-reviewed research of the community of researchers in plasma astrophysics; APS Topical Group and others).

Recent observations indicate the presence and importance of plasmas at all redshifts (z) and all scale lengths (e.g., observations of plasmas at both low and high redshift, both for interstellar and intergalactic plasmas; hot halos around high-z protogalaxies, strong X-ray galaxy clusters, etc.).

Without substantial shielding, electromagnetic forces are far stronger than weak gravitational forces (indeed, stronger by 10^{39}!); fortunately, this large imbalance is mostly shielded out by the rapid movement of charges that assures quick responses to maintain a condition very close to charge neutrality (most space plasmas are thus "quasi-neutral"). However, such "Debye shielding" is rarely absolute. Indeed, as stated by Goedbloed and Poedts (2004):

> By definition, plasmas are an interactive mix of charged particles, neutrals, and fields that exhibits collective effects. In plasmas, charged particles are subject to long-range, collective Coulomb interactions with many distant encounters. Although the electrostatic force drops with distance ($\sim 1/r^2$), the combined effect of all charged particles might not decay because the interacting volume increases as r^3. Magnetic field effects are often global with their connections reaching to galactic scales and beyond.

Thus, space plasmas will carry currents and generate magnetic fields at stellar scales (as with our own heliosphere), galactic scales and beyond.

When the standard Big Bang model was first hypothesized and formulated (1920s through early 1950s), a common assumption was that the intervening space between stars, and especially between galaxies, is empty. However, beginning in the 1950s, the field of space plasma physics was created in conjunction with new discoveries that space is not empty (viz. Van Allen's discovery of the radiation belts and numerous other results over the next half century); indeed, the current understanding among researchers in space plasma physics and plasma astrophysics (and others) is that nowhere in the universe is space truly empty (plasmas, including their neutral component, and fields permeate all space environments and all scales); of course, in most such domains, except within and near stars, the plasma density is very low (at the same time, the associated scale lengths are very large).

Very promising, yet preliminary modeling of galactic evolution using relatively simple MHD models has been carried out by Dr. Anthony Peratt of Los Alamos National Laboratory, yielding galactic formations roughly equivalent to observed configurations. These results are comparable to the best gravity-only model results, which require far more adjustments in the simulations, including ad hoc inclusions of dark matter and dark energy components [as discussed in the first two installments of this series of interviews]. Instead of limiting models to these two extreme cases, sophisticated models incorporating both gravity and EM/plasma processes need to be carried out - such work may lead to results that no longer require some of the ad hoc strategies currently used.

Standard cosmology at present is based on the assumption that redshifts (z) are created exclusively by "cosmic expansion" and Doppler redshifts. However, recent research has revealed a number of physically viable non-expansion redshift mechanisms, some of which can be directly tested in the laboratory.[3] Some effort toward testing such frequency transfer processes is emerging but has been discouraged under the [circular] assumption that redshift is necessarily due to cosmic expansion.

Substantial evidence has emerged in recent decades leading many researchers to seriously question the standard Big Bang cosmology, including its most recent version, the Lambda-CDM model. Recently I examined the literature on this question and compared results, pro and con. My conclusion was basically inconclusive, and summarized in the invited paper "Cosmic Agnosticism, Revisited" (*Journal of Cosmology*, Vol. 4, 655-663, 2010).

For those committed to the standard Big Bang research program, the facile dismissal of any dynamically important role for EM/plasmas characterizes a core commitment to the standard program, but this commitment can undermine good scientific methodology. In cosmology, we need greater attention to evidence-based research that actively seeks testing between alternative hypotheses versus just gathering more "confirmation" instances; efforts are needed that are more evidence-based and less theory-driven.

Your responses sound very reasonable and will prompt most lay readers to ask the obvious question: if the facts are so supportive of a strong role for EM/plasmas having an important role in cosmology why is plasma astrophysics/cosmology dismissed so readily by the large majority of physicists as an alternative to the Big Bang cosmology?

Once again, let me return to my response to your first question concerning "plasma cosmology." As I explained there, plasma astrophysics is a well-established, mainstream component of modern astrophysics. Already such research has revealed how both gravity and EM/plasmas are very important for astrophysical systems at stellar and galactic scale, and beyond. It's an ongoing research program as to how these results can be extended to basic cosmology questions. In that sense, as with many other colleagues who work in space plasma physics and plasma astrophysics, I wish to remain open about cosmology issues; i.e., please don't put me in any "box" about these issues, even the "plasma" box. In my "Cosmic Agnosticism", I show that leading experts continue to disagree on fundamental cosmology questions, which to me indicates that we should be generous in the consideration of alternative hypotheses (well represented by your first two installments about "Alternative Cosmologies") and skeptical about claims to final knowledge.

More generally, with respect to the philosophy of science are you a Kuhnian? In other words, do you agree with Kuhn that even sciences as purportedly hard-nosed as physics don't operate strictly on a facts-and-observation-based model, but, instead, as much on the basis of entrenched interests, funding, politics and plain old ego?

Kuhn's historical approach has demonstrated the importance of such non-scientific factors. However, as with most scientists, I apply an evidence-based critical realism that recognizes the overall "progress" of scientific knowledge.

With regard to methodology and trying to maintain open scientific dialogue, I'm uneasy about your framing of the questions. Although useful for some pedagogical purposes, such presumed dichotomies are too easily plugged into the standard narrative. For example, Steady State vs. Big Bang was the classic debate in earlier decades, presumably "settled" in favor of the latter. However, with their quasi-steady-state model, that result is seriously questioned in later works by Narlikar, Hoyle, Arp and others (see your Alternative Cosmologies, Part II). Standard accounts often feature the earlier debate, but rarely discuss comparisons with the latter model. Another example is the seemingly neutral "Plasma Cosmology" write-up in Wikipedia, which highlights Alfven's limited and flawed model and barely mentions results within the past decade. This obvious strawman leads the average reader to affirm the standard model. (Note: I have been informed that several efforts to update this flawed write-up have been consistently blocked).

I understand that you advocate a cosmological "agnosticism" at this time, but it does seem that you agree with much of what plasma cosmology suggests about large-scale dynamics. If plasma cosmology were a superior approach to understanding the large-scale dynamics of our universe, what would be the best ways, in your view, to achieve the necessary paradigm shift away from strict adherence to the Big Bang Cosmology?

In my view, the very best research today, relevant to these questions, is being carried out by a diverse community of researchers pursuing data-driven space plasma and observational astrophysics research. Such mainstream research has achieved many excellent advances in the past few decades, and promises to indefinitely continue such scientific "progress." To the extent that related theoretical work fails to consider, as appropriate, both gravity and EM/plasmas in astrophysical processes, such work, in my view, is simply not relevant to the real world.

Does the recent data supporting the existence of the Higgs boson have any impact on plasma physics?

For this question, I refer the reader to the answer provided by Professor Cahill (see Alternative Cosmologies, Part I).

Does Plasma Cosmology support the notion of an eternal universe, with no beginning? If so, where did the matter and energy in the universe come from?

In the past few decades, research in complex systems, from space plasmas to biology and ecology, has demonstrated the emergence (indeed, "creation") of new structures and coupled entities at multiple levels (micro-, meso-, macro-). Such creativity in the cosmos is pervasive. However, there are many unresolved difficulties in applying such a "creation" concept to the cosmos itself (as done in Big Bang theory). Finally, I'm inclined to avoid the word "eternal" and simply suggest that the age of the universe is indefinite. For an excellent book on this question, I recommend Hilton Ratclliffe The Static Universe (Montreal: Apeiron, 2010).

What books or other resources would you recommend to readers interested in exploring the pros and cons of various cosmological theories themselves?

Google search terms: plasma physics, space plasmas, plasma astrophysics. (Caution: "plasmacosmology.net" and related links are not sufficiently cautious about shielding effects, in contrast to standard accounts, which often presume that electromagnetism is completely shielded out except at very small scale (in conflict with the quote above from Goedbloed and Poedts (2004) – the real world strikes a balance between these two extremes.) Indeed, it's appropriate to think of our universe as a "plasma universe," as first coined by Tony Peratt.

Some books I recommend are:

Plasma Science: Basic Physics of the Local Cosmos, National Academy
    Press, Washington, D.C. 2004
Heliophysics: Plasma physics of the Local Cosmos, C. Schrijver and Siscoe,
    eds., Cambridge, 2009.
Walfgang Kundt, *Astrophysics: A New Approach*, Springer-Verlag, 2005.
Goedbloed and Poedts, *Principles of Magnetohydrodynamics: With
    Applications to Laboratory and Astrophysical Plasmas*,
    Cambridge, 2004.
Anthony Peratt, *Plasma Cosmology: Evolution of the Plasma Universe*,

Springer Press, 2013 (in press); update to "Physics of the Plasma Universe" Springer, 1992.

And some websites:

- References via Wikipedia entries "Plasma physics" and "Astrophysical plasma"
- Perspectives on Plasmas: www.plasmas.org/basics.htm (links, references)
- Space Plasma Sites:
  - o Solar Dynamics Observatory: www.nasa.gov/sdo/
  - o http://www.nasa.gov/mission_pages/rbsp/news/electric-atmosphere.html
- Alternative Cosmology Group: www.cosmology.info
- Eric Lerner's Web site: www.bigbangneverhappened.org
- Tony Peratt's Web site: www.plasmauniverse.info
- Halton Arp's Web site: www.haltonarp.com
- Hilton Ratcliffe's Web site: www.hiltonratcliffe.com

Are you optimistic that cosmology will evolve in the next decade or two to take EM/plasmas more seriously?

From what I've seen lately, EM/plasmas are already being taken seriously in certain areas of mainstream astrophysics (e.g., from basic understanding of solar and stellar plasma outflows to applying MHD models to interstellar and intergalactic "gas" (i.e., plasma) flows), and many astrophysicists maintain a careful distance from cosmological speculations.

Similar to the evolution of ideas over the past century, the "mainstream" view will continue to evolve, and some changes affecting cosmology issues will likely come from unexpected quarters. For example, as reflected in the current debate about quantum gravity models [quantum gravity theories attempt to meld quantum mechanics and gravity, which are currently incompatible, into a single theory], it's widely recognized that physics lacks a unified theory encompassing both quantum physics and relativity, and for many the weak link in that combination is general relativity (which unlike quantum physics lacks experimental testing on the relevant scales).

In unifying these theories, any presumed metric likely needs to be transformed into a dynamical entity characterized solely by solutions of the relevant equations. It remains an open question how best to address this problem. Some researchers are taking a new look at emergent gravity approaches of which one example is that proposed by Reginald Cahill in his "Process Physics." By mid-century, I predict that the current focus on the Big Bang hypothesis, and related fashions such as string theory and multiverses, will steadily decline as new discoveries will force their exponents to adopt even more ad hoc hypotheses.

The methodology and results of well-tested, mainstream observational astrophysics will gradually expand and shine new light on domains now dominated by untested speculation. Eventually a new paradigm will emerge, participants will gradually cease converting coefficients of highly abstract models into the latest grand speculation (e.g., dark energy), and cosmology will finally become a mature science. At that stage, the best of prior work, including quasi-steady-state, plasma astrophysics, and others, will be gradually integrated because of their effectiveness in providing enhanced predictive success and understanding.

Finally, what is the ultimate fate of the universe if both plasmas and gravity are relevant on the cosmological scale?

To date, the only comprehensive models that have been carried out are based on gravity-only assumptions usually within the context of the Big Bang paradigm (with ad hoc coefficients added for consistency; viz. dark matter and dark energy). As yet, no one has attempted the much more complex task of formulating a cosmic-scale model based on <u>both</u> gravity <u>and</u> EM/plasmas, a task possibly beyond capabilities of the current generation of supercomputers. Following Hilton Ratcliffe and many other astrophysicists who question the cosmic expansion hypothesis, I imagine that the universe on a sufficiently large spatial scale is relatively constant in structure over a sufficiently long time scale, thus perhaps exemplifying the "perfect cosmological principle" (i.e., at sufficiently large scales, no substantial differences in either space, time, or their combination). Nevertheless, significant differences as observed would be expected on more limited space and time scales. For me this is much more satisfactory than treating as pure "coincidence" that the time since the Big Bang (a contingency of nature) just happens "now" to be nearly identical to the inverse Hubble time (based on a presumed "constant" of nature). To me such coincidences are strong indicators that a new and deeper understanding is needed.

Chapter 40

Survival of the Beautiful:

A Conversation With David Rothenberg About Evolution and Beauty

Courage, pugnacity, perseverance, strength and size of body, weapons of all kinds, musical organs, both vocal and instrumental, bright colors and ornamental appendages, have all been indirectly gained by the one sex or the other, through the exertion of choice, the influence of love and jealousy, and the appreciation of the beautiful ...

Charles Darwin, 1871, *The Descent of Man*

Plato considered beauty to be so important that he enshrined it as one of the three objective values, which transcended individual foibles. Plato's triumvirate of beauty, truth and goodness was influential for some time.

In the modern era, a more relativist view has become dominant. In this view, all values are ultimately subjective and there is nothing inherent in nature that reflects things such as beauty, truth or goodness. Rather, these values emerge at the human level of complexity. As with many intellectual trends, however, the modern era has gone a bit too far in its relativism. It is undeniable that values in general are relative and subjective. But to conclude, as is often argued today, that all such values are entirely emergent – that is, not present at all at lower levels of complexity – with human consciousness or culture is unwarranted.

With respect to beauty, there is a growing awareness that even though determinations of beauty in particular cases shall remain entirely subjective, there is indeed a movement toward beauty in all animals and perhaps in all things. The somewhat misleading phrase that captures this truth in biology is "sexual selection." And sexual attraction is indeed its primary mechanism, but we can infer, through the observed behaviors of animals and even in plants at a far more rudimentary level, that there is an appreciation for beauty that goes beyond sex itself.

This is a controversial area, partly because of what I call "the behaviorist hangover." Behaviorism held sway in much of the 20th Century and its proponents argued that we shouldn't infer thoughts/feelings in animals or even other humans. Rather, we should stick entirely to observed behaviors and avoid explanations that rely on inferred mental states. This view has rightly been refuted not only because it is de-humanizing but because anyone who has a pet or is around non-human animals for much time knows full well that other animals have rich inner lives, mood states, preferences, etc.

Even though behaviorism has been largely rejected there is still a tendency in many scientists and other intellectuals today to denigrate reasonable inferences about mental and emotional states.

Do animals truly appreciate beauty? This is a good debate. Darwin believed that other animals have a keen sense for beauty, as the opening quote shows. Many of today's biologists would take a different view. David Rothenberg argues in his book *Survival of the Beautiful* that they do indeed and that an attraction to beauty is important at many different levels in the animal kingdom. Rothenberg's book was inspired by the finding that the complex nightingale's song shows a very similar structure to the humpback whale's song. Why would this be the case? Well, that's one of the topics tackled in this immensely interesting book.

Rothenberg suggests that "beauty selection" would be a more accurate term than "sexual selection." I like this suggestion very much and it makes me happy to think that the animal world, and possibly the universe more generally, is indeed a movement toward beauty. I've speculated a bit about the place of beauty in the universe (A Science of Beauty Part I, and Part II) and was pleased to find that thinkers like Rothenberg are also helping to blaze this necessary trail.

I had the privilege of interviewing Rothenberg by email. This interview took place before his new book, *Bug Music: How Insects Gave Us Rhythm and Noise*, came out. His new book looks in detail at how insects have influenced human music.

What do you mean by the phrase "survival of the beautiful"? What inspired you to write this book, the latest in a series of books on art in nature?

We tend to think that evolution means survival of the fittest, but that's only part of the story. Charles Darwin remarked that the peacock's tail "made him sick," because he couldn't explain it by natural selection alone. He had to uncover the process of sexual selection, where some traits survive just because one sex prefers it in the other, just because they like it. That's how we get survival of the weird, the cool, the extreme, the strange and seemingly useless in nature. Sometimes the beautiful survives just because the females like it. (That's the way it usually works in nature, but sometimes it goes the other way around...)

How did you come to study art in nature, sexual selection and music (some of which is inspired by your study of bird and whale song)?

I wanted to combine my interest in the beautiful music that nature has evolved with a larger sense of the role of beauty in nature, so I decided to consider the visual as well, about which so much more has been written. Plus, I was intrigued by the fact that a sped-up humpback whale song sounds so much like a nightingale song, and these creatures are not at all related to one another. Might nature have some kind of absolute standard of beauty, rather than the arbitrariness that evolution likes to talk about? On this topic, there is much more written on the visual than the aural.

Why did it take so long for biology to come to terms with Darwin's ideas on sexual selection? And why do most biologists still refuse to take Darwin seriously when he talks about birds and other animals having a sense for aesthetics?

That is a great question. One reason is that science is suspicious of qualities in nature that seem like they might not be useful, efficient, or practical. Most biologists today consider sexual selection, the evolution of beauty, to be a subset of natural selection, the evolution of practical traits. They want to say that the beautiful is practical, but Darwin didn't believe that aesthetics should be so pigeonholed. I profile the work of Richard Prum, one of few biologists who think that beauty in evolution should be studied on its own terms.

It's struck me as very odd, for a while now, that sexual selection is classified by modern biologists as a type of natural selection. Darwin proposed sexual selection, in his 1872 book, The Descent of Man, *primarily to explain things that he felt natural selection couldn't explain. So if sexual selection works at cross-purposes to natural selection in most cases, how is it logical to classify sexual selection as a type of natural selection?*

It really doesn't work at <u>cross</u>-purposes, but in addition to natural selection. It explains why some features evolve that seem extravagant, not efficient. It is important for us to realize that nature is not engineered for practicality, but has evolved upon a mix of practicality and caprice.

Darwin is famous for making the statement that the peacock's tail made him sick because natural selection couldn't explain it. Natural selection would, rather, suggest a far smaller and more maneuverable tail. But sexual selection has nevertheless favored larger and ungainly tails. So isn't this a clear example (with thousands more readily available) of sexual selection working at cross-purposes to natural selection?

In that sense you are right, sexual selection does work against natural selection. But mainstream biology doesn't admit that. The average textbook says that, even if a trait looks impractical, it really does indicate good genes and good health. Yet Richard Prum argues, and I take up his argument in Survival of the Beautiful, that there really is little evidence for that view, and the arbitrariness of sexually selected traits should be taken more seriously. He, and Darwin, tend to take the arbitrariness a bit too seriously; I'm also interested in the idea that there are certain natural tendencies in aesthetics, nothing too simple or easy, but certain vague rules at work beneath everything, as I mentioned to you earlier.

It also seems to me that the reticence to accept sexual selection the terms that Darwin proposed it - based on a feeling for beauty among all creatures, to varying degrees - relates to the Behaviorist movement in the first half of the 20th Century, which literally denied any type of mind or subjectivity to animals and, often, to humans too. Are we still in a Behaviorist hangover?

Darwin certainly didn't consider animals to be mindless nonsubjects... you may have a point, but I don't think that most of us are in a behaviorist hangover, though certainly plenty of biologists are!

You mention many times in your book what I call "principles of beauty," similar perhaps to the "laws of form" championed by Darcy Thompson and other biologists who have tried to describe the underlying structures that guide biological forms. The idea is that sexual selection may not be entirely arbitrary and, instead, be based ultimately on physical and chemical principles that guide biology - or perhaps there are even deeper principles of beauty that all organisms tap into. I've proposed some principles of beauty here and I'm curious what you think of the effort to develop principles of beauty in a scientific manner, through hypothesis and data, as I suggest in my essay?

You're definitely on to something, but in my book I caution against putting too much weight on symmetry and elegance alone. Nature always has a certain amount of messiness, inexactness, and surprising messiness as well... check out all those references I talk about in chapter four; I don't trust any such list that is too simple or claims to be comprehensive. The answer is in the details: in the mathematics of Wolfram and the chemistry and physics that Philip Ball talks about. Probably his trilogy on shape and pattern is the best book on the subject in my opinion.

I certainly agree that symmetry is just one of many principles of beauty, though it does seem to be an important one. Why is symmetry attractive to us and other animals, as well as, apparently, nature more generally?

I think symmetry is one of those features of nature determined by mathematics, chemistry, and physics, principles beneath sexual selection and the whims of evolution. I find Philip Ball's writing in *Shapes* to be the most helpful in understanding this.

You mention Birkhoff's attempts to quantify artistic quality. This is a wonky scientific way to approach art, admittedly, but I must admit I like the attempt. There's always a risk in de-mystifying art by being too literal – too quantitative, in this case – but, more technically, isn't Birkhoff's approach flawed in that under his suggested equation ($M = O/C$, where M is aesthetic measure or value, O is aesthetic order, and C is complexity) a blank canvas would have the highest possible "M" (artistic quality)?

Of course it's too easy, but at least he tried! He should be congratulated for his attempt.

You have a very eclectic background, including in music. You've literally recorded music with whales and birds. Can you describe your process for engaging in this inter-species creative process?

I've been asked this question many times in interviews all over the world, and it's the one question my answer never seems to satisfy. I clam up and don't know what to say, retreating into cautious defense. "Of course I don't know what the whale is feeling, so how can I know what I feel..." I'm immediately suspicious of people who claim a deep connection with whales the minute they look into the giant animal's eye, or feel his deep chant reverberate through sound waves under the sea. "I knew," they say, "the animal had something deeply important to say to me," and they sigh with reverence.

When I'm playing with whales I'm never sure of anything, being so wrapped up in the music and trying to play in a unique way halfway between human and cetacean. First of all, it's a strange technological process. I'm playing my clarinet onboard a boat into a microphone that's plugged into an underwater speaker, so the notes I play are being broadcast out into the soundworld of the whales. Then I'm wearing headphones which are attached to an underwater microphone, called a hydrophone, which is listening live to the underwater sound environment, which includes the singing whale and my deep sea burbling clarinet, altogether. It's kind of like a recording studio where each player is isolated in a separate booth, except one booth is the whole ocean with a forty foot whale in it, singing the one song he needs to know.

Why even try such a stunt? To make music that can be made no other way. As a jazz musician I know how exciting it is to jam with a musician who can't speak my language, but can make sense of my music as I play along with theirs. It's astonishing to realize this can also work with other species—from birds, to bugs, and even to humpback whales, the animal with the longest, most moving music in the natural world, a sound that can be heard underwater from ten miles away, a song with clear melodies, phrases, rhythms and parts that takes the whale twenty minutes to sing before he starts the cycle over again, in performances that last up to twenty three hours.

Playing along with a whale, wearing headphones and listening to the strange reverberations of underwater sound where you can't tell where any sound is coming from because there is no sense of stereo space, is a kind of out-of-body experience, thrusting the human sound of a clarinet into a world where it doesn't really belong, because there's no way a clarinet could be blown underwater. What use is a whale song in our human world? It reminds us that we are not the only musicians on Earth, and that if we want to understand the natural world beyond our narrow human concerns, we have to listen to and appreciate the full range of animal musics that have been on this planet for millions of years before humans ever got here. It's a very humbling feeling.

So I don't jam along with whales to make me feel special, but to make music that is special. Half-human and half-whale? Perhaps no one's gonna like it!

Maybe not at first. Most of the time the whales are not interested. But every once in a while, when the sea is calm and one great beast is right under the boat, so close that his moans can be felt right through the hull, then sometimes he changes his song when he hears what I play. At those moments I feel a true sense of awe, that music is something really big. Bigger than our whole species, something written right into the fabric of all life whose beauty is far beyond our ability to explain, or even feel its purpose. Touching a piece of the melody of the universe, it's no longer about me at all, but something I feel privileged to be a tiny part of.

You write that your book was inspired by the discovery that a slowed down mockingbird song has pretty much the same structure as a whale song. This is remarkable, but what does it mean? Is it coincidence, or is there really a deep structure to art/creativity that can span the yawning gap between a whale and a mockingbird?

It means there are principles of order at work beneath the whims of sexual selection, and we don't really know why.

In terms of sexual selection and the "survival of the beautiful," what does the mockingbird song mean to the female mockingbird (only the male mockingbirds sing)? I know we can't ever know with certainty, but what do you think it feels like to be a female mockingbird hearing the song?

We don't really know... we believe the male sings to attract the attention of females, but there isn't much evidence that the females are paying attention, or that anyone is paying attention, and no clear reason that birds like nightingales, mockingbirds, thrashers, butcherbirds, and shama thrushes need such exceedingly complicated songs.

The possibility for extremely complicated and beautiful sexually selected traits is out there, and sometimes it cuts through the constraints of sexual selection.

Last, what do you think of efforts to get animals to create art with human help, like the elephants who formerly worked in the timber industry in India who have been re-trained to paint self-portraits and other such efforts?

I have a chapter on this in *Survival of the Beautiful*. I much prefer the more abstract efforts of the elephant Siri in the Syracuse Zoo (as depicted in the wonderful book *To Whom It May Concern*) than I do those elephants who can paint realistic pictures of elephants. There are some good abstract elephant painters in Thailand as well, but my bias is that art made by animals should look new and different, and teach us humans something unexpected, rather than showing us just what we want to see.

Chapter 41

Something From Nothing:

A Conversation With Lawrence Krauss About Nothing

In conducting a number of interviews with various experts over the last couple of years – and requesting interviews from some who have turned me down – I've learned, perhaps unsurprisingly, that people are far more inclined to be interviewed by someone who they expect is friendly to their ideas.

Lawrence Krauss knew going in to our interview that I wasn't very receptive to his ideas with respect to the roles of science and philosophy in our public discourse. I previously wrote a column on Krauss's 2012 book, *A Universe from Nothing*, and his public spat with Columbia University philosopher of science (with a Ph.D in theoretical physics) David Albert. My column was critical of Krauss's views on the value of philosophy versus science and Krauss's debating style. My main point was that there is no real dividing line between science and philosophy and that every scientist is implicitly a philosopher.

That said, I was happy to find that Krauss, while requiring some (polite) pestering to get our interview finished, was willing to address criticism and contrary views in the below interview.

A Universe from Nothing is a very interesting read from a foremost physicist of our time. Krauss's goal is to show our universe could literally have come from nothing. He seeks to show plausibility rather than any kind of proof, recognizing that it is far too early in our understanding of cosmology to attempt any proof in such matters. I didn't find the effort entirely convincing, personally, as I discus in the interview below. My feeling is that it is more plausible that there has always been something, rather than a literal nothing, and our universe sprang in some manner from this eternal something. Regardless of my personal views, I can recommend Krauss's book as a good read and great overview of modern cosmology and physics more generally.

I don't know Krauss personally, though I did meet him briefly at a talk he gave at UC Santa Barbara earlier this year. He exudes a no-nonsense ultra-intelligent confidence. But as I wrote in my previous column, I feel like Krauss and his co-thinkers exemplify well the perils of scientism – the view that science can, at least potentially, answer all meaningful questions about life, the universe, and everything.

For me, the middle ground between muddled mysticism, dogmatic theism and scientism is an acceptance of the ultimate mystery behind it all. We'll never know the full extent of what we don't know and, despite the amazing successes of science and technology in our modern world, this mystery should forever keep us humble. The ocean is deep and we'll never exhaust the pleasures of discovering new things in those depths.

I had the pleasure of interviewing Krauss via email. Krauss lives in Arizona and Australia.

What makes you tick as a physicist and as a person?

I enjoy experiencing life, and the universe, in every way I can. I enjoy being surprised and astounded, and I like to have fun.

In your recent book, A Universe From Nothing, *you argue that modern physics has provided a plausible narrative for how the entire universe could have arisen from literally nothing, which undermines yet another key traditional reason for religion: to explain the origin of the universe. Are you personally an atheist or an agnostic? What led you to this view?*

I am a scientist, and therefore I don't buy into absolutes. Things are either likely or unlikely. Everything I know about the universe tells me it is extremely unlikely, to the point of near certainty, that there is any divine guidance. I don't classify myself by labels.

Many scientists have suggested ways to reconcile science and spirituality, such as Stephen Jay Gould, Alfred North Whitehead, and Alan Barbour. Do you think it's possible to reconcile modern physics and spiritual views of the world? Or do spiritual/religious views simply need to be jettisoned? Would we be better off if they were jettisoned?

Science is spiritual. Religious views should be jettisoned because they are wrong.

How is science spiritual?

Science encourages awe and wonder, and the sense that there is more to the universe than we directly experience. The advantage of the spirituality of science is that it is real.

While your book attempts to present a plausible picture of how the universe could have come from nothing, don't you gloss over what most people really mean by "nothing" - that is, nothing at all, nada, zilch? The types of nothing you address aren't this type of nothing, so your approach seems to beg the question as to where this original something, whether it's the laws of physics or what have you, came from.

No I don't. I describe initial conditions with no space, no time, no matter, no radiation, no laws. That is a good definition of nothing as far as I cam concerned.

Following up on what "nothing" really means, you write in the Q&A section of the paperback edition of your book: "I then describe how it is possible that space and time themselves could have arisen from no space and time, which is certainly closer to absolute nothing. Needless to say, one can nevertheless question whether that is nothing, because the transition is mediated by some physical laws. Where did they come from? That is a good question, and one of the more modern answers is that even the laws themselves may be random, coming into existence along with universes that may arise. This may still beg the question of what allows any of this to be possible, but at some level it is, as I describe at the beginning of the book, 'turtles all the way down.'" I'm not trying to play gotcha (frankly I hadn't seen your Q&A when I asked the previous question), but it seems that you've changed your position since writing that Q&A. If so, what prompted the change of mind? And isn't the point of science and physics more specifically to avoid the "turtles all the way down" argument, which was exactly the point of this well-known metaphor!

I haven't changed my mind at all. I simply tried to succinctly summarize my argument, and said it is possible. It could be that there was precisely no existence, before our universe's existence, or not. We don't know. And, indeed, the turtles all the way down argument is a red herring, and is a debate about something that we have no idea about, and may not exist. It doesn't matter. The point is that our universe didn't exist, then came into existence, and we want to understand how that can happen. And we now have a plausible picture of how that can happen. So the non-existence of our universe is the 'nothing' that matters. The rest is metaphysics and semantics and irrelevant to science, at least at the moment.

Isn't a more helpful answer to how the universe came to be - which is the question your book addresses - simply that there has always been something, even if we don't know what that something is or was? This answer avoids entirely the infinite regress and bickering over whether God was the first mover or whether the universe really came from absolutely nothing.

Science isn't based on what we would like. We don't know the answer yet. To assume 'something' is to make an *a priori* decision, which has no empirical basis.

I don't follow why you think it is an a priori assumption that there has always been "something." Clearly, we have something - an entire universe - and isn't it pretty rational and empirical (that is, not really a priori) to assume that that something, the entire universe, didn't come from literally nothing since we haven't witnessed anything coming from literally nothing in the entire history of scientific exploration?

No. We witness things coming into existence, that didn't exist before, all the time in physics. Our universe could be one of them. So you are assuming because you haven't witnessed it that it cannot happen. That is an assumption, and indeed even if we hadn't witnessed it, it is a pretty small-minded assumption that that has to be the case universally – a small-minded assumption that science teaches us not to have.

With respect to the first type of nothing that you address - empty space and the laws of physics that come with empty space - you rely on the theory of inflation for your argument that this type of nothing can produce our universe. Yet Paul Steinhardt, one of the creators of inflationary theory, has recently <u>repudiated</u> his theory. Do you think he's wrong in repudiating inflation? Would your arguments still work if inflation was wrong?

Yes to both: I do think he's wrong and my arguments still work even if inflation is wrong.

Doesn't your book slide into philosophical territory more than science territory since you're discussing ideas that are inherently unfalsifiable and speculative?

The ideas I discuss are speculative, but not necessary unfalsifiable. Even multiverses might, in principle, be probed, as I describe in the book.

You've criticized modern philosophy pretty definitively, so I'm curious where you draw the line between philosophy and science? Are you a Popperian or do you prefer some other criterion of scientific soundness than falsifiability?

I am not an anything. Unlike philosophers, I don't classify myself by some 'ism' or 'ian' based on someone's classification. Science derives knowledge from empirical inquiry. Philosophy, at its best, reflects on that knowledge, but doesn't add to it.

Do you think traditional philosophical criteria of soundness (for example: logical coherence, adherence to known facts, and parsimony) are sufficient for rigorous thinking? Or do we need the stronger criterion of falsifiability?

Logical coherence derives from empirical investigation. Things that don't seem logical classically may in fact occur, like an electron doing many different things at the same time.

Last, what is your response to those who suggest, like Kuhn, that science isn't really that rational in how it operates – that is, that paradigms shift not because of incremental logical changes but, instead, in large shifts that are generally resisted by the old guard until the weight of evidence simply can't be ignored anymore?

I think this is a simplistic view that has been discredited by all of my experience in science, and I am not alone in this view as far as I can tell. Scientists are skeptical, and do not change viewpoints easily, but the weight of any sound evidence cannot be ignored and is not generally ignored.

Chapter 42

The Romantic Reductionist:

A Conversation with Christof Koch

Reductionism is one of the primary methods of modern science. The key idea is that previously intractable problems – like the mind/body problem – are in theory tractable by breaking the problem into smaller parts and solving the smaller problems. Solving the smaller problems will, then, allow the larger problem to be solved. Or so the idea goes.

Christof Koch, for the past 27 years a professor of cognitive and behavioral biology at Caltech, but who has now moved to be the chief scientific officer of the Allen Institute for Brain Science in Seattle, is a lifelong reductionist. He's written extensively on biophysics and neuroscience. His best-known book, a detailed and scholarly examination of the physical basis for consciousness, is The Quest for Consciousness: A Neurobiological Approach.

Koch's new book, *Consciousness: Confessions of a Romantic Reductionist*, is far more accessible. It's a lively and interesting account of Koch's evolution as a thinker, including his changing views in neuroscience, philosophy and spirituality.

Koch stated just a few years ago, in an article co-authored with his long-time mentor the Nobel Prize-winning co-discoverer of DNA, Francis Crick: "Neuroscientists do not yet understand enough about the brain's inner workings to spell out exactly how consciousness arises from the electrical and chemical activity of neurons. Thus, the big first step is to determine the best 'neuronal correlates of consciousness' – the brain activity that matches up with specific conscious experiences." This is a good example of the reductionist approach to understanding the brain basis of consciousness because it intentionally ignores – for now – the over-arching metaphysical issue of "how consciousness arises" and focuses instead on understanding how the brain and its components work.

In his latest book, however, Koch is willing to indulge his more "romantic" side. The self-professed romantic reductionist goes far beyond his earlier statement and does discuss his current views on how consciousness arises. Perhaps most significantly, Koch supports panpsychism as probably the best candidate for explaining how consciousness arises. Panpsychism suggests that all matter has some modicum of mind, and vice versa.

"Romantic" doesn't mean anti-rational. To me the term means simply that we recognize the mystery of the universe and the fact that the universe will always remain mysterious to some degree. For Koch, it means that we can discern patterns of meaning in the universe, meaning that can't be drawn from mere scientific facts and theories.

But panpsychism can also be intellectually rigorous, particularly when we recognize that it's about as simple (parsimonious) as a theory can be while also including the reality of conscious experience – rather than simply ignoring it as some approaches do (what the physicist Erwin Schrödinger described as "objectivation" – the tendency to forget the reality of the subject while the subject itself engages in its theory-making).

Specifically, Koch supports Giulio Tononi's version of panpsychism (described in his new book, *Phi: A Voyage from the Brain to the Soul*), which views any system, biological or artificial, that has at least some bits of "integrated information" as possessing at least some minimum level of consciousness. As integrated information increases, so does consciousness.

Some have decried this apparent evolution in Koch's thinking. Stanislas Dehaene, a prominent neuroscientist, wrote in a review of Koch's book:

> [For Koch] evolution implies a progressive amplification of global consciousness, with computers and the Internet as its most recent avatars. Openly confessing his recent familial turmoil and his loss of Christian faith, Koch finds solace in this view of life. He also admits that his long-time mentor and collaborator on the mind-body problem, Francis Crick, would have cringed. An avid reader of Jacques Monod's *Chance and Necessity*, I too was stunned: Rare are contemporary biologists who confess such thoughts, and they are even rarer, I thought, among those who study consciousness.

As a card-carrying panpsychist, I find Koch's "confessions" refreshing and encouraging. Recognizing that all matter very likely has some modicum of consciousness and that the universe is, as a general matter, evolving toward higher consciousness is an entirely fact-based, rational and rigorous position. But, contrary to the prevailing reductionist materialism in neuroscience and other sciences, it also provides room for more spiritual approaches to the world – which recognize the inherent mystery behind the world around us.

I had the pleasure of interviewing Koch via email from his former home in Pasadena, California.

You've studied the mind for decades but only until recently have you been willing to publicly discuss the problem of consciousness itself. What prompted this change of heart?

Well, that's not really true. I started to give public talks on the brain correlates of consciousness, including a very popular Caltech class on The Neurobiology of Consciousness, since roughly the early 1990s. What has changed over the past several decades is the attitude the audience brings to the topic. Early on, I always had to justify why natural scientists can, and should, study consciousness and that the quest for the material roots of consciousness should not just be left to philosophers, religious people or the retired. This view, that consciousness can be investigated in a scientific manner, has now become much more widely accepted.

Your new book, Consciousness: Confessions of a Romantic Reductionist, is a great and accessible read on your career studying the brain and mind. You surprised me with a sort of "coming out" as a panpsychist, in that you suggest the most natural and simple of solutions to the mind/body problem is the idea that all matter has some associated consciousness. Can you explain your reasoning behind this position? And what does it mean in practical terms to have a panpsychist view of the world?

There are two main sources for my attraction to a panpsychist position.

First, many species – bees, octopuses, ravens, crows, magpies, parrots, tuna, cichlid and other fish, mice, cetaceans, dogs and monkeys - are capable of sophisticated, learned, non-stereotyped behaviors that would be associated with consciousness if a human were to carry out such actions. The nervous system of these creatures, while typically smaller than that of humans, are highly complex, with neuronal circuits as complex as anything seen in the human brain. When studying mammalian brains, it is difficult to observe anything exceptional about the human brain, except possibly its large size (note that the brains of whales are up to five times bigger than the human brain). From this I conclude that consciousness is vastly more widespread than commonly assumed. What makes humans special is the emergence of self-consciousness, consciousness reflecting upon itself. But all the current evidence suggests that many animal species, and perhaps all multi-cellular animals, experience the sounds and sights of life. This opens the way to reconsider the old philosophical position of panpsychism.

Panpsychism is the belief that anything physical has a mental aspect or that the mental is fundamental and ubiquitous, from electrons to brains. It has two major flaws. One is known as the problem of aggregates as recognized already by Leibniz. As the philosopher John Searle puts it well in his review of my book in the New York Review of Books "Consciousness cannot spread over the universe like a thin veneer jam; there has to be a point where my consciousness ends and yours begins." Indeed, if consciousness is everywhere, why should it not animate the iPhone, the Internet, or the United States of America? A second flaw was that earlier versions of panpsychism did not explain why a healthy brain is conscious while the same brain, placed inside a blender and reduced to a goo would not be. That is, it does not explain how aggregates combine to produce specific conscious experience.

Second, I have in recent years been swayed by the conceptual framework of the Integrated Information Theory (IIT) of Giulio Tononi, which postulates that conscious experience is a fundamental aspect of reality and is identical to a particular type of information (integrated information). Consciousness depends on a physical substrate but is not reducible to it. Any system that possesses some non-zero amount of integrated information, whether it hails from the ancient kingdom of animalia or from its recent silicon offspring, experiences something. While it feels like nothing to be a heap of sand or a black hole, it feel like something to be a bee or the Internet. IIT addresses the problem of aggregates by postulating that only 'local maxima' of integrated information exist (over elements, spatial and temporal scales): my consciousness, your consciousness, but nothing in between; each individual consciousness in the US, but no superordinate US consciousness. And it explains why some types of brain circuits, say the cerebellum, contribute little to consciousness while others, such as neocortex, contribute much more. Unlike classical panpsychism, not all physical objects are mental (an electron, a black hole or a heap of sand would not be). Thus, Tononi's theory offers a scientific, constructive, predictive, and mathematically precise form of (integrated) panpsychism for the 21st century.

Is cognitive neuroscience a mature science at this point? Or are we still in the early days of understanding the brain and mind, with many competing theories still presenting credible but competing views?

A final true science of the mind will have to be built out of a deep understanding of nerve cells, and the amazingly complex circuits they form in the brain. For it is neurons that are the atoms of perception, memory, behavior, thought and consciousness. To paraphrase Winston Churchill - cognitive neuroscience is at the end of the beginning of the quest to understand our brain and mind. So it will still be a while.

I'm familiar with Tononi's work and also find it pretty appealing. You write that "consciousness depends on a physical substrate but cannot be reduced to it." Can you elaborate on what this means? This sounds kind of dualistic to me but I don't think that's what you mean.

Exactly what I say. Experience utterly depends on a brain but is not the same as the brain that produces this experience. It is experience, after all, which I am more certain about than anything else. Brain I can only infer indirectly. I have no direct experience of my brain. It is the mind that feels the heavy heart after falling out with a loved one, not the neurons making up the brain. Without the neurons, there would no sadness but it is not the neurons that are sad.

As you state in your own writings, that you don't believe in philosophical labels, so I won't answer into what sort of exact philosophical camp this position falls and the extent to which it is a dualistic position. The world is too complex to be easily labeled.

Staying with Tononi's ideas, can you explain Tononi's solution to the "boundary problem" (also known as the "combination problem")? That is, how is it that, as you write, all Americans have individual minds but there is no "American mind" in the literal sense as an aggregate of all the smaller minds? How are "local maxima" determined?

One of the central notions of integrated information theory is exactly this: that only 'local maxima' of integrated information exist (over elements, spatial and temporal scales): my consciousness, your consciousness, but nothing in between; each individual consciousness in the US, but no superordinate [aggregated] US consciousness. The local maxima themselves are determined by the extent to which some neural network carried information that is both integrated and differentiated. Even though it may be residing within a larger network, the larger network of which it is a part can have a lower degree of integration and differentiation. It is all a question of the wealth and strength of the connections among the subcomponents.

More fundamentally, why would consciousness be tied to integrated information, or information at all?

That, my friend, I couldn't tell you. This might well fall into the same category of fundamentally unanswerable (but utterable) questions as "why is there something rather than nothing"! You and I find ourselves in a universe where integrated information is consciousness.

You delve into the spiritual arena a little in your book and I wanted to ask if you could briefly describe your own spiritual evolution – the "romantic" aspect of the "romantic reductionist" that you describe yourself as?

I was raised by my parents in the best liberal Catholic tradition, in which science—including evolution by natural selection—was by and large accepted as explaining the material world. I was an altar boy, reciting prayers in Latin and listening to Gregorian chants and the masses, passions, and requiems of Orlande de Lassus, Bach, Vivaldi, Haydn, Mozart, Brahms, and Bruckner.

Mother Church was an erudite, globe-spanning, culturally fecund, and morally unassailable institution with an unbroken lineage extending across two millennia to Rome and Jerusalem. Its catechism offered a time-honored and reassuring account of life that made sense to me. So strong was the comfort religion provided that I passed it on. My then wife and I raised our children in the faith, baptizing them, saying grace before meals, attending church on Sundays, and taking them through the rites of First Communion.

Yet over the years, I began to reject more and more of the church's teachings. The traditional answers I was given were incompatible with a scientific worldview. I was taught one set of values by my parents and by my Jesuit and Oblate teachers, but I heard the beat of a different drummer in books, lectures, and the laboratory. This tension left me with a split view of reality. Outside of Mass, I didn't give much thought to the questions of sin, sacrifice, salvation, and the hereafter. I reasoned about the world, the people in it, and myself in entirely natural terms. These two frameworks, one divine and one secular, one for Sunday and one for the rest of the week, did not intersect. The church provided meaning by placing my puny life in the context of the vastness of God's creation and his Son's sacrifice for humankind. Science explained facts about the actual universe I found myself in and how it came to be.

Harboring two distinct accounts, one for the supralunar and one for the sublunar world, to use Aristotelian imagery, is not a serious intellectual stance. The resultant clash was my constant companion for decades. Yet I knew that there is but a single reality out there, and science is getting increasingly better at describing it. Humanity is not condemned to wander forever in an epistemological fog, knowing only the surface appearance of things but never their true nature. We can see something; and the longer we gaze, the better we comprehend.

In a mid-life crisis (that erupted late, at age 50), I resolved the conflict between these two types of explanations, by rejecting Catholic, and, indeed, all Christian precepts.

I do believe that some deep and elemental organizing principle created the universe and set it in motion for a purpose I cannot comprehend. I grew up calling this entity God. It is much closer to Spinoza's God than to the God of Michelangelo's painting. The mystic Angelus Silesius, a contemporary of Descartes, captures the paradoxical essence of the self-caused Prime Mover as "Gott ist ein lauter Nichts, ihn rührt kein Nun noch Hier" (God is a lucent nothing, no Now nor Here can touch him).

The rise of sentient life within time's wide circuit was inevitable. Teilhard de Chardin is correct in his view that islands within the universe—if not the whole cosmos—are evolving toward ever-greater complexity and self-knowledge. I am not saying that Earth had to bear life or that bipedal, big-brained primates had to walk the African grasslands. But I do believe that the laws of physics overwhelmingly favored the emergence of consciousness. The universe is a work in progress. Such a belief evokes jeremiads from many biologists and philosophers, but the evidence from cosmology, biology, and history is compelling.

Spiritual traditions encourage us to reach out to our fellow travelers on the river of time. More than most secular ideologies, religions emphasize the common bond among people: love thy neighbor as thyself. Religious sentiments, as expressed through music, literature, architecture, and the visual arts, bring out some of what is best in humankind. Yet collectively, they are only of limited use in making sense of the puzzle of our existence. The only certain answers we can obtain come from science. What I find most appealing from an intellectual and ethical point of view are certain strands of Buddhism.

I am saddened by the loss of my religious belief, like leaving forever the comfort of my childhood home, suffused with a warm glow and fond memories. I still have feelings of awe when entering a high-vaulted cathedral or listening to Bach's St. Matthew Passion. Nor can I escape the emotional thrall, the splendor and pageantry, of high Mass. But my loss of faith is an inescapable part of growing up, of maturing and seeing the world as it is. Science is a story for grown men, not a consoling tale for children.

I'm cast out into the universe, a strange, scary, and often lonely place. I strive to discern through its noisy manifestations—its people, dogs, trees, mountains, and stars—the eternal Music of the Spheres.

Do you think we'll be able to satisfactorily integrate science and spirituality in the not-too-distant future? Do you find Ken Wilber's attempted integration (in works like The Marriage of Sense and Soul *and* Sex, Ecology, Spirituality*) at all compelling?*

I truly do not know. But I know I will not give up striving to reunite a scientific with a spiritual perspective.

You state toward the end of your book: "The universe is a work in progress." Waxing romantic, would you agree that "God is a work in progress"?

I do not know what this means!

Last, how large a role in your own peace of mind and spiritual practice do activities like rock climbing and meditation play?

So far, meditation, while appealing from an intellectual point of view, is not for me. I lack the discipline and the desire to contemplate for hours, attending to "no awareness". I thrive on running, biking and climbing for hours, hyperkinetic. For me, life is motion. I can rest when I'm dead.

Chapter 43

Hi Phi:

A Conversation With Giulio Tononi About

the Nature of Consciousness

So many questions. How does matter produce mind? Or does it? Is there a soul? What happens when we die? These questions and more are tackled in Giulio Tononi's 2012 book, *Phi: A Journey from the Brain to the Soul*.

Tononi is a psychiatrist and neuroscientist at the University of Wisconsin, Madison. He collaborated for a number of years with Nobel Prize winner Gerald Edelman, developing with Edelman what was first known as the Dynamic Core Hypothesis, a theory of human consciousness, and later working on his own to develop the Integrated Information Theory (IIT) of consciousness. The essence of IIT is that integrated information is consciousness. As such, it can be quantified and characterized in great detail – but for now it can be quantified only in principle for most systems because doing so in practice is extremely difficult for any conscious system above the most basic level of complexity.

I've followed Tononi's work for a number of years, drawing from his ideas in my own work on theories of consciousness. In particular, I found Edelman and Tononi's book *A Universe of Consciousness* (1998) very helpful in shedding light on approaches to quantifying consciousness and I have enjoyed and appreciated Tononi's later work on consciousness, even if I don't agree on all the details.

The key concepts of IIT, discussed in poetic and metaphorical terms in Phi, and in detail in Tononi's more technical work, may be summarized as: 1) causation is information; 2) information is "integrated" when the whole consists of more than its parts, that is, the whole is irreducible to its parts because information would be lost through such reduction; 3) integrated information is consciousness; 4) we can quantify integrated information, at least in theory, if not in practice at this time; 5) we can quantify and characterize actual qualia based on a translation of qualia to a certain type of information space.

IIT is catching on, but it's taking a while: Tononi's first publication on IIT was in 1998. This is, perhaps, to be expected for a theory as profound as a comprehensive theory of consciousness. Tononi has some high-profile supporters, including Christof Koch (see here for my interview with Koch), formerly at CalTech and now at the Allen Institute for Brain Science. Even the arch-materialist Daniel Dennett expressed some sympathy for IIT when I asked Dennett about IIT a couple of years ago.

I attended the Association for the Scientific Study of Consciousness (ASSC) 17th annual meeting in San Diego in July of this year, where I saw Tononi speak twice. I also interviewed him one on one as part of my ongoing series of interviews with experts in various fields – see below. The ASSC meeting is the most prominent annual meeting of scientists who study consciousness. I felt like I was witnessing a paradigm shift as it happened, the beginning of a shift from materialist views to frameworks that, while no less scientific, are not strictly materialist because they explicitly include consciousness as a fundamental property – with Tononi's model being the most prominent in this latter category.

IIT had an extended moment in the sun at this conference, with a three-hour "tutorial" before the conference officially kicked off, a two-hour roundtable discussion midway through the conference, and a poster session by Tononi's lab colleagues Larissa Albantakis and Masafumi Oizumi, who also took part in the tutorials. That's some good coverage. Time will tell if IIT is getting a fleeting moment in the sun or it is truly the mark of a nascent paradigm shift in this exciting field.

A final personal note, while not often mentioned in academic discussions, is that I couldn't avoid, during my time with Tononi, the impression of being in the presence of a great man. I was able to get a good feel for Tononi's personality and abilities during his talks, our interview, and over dinner. Tononi is obviously incredibly intelligent, highly articulate to the point of rattling off very long numerically differentiated paragraphs about all sorts of topics, and highly accomplished in his two main fields (sleep science and consciousness). But he is also highly affable, likeable and egalitarian. I place great stock in these latter qualities.

Why is understanding consciousness important? Why should we care?

Because that's what we are. I usually say, to define consciousness, that it is what goes away when you when you fall asleep or when you undergo general anesthesia. You ask yourself what goes away; everything goes away. Nothing is left. Colors and sounds and shapes and feelings and thoughts, everything is gone. You are gone, your friends are gone, your country is gone, your universe is gone, as far as you are concerned. It's a rather important thing. When you wake up, or even when you dream, it all comes back. Consciousness is the only thing you're certain of, and the rest is what we imagine the world to be. We've taken thousands of years to understand better how the world is; no doubt the world exists. For me and for you, however, the only thing that really exists is my and your consciousness, and that's it.

Can we ever know what it is like to be a different kind of consciousness, for example, a bat? How about even another human being?

You are referring to Thomas Nagel's famous essay in which he very potently says that we'll probably never know if a bat is conscious. Even if we did, we certainly would never understand how it feels like to be a bat, especially given that bats have very strange sensory systems, from our point of view, and who knows how a bat sees the world, given that they use sonar. We'll never know in fact, Nagel's essay says, because it's impossible. It's your own private thing and a bat's private thing. It's hard enough to know what your wife or your brother or your friend's consciousness really is like and sort of empathize. It's impossible to know what being a bat is like. Integrated information theory (IIT) doesn't tell us yet how a bat feels because we haven't been able to model that complex a system yet. IIT does, however, tell us that it is a scientifically meaningful question to ask what it is like to be a bat, and it provides a way to take any physical system and ask, at least in principle, "Is there anything it is like to be this system?" The answer is going to be measured in terms of a quantifiable framework. A little bit, quite a lot, almost as much as us, more. A bat would probably place somewhere along the lines of not as much as us, but not like nothing. You would have a feeling at least for, "Does it feel like much?" Would it be like when you are fully conscious and awake or would it feel just like when you are sort of sleepy and almost gone, or more like the consciousness you have when you are drunk? IIT allows us in theory to quantify the consciousness present in a bat, but also to describe it qualitatively through a mapping of experience onto different complex shapes, which can be compared.

What are the basic concepts of your Integrated Information Theory?

The idea actually comes from literally sitting in your armchair, as a philosopher typically does, and wondering, "I'm conscious. What are the essential properties of consciousness?" The most important part of the theory is identifying those essential properties, those things that experience must have, every experience, in order to be an experience. The most important ones are, first, that every experience is unified. When you have an experience, whatever experience, it's always one experience, and you cannot divide it into pieces. You cannot have the experience of the left side of what is in front of you independently of the right side. It doesn't even make sense. Either there are two people, one is seeing left and one is seeing right, or you have one person, you, and you have to see both. You can talk about the left and the right, but they're always there together. Similarly, you cannot separate the color from the shape. I cannot look at your shirt and see its shape and not, at the same time, see its color . . . there's no way to do it. Nor can you listen to my voice and hear the sound without understanding the meaning. So there is always a unity, and that unity says that, in some sense, if there is a physical system that generates your consciousness, it must be something that actually works like a single entity. It cannot be divided into pieces. The other key property is the information contained in each experience. Information" means that a particular experience is one out of many possible experiences, which differs from every other one in its particular way. Imagine, let's say, a complicated, buzzing street scene in New York or, conversely, just lying on the beach in Southern California and watching the sky, purely blue, hearing nothing, totally relaxed. The second experience is a very simple experience, just pure you, and the New York scene is very complicated. Well, according to the theory, they're both equally informative even though it may seem like there is a lot more information coming at you in the New York street scene. Not because of how many pieces there are in each, but because they both are that particular experience by the fact that they rule out all the other possible experiences you could have had in that moment. Imagine watching a movie. For every frame of the movie, you have a different experience. No effort whatsoever. It's the simplest thing in the world for us. And there are, of course, thousands of frames in one movie, millions of movies, and all the movies that have not yet been done. And for each of them, you could have a different experience. So the repertoire of possible experiences is immense; nobody has counted it, and they are all different, each in its particular way.

These are the two key points. Now, of course, we all believe there's an outside world. It's made of things. We don't know exactly what these things are because our physical theories are still uncertain about exactly what the ultimate nature of nature is. But, in the end, the constituents of nature form atoms, molecules, and neurons, and brains, and these can do certain things and not others. And the idea here is that whatever physical system is in your brain, made of neurons, for it to be able to generate the experience, it must be able to work as a single identity -- that's the integration part of "integrated information" -- and, at the same time, a single entity that can specify trillions and trillions of different experiences, each different in its particular way. So that is what you need to generate consciousness, and that's what the theory tries to pursue. IIT suggests that we can quantify the integrated information in any given system (a quantity called phi), which is a measure of the consciousness present in that system.

We're here at a conference where you've got two major sessions on your theory – a tutorial, today's round table, and Larissa Albantakis [one of Tononi's postdocs] has a poster presentation tomorrow. So, there's a lot of attention to your theory now, more than a decade after you proposed it. Do you feel like we're in the middle of a paradigm shift in theories of consciousness?

I don't really think too much about that. What certainly happened was, as everybody knows, that until 20 years ago, it was essentially forbidden to talk about consciousness. I decided when I was 16 that I wanted to study consciousness for ethical reasons, but there was not much on it, and certainly not much being studied scientifically. So I studied medicine, psychiatry, and neurology in order to get closer to the real thing and know a bit more. But you couldn't really say at that time "I want to study consciousness," and still be taken seriously as an academic. So we are definitely in the middle of something new in the study of consciousness. There is a society [the Association for the Scientific Study of Consciousness]; there are lots of new presentations. It's wonderful to see, and lots of young people now say "I want to study consciousness," and they don't think it's impossible or should be. That has been a real shift. With respect to IIT itself, I really don't worry about these issues because, the thing is, with consciousness, especially if you try to address what people call the mind-body problem, the "hard problem," you're going to get a lot of flack anyway. And if you worry about people's conceptions, misconceptions, and reactions, you'll never make it far.

In terms of strategy, you say you don't worry about the day-to-day misunderstandings or reception of your theory, but clearly, you want your theory to catch on. You wouldn't be doing what you're doing if you didn't. So do you think much about strategy as to how to best get your theory a fair hearing and if you think it's correct, as I imagine you do, position it so it will one day become the dominant theory of consciousness?

I do worry about it to the extent that, for instance, you can get money to work on these issues. I must say, my record so far hasn't been good. Maybe it will change. So far, I had not gotten a dime for studying consciousness qua consciousness. Some entities are now funding research on consciousness, which makes me hopeful. I'm happy that IIT is beginning to get some notoriety. As you said, here there was a tutorial, a round table, some scouting attention, which is good. But, at the same time, for the past 30 years, when I was struggling with the theory, if I had to depend on people's reception of, "Is it worth studying consciousness? Is consciousness integrated information," and so on and so forth, I would never have been able to do anything. At some point, you have to trust your intuition.

Do you get tired of defending the theory?

Sometimes, yes, in the sense that, through experience, I know now that it takes some time to truly understand IIT. I think I know the reason roughly, which is, you have to step back to get the big picture first. You have to start from consciousness and ask, "What are its essential properties?," and then map it onto the outside world. I call this the intrinsic perspective. It's very hard to take the intrinsic perspective. Second, IIT uses the word "information" because there is no better word one could use. IIT uses the term in a very different sense than "information" normally means to people, or even in information theory. That's where many of the problems lie. The information of information theory is a very different thing – it is information from the extrinsic perspective of an observer, for whom the meaning is already given and it simply needs to be communicated across a channel or stored in a memory. So everybody misunderstands IIT usually at first. I find that it's a bit easier with younger people, who are more open. They come at the questions fresh and ask, "Okay, what is this?" and then it's a bit easier to explain and convey the key ideas of IIT.

Do you feel like, in your experience, this field follows a Kuhnian model -- where it's not really that rational in terms of how theories change over time – or do you think it's more Popperian, in that it really is about the rational debate of ideas, getting a fair hearing, and people considering the pros and cons?

I don't know, really. I can tell you that, by looking at some of the people who are now more-or-less sympathetic to IIT, or actually developing it and obviously know perfectly well its key aspects, it looks a lot like a transition. At first, one may not really get it, and then suddenly one begins to get it. Maybe not yet in full or so, but it begins to make sense. What happens, I have been told more than once, is that one hears the same words, sees the same evidence, hears the same talk, and then, at some point [snaps fingers], one gets what it really means, and then it makes a big difference. So, the process of change is probably more Kuhnian than Popperian.

You mentioned information and the confusion about the meaning of "information" in your theory, and I've heard this critique from others already, about your theory. The idea is that information is, in its basic sense, a product of consciousness. Searle, for example, argues that it's a category error to suggest that consciousness is actually equivalent to information. What's your response?

Well, this is quite a long story. Let's take Searle. The point he was making was essentially: "Ah, it's the usual mistake." You take information from the extrinsic, the observer's, perspective and you think you're measuring consciousness. It was really funny when I read Searle's critique. It was really funny because one of the foundations of IIT is that everything is to be done from the intrinsic perspective. And, in fact, it's completely against taking the extrinsic perspective on information. Information in IIT refers, essentially, to the differences that make a difference in the system itself. If you are the thing at issue, what makes a difference to you? If I am this little maggot's brain, or if I am this complicated human brain, what makes a difference to me? From the extrinsic perspective, an observer, you can describe molecules, atoms, quarks, signaling, treat the brain as a channel through which symbols flow, but you never get meaning out of the brain under this view. This was one of Searle's classic arguments. When he used his very profound, but very criticized, Chinese room argument, he essentially was saying as follows: you are in a room, you get questions in Chinese, you follow some very complicated rules that you don't actually understand, and finally you produce an answer, in Chinese, that you hand back out of the room. And what happens throughout this thought experiment scenario is, of course, this: the answer comes out of the room as if you, inside the room manipulating Chinese characters based on rules that you follow but don't understand, understood Chinese. So to an external observer you understand Chinese. But, of course, you in the room -- that was Searle's stroke of genius -- doing all that complicated processing, have not the slightest understanding of Chinese. You're just manipulating symbols. So Searle thinks you can't get semantics from syntax -- that is, you can't get meaning out of doing procedures -- so the computer won't do that. Somehow, however, we humans do that.

IIT says that on this Searle is right. Information has to be meaningful for the system, not for an outside observer, and the only meaning there is for a system, me, for example, comes from differences that make a difference to me, intrinsically. "Integrated information" refers to the fact that there are lots of differences that make a difference to the same entity, and the more of that, the more there is consciousness.

In terms of strategy and getting your ideas across, you've written a new book, Phi: A Voyage from the Brain to the Soul, *and you pursue kind of a poetic literary approach to your theory. It's not very technical, intentionally. Is that because you wanted to reach a wider audience, or because you thought that this is another way to convey your ideas in a different form that would be effective?*

There are many reasons, as often in life. I started writing Phi for my own sake. Obviously, you need scientific papers, which we're doing, and then tests, which we are doing. The book is a complementary side to the normal scientific approach. I thought this theory of consciousness offered a unique opportunity to be presented that way. The first part of the book is about the evidence, the second part is about the theory itself, the third part is about the implications.

If you had to write a theory of immunology, you wouldn't be able to do it poetically. Consciousness is different because it's where science and the humanities come together. It's where you and the world come together, so it's a very special place and it would be a wasted opportunity not to try it.

There are some things that are perhaps best conveyed poetically or maybe, I was hoping, better understood poetically. I'll give you one example that I tried to convey in the book; I don't know if it succeeded. Assuming IIT is roughly in the right direction, assuming that you could measure consciousness properly for complex systems -- which we can't right now, but you can imagine -- then if you were to take the universe, or the solar system, or even people in a city and you were to run these entities through the program you would find out where there is consciousness, how much, and what kind. What the universe would condense down to under this analysis is something that is very different from the way we have been used to thinking since Galileo and since Darwin. One chapter in Phi, at the beginning, is called Displacements and it says what happened in the course of science has been that, first, we realized that we are not at the center of the universe, the physical universe. That was the Copernican Revolution. Second, we realized that we were not even the pinnacle of creation or anything like that, but are probably the end result of a lot of steps of trial and error, evolution by natural selection. That was Darwin. Third -- I credit Francis Crick for this, a conclusion that most neuroscientists keep telling us every day – we are just the product of neurons buzzing in our brain, and that's it. There is nothing more to it that; there is no soul. That's the biggest and worst displacement of all. I would say this is the standard view of the universe that we now have through science. Now if you take IIT to be, for a moment, roughly correct, it actually very much changes this view of humans and our place in nature. It truly turns it around. Not because I wanted it to do so -- there's no romantic attempt to salvage our former position in the universe.

If you take this "displaced" view seriously, it says, that mass, energy, charge, etc., are fundamental properties of the universe. We know there is a lot of this stuff around in the universe, and there is much more out in the universe than there is in the Solar System, on our Sun, on our planet, and certainly in my head. My brain has a trivial amount of mass and energy, this is true. That is, it is true that from the viewpoint of mass, energy, and charge, we are trivial, trivial, trivial. But according to IIT integrated information, that is, consciousness itself, is at least as fundamental as mass or energy. And it turns out that, lo and behold, we have a very special structure here in our brains. It may not have been created by a deity, but it's very, very special. It's small, but it's very special because of the large amount of integrated information it generates in our heads. If we had what I call a qualiascope, instead of a telescope or a microscope, and we could look at the universe with this qualiascope that doesn't look for mass or energy, but it looks for integrated information, the universe would look very different. It would look primarily empty. Where you see the great galaxies, for a moment, you would see dust. Very little integrated information, I would imagine. Through the qualiascope, you would look at the Sun, this big, big star-which is not even that big in the great cosmic scale of things and also turns out to be primarily dust. You wouldn't see anything through the qualiascope in looking at the Sun. Then you turn the scope down and you look at the mountains, and they're also dust . . . and the ocean, itself, is sort of dust. Then you look at animals, and within those animals, in a body which is also mainly dust, there is going to be this gigantic object, this fantastic constellation,. . . which is a constellation made of integrated information, not of mass and energy, but it is just as fundamental. Now, suddenly you can see that your friend and yourself are two giant constellations. That child is also like that, maybe a little bit smaller, but it's like a giant constellation too. Animals, in various ways which you can only begin to appreciate, are big constellations too. Suddenly, you have a very different view of the universe. It is a very empty place, but inside it are these gigantic constellations. Each of them is a different shape, an extraordinary shape-and each of them is a universe of consciousness. Now, this is a poetic image. The universe is not an empty place with gigantic masses where we are a speck on the periphery. The universe is an empty place where there are giant constellations, and as far as we know right now, we are the biggest constellations of all in a very profound scientific sense, and this is just as real as that there are big stars and big mountains in the traditional sense.

Shifting gears a bit, you write about Bruno, Leibniz, Spinoza, all of whom were panpsychists of various stripes. Christof Koch has come out recently, publicly, saying, essentially, "Sure, I'm a panpsychist. I'm not going to put a lot of weight in that label, but I'm okay with that label now." You have, historically, shied away from that label. Have you changed your views, or do you still dislike this term?

No, I have not changed my views. Panpsychism is a vague term, but IIT is not vague at all, so it is dangerous to simply call it panpsychist, just because it says that consciousness is graded, and animals, including simple animals, even some artificial system, may have some of it.

Many of the greatest philosophers were panpsychists, and I have great respect for them. They were, essentially, monists who, instead of saying that the world divides into two things, would say, "No, it's one thing." Rather than saying that there is the physical world-which, of course, exists-and then somehow ignoring mind, they took mind seriously and said, "There is this thing, which is both." Many of the great philosophers took that position because it's more elegant and not absurd like materialism or dualism. The problem traditionally with panpsychists -- even the very best, like Leibniz, as he recognized himself -- was that beyond saying that everything is pervaded with soul or psyche in some way or another, they have no way to understand why some things seem to be more pervaded with soul than other things. Why are our brains clearly pervaded with that full soul that is human consciousness, and a heap of sand apparently not? What was the key difference? This he called the problem of aggregates, and that problem has always been there.

Second, these thinkers had nothing constructive to say about the quality of consciousness. Yeah, maybe everything is pervaded with soul, but why does the way I'm pervaded right now look red as opposed to green, or sound like a trumpet? Nothing to say about that, so it was empty. IIT says that, first of all, not everything is pervaded with soul -- there are things that definitely, according to IIT, have no soul whatsoever, no consciousness. What are those things? Feed-forward networks, simulations in the computer, crowds, and many other things. A crowd doesn't exist in and of itself as a conscious entity; only the people exist.

For some cases it's pretty clear that there's no consciousness present; for others we would have to do some analysis. A heap of sand definitely does not have a soul. Very special parts of your brain do, but cerebella don't. IIT goes further and asks: "What kind of consciousness is present?" So, you can't say IIT is "pan" because not everything is conscious in IIT. But IIT does share with panpsychism the notion that consciousness is an intrinsic property of certain things. It's a fundamental property of nature, it's not an add-on, an epiphenomenon, or a different kind of thing altogether.

You talk about a photodiode having one bit of integrated information, therefore having one bit of phi, consciousness. Koch has written about a proton or neutron having some integrated information because it's comprised of quarks that have a certain relationship. So is it fair to say that all stuff has some consciousness, but it's really about the level of consciousness? You talked about a crowd or the Internet not having its own consciousness, but the constituents do. Is that fair?

That's correct, a crowd wouldn't, but the individual people would. The whole brain wouldn't, but certain parts of the cortex would, and so on and so forth. I've never talked about neutrons, but let's talk about the photodiode, which I've used so much that it's become an easy target for making fun of the theory.

To be precise, for a photodiode to be conscious, it has to have at least two elements that interact, in both directions. It's a minimally conscious photodiode. It's terribly simple, but not just one element . . . and the theory would say: "Yes, the photodiode has a non-zero value of consciousness, one bit of consciousness," and IIT would actually tell you what kind of consciousness that would be. It's very, very simple. One thing to realize is, first, that this is incredibly little consciousness. How little? I used the example of absolute zero today . . . it's like saying -271 degrees kelvin is hot. Well, it's hotter than absolute zero, but it's definitely damn cold. A photodiode with one bit of consciousness is indeed conscious, but it's damn little.

So when Christof Koch, for example, says, "IIT is a species of panpsychism," do you wince a bit?

Well, I would have to go through all of these qualifications. Basically, I don't think it's panpsychist in the most common sense. "Panpsychist" means "everything," and there can definitely be things like a purely feed-forward system that has no soul whatsoever. Now, some of its constituents at the lower level might have it, but this is a very different way of talking about things than traditional panpsychism.

Along the same lines, we've had a long debate about the combination problem and the boundary problem (two sides of the same problem, really). As solutions to these problems, you've talked about local maxima, you've talked about singularities, so could you explain how IIT does, in fact, delineate the boundaries of each unitary consciousness?

This is what is called in IIT the exclusion axiom. One of the key features of consciousness, I believe, beyond integration and information. I usually mention it by saying, okay, experience is one, it's one of many possible experiences, but it is also the <u>only</u> one. So, at any given time, I'm having only one experience -- which right now is seeing you and giving you answers in this place in this world -- and there is not, at the same time, another me which experiences exactly the same except for color, a color-blind version of me, and, one that does so except for perceiving faces, like a prosopagnosic patient. There is not an infinite number of slightly, or more, defective versions of my own consciousness, there is only one me -- or full me, the full experience -- not all these superimposed partial consciousnesses. Looking at time, there is also a similar exclusion. Consciousness doesn't flow every microsecond and it doesn't flow over the course of days. It's in the middle somewhere, in a fairly defined range. That's the exclusion axiom, that's a property of consciousness which I dare anybody to deny. That's the way it is.

This boils down to assuming that in any physical system, integrated information is a causal form of information. It's differences that make a difference [the Batesonian definition of information], and you cannot have a multiplication of causes. If this were a version of Occam's razor, it would be something like "causes should not be multiplied beyond necessity." With respect to consciousness, however, it becomes "entities should not be multiplied beyond necessity." There's a beautiful fit between Occam's razor and consciousness. So we say, you cannot have a multiplication of consciousness over the same elements or over different spatiotemporal scales. How do we decide which one actually becomes dominant, to the exclusion of others? Well, since integrated information is a form of causation, we say the dominant consciousness is the one that's maximally potent. Whatever does most of the job in terms of causation is the dominant consciousness. This is based on the principle that, if something does exist, it exists to the extent that it can do things.

In the case of the mind, if we have multiple candidates for conscious and causal entities, which consciousness really exists? Well, the one that does the most. It's just an extension. If you do nothing, you don't exist. If you do, you might. But if there are multiple things that do things superimposed on each other, which one exists? Well, the one that does the most.

Ok. If we take an iPhone, which you've talked about here, and you actually could operationalize your equations to calculate phi for that iPhone, wouldn't yet get a non-trivial phi?

No.

No? You're saying no?

Probably. We haven't done it, and it can't be done right now.

Why wouldn't you get a non-trivial phi?

I premise this by saying, we haven't even been remotely capable of measuring phi for an iPhone . . . but, based on what we have done with small systems and what we sort of know about how an iPhone is organized, there are two main problems, which is why, I think, an iPhone would have either minimal or no phi, in just some components, or maybe a very small "dot" of phi. So, under IIT, there is nothing it is like to be an iPhone. The number one argument for this conclusion is that anything that's essentially a look-up table, a feed-forward look-up table -- which many search engines, for instances, are like -- would have zero phi, because we know you need to have a system where everybody can interact with everybody else to have a non-zero phi. Computers, typically, are not built in such a way that everything can interact internally, because otherwise it wouldn't work. It follows a set of steps. So, usually, in feed-forward architectures and-to the extent that these are implemented into a computer, there is no consciousness at the level of the computer itself.

So the iPhone, as a whole, has not much more phi than a photodiode by itself?

Yeah, probably not. Maybe nothing because it breaks into pieces, and the pieces might have very little value of phi.

What, then, would be required of the broad-level architecture in order to construct a high-phi iPhone?

If we were to do this in hardware, there's probably a lot of biological details that are irrelevant to generating your own consciousness. We could throw away a lot of those particular details. What matters is the difference that makes the difference in the dominant consciousness, which is the one that reaches the maximum. We just need to emulate the power of that, and we'll have you. You can simplify a lot but, of course, it might end up a lot like us. This doesn't mean that we can create artificial consciousness today – we clearly can't – but under the framework of IIT, it would have to be made of real things, and they would have to have the right spatiotemporal scale. You need, as a simple recipe, a lot of specialists that talk to each other and that's hard, as we know, even in human societies.

Shifting gears and wrapping up, what are the spiritual implications of IIT, if any? You've mentioned already the idea of phi stars, kind of a backing-away from the Copernican idea that humans aren't really important in the grand scheme of things. Is there more to it for you personally?

There are many implications and in my book, of course, I tried to go through what IIT implies for what death means and what dementia means, what pain means. By knowing more about science and what consciousness is, we can make more informed decisions. Some of these life or death decisions are not decisions that we make scientifically, but they can be informed by science, and that's one of the key implications of IIT. If we have a better understanding of consciousness, we'll be able to use ethics and the law to do a better job because we'll understand better what's going on, like we do with coma patients. If we know for sure that there is nobody there -- or it's as little there is as in the iPhone -- and it will not be recoverable because of permanent damage -- then I think you can act based on that, as opposed to saying, "We'll never know, there could somebody there," which is our status right now. The other aspect is that when I say each of us is a giant constellation of consciousness in a universe generally empty of consciousness -- and so are many animals, although not as big as us – these "phi constellations" are much bigger than mountains and suns and planets. I mean that. It means that everyone is extraordinarily important. Once somebody dies, one can really say, an entire universe is destroyed. It's really true. It's an entire universe. Something it is like to be you, something that's really real, something that doesn't require an observer to exist, does at some point cease to exist.

Printed in Great Britain
by Amazon